Mexican Rural Development and the Plumed Serpent

Mexican Rural Development and the Plumed Serpent

Technology and Maya Cosmology in the Tropical Forest of Campeche, Mexico

Betty Bernice Faust

Foreword by Betty J. Meggers

BERGIN & GARVEY
Westport, Connecticut • London

Library of Congress Cataloging-in-Publication Data

Faust, Betty Bernice.
    Mexican rural development and the plumed serpent : technology and
  Maya cosmology in the tropical forest of Campeche, Mexico / Betty
  Bernice Faust ; foreword by Betty J. Meggers.
        p.   cm.
    Includes bibliographical references and index.
    ISBN 0–89789–482–0 (alk. paper)—ISBN 0–89789–699–8 (pbk.)
    1. Mayas—Agriculture.   2. Maya philosophy.   3. Mayas—
  Antiquities.   4. Human ecology—Mexico—Campeche (State)   5. Biotic
  communities—Mexico—Campeche (State)   6. Technology and
  civilization.   7. Rural development—Yucatán Peninsula.   8. Water
  resources development—Mexico—Campeche (State)   9. Campeche (Mexico :
  State)—Social conditions.   10. Campeche (Mexico : State)—
  Environmental conditions.   11. Campeche (Mexico : State)—
  Antiquities.   I. Title.
  F1435.3.A37F38   1998
  306.3′49′089974—dc20   96–28277

British Library Cataloguing in Publication Data is available.

Library of Congress Catalog Card Number: 96–28277
ISBN: 0–89789–482–0
ISBN: 0–89789–699–8 (pbk.)

First published in 1998

Bergin & Garvey, 88 Post Road West, Westport, CT 06881
An imprint of Greenwood Publishing Group, Inc.
www.greenwood.com

Printed in the United States of America

The paper used in this book complies with the
Permanent Paper Standard issued by the National
Information Standards Organization (Z39.48–1984).

10 9 8 7 6 5 4 3 2 1

Copyright Acknowledgments

The author and publisher gratefully acknowledge the following for permission to use materials from their publications:

Stanford University Press to modify Plate 19 from *The Ancient Maya* by Sylvanus G. Morley (1946), for the map which appears as Figure 1.2 in the present book.

Waveland Press to reprint Figure 2 from *Chamulas in the World of the Sun: Time and Space in a Maya Oral Tradition* by Gary Gossen, which appears as Figure 2.2 in the present book.

University of New Mexico Press to reprint Figures 6.1 and 6.10 from *Pre-Hispanic Maya Agriculture* by Peter D. Harrison and B. L. Turner II, eds. 1977, as Figures 3.2 and 3.1, respectively, in the present book.

Brigham Young University Press to reprint Figure 169 from *Investigations at Edzná Campeche, Mexico*, vol. 1, part 1 by Ray T. Matheny et al. as Figure 3.5 in the present book.

Academic Press to reprint Figure 3 from "Maya Development and Collapse: An Economic Perspective" by Patrick T. Culbert in *Social Process in Maya Prehistory: Studies in Honor of Sir Eric Thompson 1977*, as Figure 3.4 in the present book.

Jon Kusler and the Association of Wetlands Managers, Berne, New York to reprint Figures 1–5 from *Ecotourism and Resource Conservation: A Collection of Papers from the Ecotourism and Resource Conservation Project 1991*, as Figures 4.3, 5.1, 5.2, 5.5, and 5.6 in the present book.

Bret Diamond for the non-exclusive use of his copyrighted photographs.

National Anthropology Archives, National Museum of Natural History, Smithsonian Institution, for the use of my photographs, archived there, including some taken by Miguel Medina Yeh, working as my research assistant.

Contents

Figures and Tables

FIGURES

TABLES

Foreword

Given the problems, uncertainties, conflicts, dangers, and disruptions that daily confront us in our rapidly changing world, why should we bother to read about a small Maya community on the peninsula of Yucatán in Mexico? What can we learn that will be relevant to resolution of the ideological conflicts in Ireland, Bosnia, and Israel? Or the tribal warfare in east Africa? Or the progressive disintegration of our own society? We are vaguely aware that the demands of growing urban populations for food, shelter, and energy are degrading the habitats of isolated indigenous communities in distant regions, destroying them physically and culturally, but are inclined to consider this the inevitable consequence of "progress." Peasant communities like the one described in this book are relatively invisible. If we think of them at all, we consider them relicts of a superceded way of life and irrelevant to the solution of more important and more immediate problems. There are several reasons for suggesting that this presumption may be wrong. Superficially, the people of Pich are like us. They wear similar clothes, live in similar houses, listen to radios, send their children to school, vote in national elections, drive cars, etc. They are also experiencing the same social disruptions—alcoholism, juvenile delinquency, theft, family violence, economic insecurity, changing values—as a consequence of growing subservience to the demands of a national economy. Unlike us, however, they possess a large body of traditional knowledge accumulated during millennia of experience in maximizing the sustainable exploitation of local resources. The older members of the community recognize the relationship between the growing social and environmental deterioration and the imposition of inappropriate attitudes and procedures, but feel increasingly helpless to prevent the inevitable collapse.

During the decade in which Betty Faust has lived intermittently in Pich, she has learned by experience that overt similarities often conceal covert cultural differences. Long-term involvement has not only permitted her to describe traditional values and their implementation, but also to observe their relevance to maintaining subsistence security during short-term climatic fluctuations. She provides detailed accounts of the manner in which primitive methods of water control, exploitation of game and forest products, beliefs, and rituals reflect and reinforce the integration of humans with other components of the ecosystem. As survivals of the sustainable systems of intensified food production that supported one of the most complex civilizations of pre-Columbian America, they deserve our serious attention.

As an archeologist concerned with the relationship between cultural evolution and environmental limitations, I have been struck by the seeming contradiction between the complexity of Maya culture and the relatively low agricultural potential of their environment. Terraces, ridged fields, and evidence of irrigation have been identified in some regions, but their capacity for continuous intensive cultivation is not clear. Major architectural complexes surrounded by small earth mounds are often separated by only a few dozen kilometers. Assuming all were contemporary, the precolumbian population density was several times greater than at present, when subsistence resources are supplemented by imported food. The imprecise nature of carbon-14 dates, absence of detailed ceramic chronologies, and assumptions based on Old World models of state formation are among the potential biases that hinder our understanding of the conditions that produced, maintained, and annihilated one of humanity's most remarkable cultural achievements. Betty Faust makes it clear that the elders in Pich (and presumably in other traditional communities) possess information that can help resolve these contradictions.

Finally, communities like Pich can inform us on basic processes of human sociocultural behavior. Biologists have turned to single-celled organisms to decipher the chemical reactions, physical interactions, molecular structures, and other processes common to all forms of life. As a consequence, we are increasingly able to enhance the productivity of domesticated plants and animals, to identify genetic sources of disease, and to understand the biological basis for aging, among other accomplishments. Peasant villages are the cultural counterpart. For some ten millennia, humans lived in small self-sufficient communities whose survival depended on maintaining a sustainable integration with resources in the immediate environment. Although storage or assistance from neighboring settlements could offset temporary local disaster, extinction or emigration was the penalty for persistent overexploitation. As a result, such communities developed detailed knowledge of long-term productivity of local resources, sometimes explicit but often encoded in rules of conduct enforced by supernatural sanctions. Practices that we dismiss as superstition often enhance long-term availablity of renewable resources and cushion the community against the impact of catastrophic events too infrequent to be experienced during living memory.

In the words of Betty Faust, "This is not only a book about a Maya community but one of reflections concerning the relationship between human beings and the natural world." The same symptoms of social, economic, and ideological disintegration manifested by modern nations are present in Pich, but their dynamics are more easily observed because the scale is smaller and the relationships between internal and external processes are consequently clearer. Biologists have suggested that parks and biological reserves are an environmental analogue of miners' canaries, where the extent of large-scale environmental changes might be evaluated (Vitousek et al. 1996:471). The community of Pich is their human counterpart. Like the miner's canary, their demise may foretoken our own.

Betty J. Meggers
Smithsonian Institution

Preface

This book is based on eleven years of "unfinished conversations" (see Sullivan 1989) with members of the modernizing Maya community of Pich, Campeche, Mexico. I began to study these Maya in May of 1985 while waiting for permission to study recently arrived Maya refugees fleeing a "hidden war" in Guatemala which included violent attacks on all peasant communities in certain zones (Manz 1988). These refugees had been settled by the United Nations and a Mexican government agency in an official camp less than 2 miles from Pich. The permission I sought was never granted.[1] I continued my study of Pich, using it as a case study to explore the relationship between rural development and Maya traditions, including cosmology, technology, social organization, and processes of adaptation. Two technologies are essential for village survival: water management and food production. I analyze these technologies with reference to archeological and historical materials and the traditional cosmological system expressed in present-day rituals. I then describe the approaches of various Pichuleños (members of the community of Pich) to modernization, and their reflections on it. The analysis of what has happened in Pich is based on an examination of the long-term processes of adaptation and change known from the archeological record, the history of the region, oral histories of the elders of Pich, and observations of daily life. I analyze these Maya traditions and perceptions with reference to possibilities for combining them with modern science and technology in ways that could help the Maya restore and maintain their resources and their cultural identity, while participating in the modern world. Fieldwork was done during fourteen months, from May 1985 to September 1986; the summers of 1990, 1992, 1993; and eleven visits from September of 1994 to April of 1996, averaging four days each.

I have at various times explained anthropological fieldwork to Pichuleños in different ways, trying to help them understand the purposes of my activities. I write down their history and what is happening in order to make comparisons with other parts of the world. I take photographs and record interviews so that my students can understand what life is like in Pich. I have told them that I was first writing a thesis and then a book. In this book, I have left out incidents that I believe might embarrass individuals, referring to patterns of behavior rather than incidents involving the behavior of particular people. I have also altered some incidents, constructing composite ones to represent the patterns. In making these adjustments to protect privacy, I have excluded some data. I have given pseudonyms to some individuals but have not changed the name of the community itself. Despite the precautions, I may have inadvertently included details that will be considered violations of privacy. For that I apologize, in advance, to those children of Pich who will someday read this. I hope that when that day comes, they will understand my intentions of making a contribution both to the survival of a culture I learned to value, and saw endangered, and to the efforts of those who are trying to protect the biological processes (including species diversity) upon which all human cultures depend (Ledec and Goodland 1988:8–9; Munro 1991:30–31; Groombridge 1992:xvi–xvii; U.S. National Research Council 1992:32; Gibbons 1993:1–3; Heywood 1995:12–13; Ehrlich and Ehrlich 1996:242–244). Pichuleños once had a vision of a future in which, as in ancient times, human beings used resources in ways that were congruent with the cycles of nature and the survival needs of other species; I hope we all can learn something from them before their traditional healer's prophecy becomes reality and "that ancient serpent rises out of the sea to end this world and start another."

SPECIAL CONVENTIONS

Dates: Some original dates of publication for references are given as "1540?" or "1500s" because in the sixteenth century the year of publication was not routinely included.

Foreign words: Italics are used for both Spanish and Mayan words. A vertical apostrophe indicates a glottal stop in Mayan words. Mayan place names carry the accent marks conventionally used with them in Mexico, representing their Hispanicized pronunciation; Mayan names of plants and animals are written with the conventions used in the *Diccionario Maya* (Barrera Vázquez 1991). "Maya" is used to refer to the ethnic identity, "Mayan" to the language. Quotes are verbatim; translations are the author's.

NOTE

1. The Comisión Mexicana de Ayuda a Refugiados (financed by the United Nations High Commission on Refugees) never answered written requests and responded to both personal visits and telephone calls with assurances that they would call me when it was "convenient," for me to do my research in the camp.

Acknowledgments

I would like to thank the Shell International Foundation for Research in Developing Countries for making possible the initial year of fieldwork conducted from September of 1985 to September of 1986 in Pich, Campeche, Mexico; the Mexican government for a research visa; and the Insitituto Nacional de Antropología e Historia (National Institute for Anthropology and History) for permission to do this anthropological research. Visits to obtain additional data on processes of change were made in the summers of 1990, 1992, and 1993. Research in the summer of 1992 was funded by the Wenner-Gren Foundation for Anthropological Research.

A preliminary feasibility study was done from May to July of 1985, with the encouragement of Dr. Gary Gossen and a grant from the Benevolent Fund of the State University of New York at Albany. Graduate course work was funded by the Danforth Foundation. Permission to do the research was kindly granted by the Mexican Consulate in Washington, D.C., and the National Institute of Anthropology and History in Mexico City.

I would like to thank many, many people in Mexico and the United States whose kindness and assistance have made this work possible. I cannot name all of them here, but I would especially like to mention the following in Mexico: Director William J. Folan and his wife, and colleague, Lynda Florey Folan, of the Centro de Investigaciones Históricas y Sociales de la Universidad Autónoma de Campeche (Research Center for Historical and Social Sciences of the Autonomous University of Campeche, Mexico), who provided friendship, advice, and access to the research center's library; the staff of the center for their encouragement and friendship; the researcher Abel Morales López, who introduced me to the local archeology and taught me a great deal as we worked together on an article interpreting the symbolism of one of these sites. Special thanks also to the anthropologist Juan Manuel Sandoval Palacios of the Instituto Nacional de Antropología e Historia for his advice and encouragement; the attorney José Aranda Alpuche and his family for their many generous acts of hospitality and assistance; Father Martín Zamora for helping me understand Mexican Catholicism, for his extensive kindness and assistance with the archives of the church, and for his friendship during some difficult times. I appreciated greatly the aid of the Honorable José Maldonado Medina, Presidente of Campeche, together with his wife, Doña Minerva, and their children, who were most helpful and kind to both my son and me during a very busy period in their own lives; the pediatrician Santiago González Ambrosio, his wife, Isabel, and their children, who have frequently shared their home in Campeche with me throughout the years of research; and my doctor, Manuel Gantús Castro, who provided medical care, friendship, and the assurance that I was not going to die from an attack of para-typhoid and amoebas.

In the United States, I want to thank my dissertation adviser, the anthropologist Susan Wadley, for her assistance and encouragement at the dissertation stage and for her support and the hospitality of her home during the rewriting effort, and also to thank her daughters, Shona and Laura, for sharing so much of their mother's time. I wish to also give special thanks to my interdisciplinary dissertation committee of the Maxwell School of Citizenship and Public Affairs at Syracuse University: the anthropologists Hans Buechler and William Mangin, the sociologist of law Richard Schwartz, and the political scientist and planner Edwin Bock. I also wish to express my gratitude to the anthropologist Gary Gossen, both for his training in Maya anthropology and for his assistance as an outside reader of my dissertation. Since graduation, Hans Buechler has read the new versions and made suggestions as I struggled to turn the dissertation into a book. He also made his office available to me to use during summer months. Other anthropologists whose advice and encouragement have been crucial include E. N. Anderson, Duncan Earle, Marilyn Gates, Ellen Kintz, Richard Leventhal, John Sosa, Alicia Re Cruz, and both Dennis and Barbara Tedlock. Earlier training in development anthropology by Glenn Cochrane has also been very helpful. Professional colleagues outside of anthropology whose suggestions have been valuable include the geographer Philip Wagner, the geologist Gary Gates, the scholar of sixteenth-century Spanish literature Helen Reed, the environmental scientists and policy analysts Richard Smardon and John Sinton, the botanists Javier Ortiz Díaz and Frank Lang, the linguist Frances Kartunnen, the historian of biology Alfred Crosby, and the psychologist Richard Pearson.

Equally essential has been the help and encouragement of my family and personal friends. To my parents, Paul and Patty Faust, I am in debt not only "for giving me life itself," as the Maya have taught me, but also for the many ways in which they have contributed to my preparation for this project from my earliest childhood. In addition, my father spent many hours helping me edit this manuscript and assisting me with the analysis. His skills as an engineer and technical writer have contributed greatly to the refinement of both analysis and writing, particularly in the areas of technology, geology, and astronomy. My mother has supported this joint effort with wonderful meals, encouragement, and reminders—keeping us on task. I am also deeply appreciative of the support I have received from my sister, Sherry Zimmer-Faust, and her family and from my daughter, Laura Lynn Fountain, and her family.

Beyond all the rest, I especially want to thank my son, Aaron Christopher Sumner, and my grandmother, Ellen Hurley Wammack Johnson: my son for his help and understanding in the field and in all the stages of preparation before and after the field, for his artistic advice concerning the drawings, and for his unwavering faith in his mother becoming an anthropologist; my grandmother for teaching me about rural poverty and the wisdom of old traditions.

In addition to those mentioned above, I would like to thank the many other people in Campeche who helped me, all of the faculty at Albany and Syracuse who prepared me for the field, and my fellow graduate students for their help and support. I also wish to express appreciation to my colleagues at Ithaca College and Southern Oregon State College. The Human Ecology Section of the Center for Research and Advanced Studies, Mérida Unit (Sección de Ecología Humana del Centro de Investigación y de Estudios Avanzados del Instituto Politécnico Nacional [CINVESTAV]) has provided support, facilities, and encouragement for the final preparation of the manuscript. The computer preparation of figures and maps was done by the biologist Diego Roberto Vázquez del Valle, who improved on my drawings. Final stages of analysis benefited greatly from many discussions with biologist John G. Frazier, researcher in conservation biology, CINVESTAV, Mérida. I also wish to express deep gratitude to Betty Meggers of the Smithsonian Institution, Washington, D.C., who has provided research support, made many valuable suggestions for improvements in the manuscript, and written a foreword for the book. In the final stages of preparation, both Drs. Meggers and Frazier have continually encouraged me, while their professional lives continue to inspire me as models of commitment to the ideals of the scientific enterprise and to the training and support of Latin American scientists.

Most of all, I would like to express my deep sense of gratitude to and continuing affection for the large, extended family in Pich who adopted me and the village elders who taught me, particularly the *h-men*, Don Pedro Ucan Itzá, to whom I am greatly indebted for his continuing guidance of my attempts to understand the Maya World and the Maya Sky (see Sosa 1986). To all my friends and neighbors in Pich who shared their lives and knowledge with me so generously, *Dios bo'otik te'ex* (may God repay all of you).

Introduction:
The Plumed Serpent and Rural Development

We had thought that the trauma of these events—the Classic-period Collapse, the Spanish Conquest, and five hundred years of colonial domination—had cut the umbilical cord linking the ancient world of the Maya to their modern descendants, . . . We were wrong.

Linda Schele, "Afterward: A Final Word on Trees"

Today's Maya traditions are related to the Plumed Serpent of the ancient Maya. This feathered snake was and is a symbolic representation of a Mesoamerican[1] understanding of the sacred relations between the natural world and human society (Freidel, Schele, and Parker 1993:78–79, 128, 427); Miller and Taube 1993:148–151). The sacred creation myth of the K'iche' (Quiché) Maya, *Popol Vuh*, refers to the Plumed Serpent in the beginnings of creation,

> Whatever might be is simply not there: only murmurs, ripples, in the dark, in the night. Only the Maker, Modeler alone, Sovereign Plumed Serpent, the Bearers, Begetters are in the water, a glittering light . . . . He [Heart of Sky] spoke with the Sovereign Plumed Serpent, and they talked, . . . They agreed with each other, they joined their words, their thoughts. Then it was clear, then they reached accord in the light, and then humanity was clear, when they conceived the growth, the generation of trees, of bushes, and the growth of life, of human kind, in the blackness, in the early dawn. So there were three of them [thunderbolts], as Heart of Sky, who came to the Sovereign Plumed Serpent, when the dawn of life was conceived. (D. Tedlock 1985: 72–73)

Such themes from the *Popol Vuh* have been clearly identified in Classic Maya ceramics (Coe 1973, 1989; Robicsek and Hales 1981). Serpents also appear in the Classic period as symbols of the role of kings as visionary mediators between this world and the Divine. During the Postclassic period, the Plumed Serpent was a "symbol of the divinity of the state," eventually becoming the mythological hero, or god, Quetzalcoatl among the Toltec and K'uk'ulkan in the Peninsula of Yucatán (Freidel, Schele, and Parker 1993:289; Schele and Freidel 1990:394–395). The Feathered Serpent moves between the sky world and the earth and the underworld. It represents the interconnections, the interdependencies, the reciprocity that is required in the natural cycles that sustain human life: weather, plants, animals, humans, deities. This snake flies in the sky and swims in the seas and underground currents. Frequently depicted as two-headed, it represents both the past and the future cycles of the solar day and the solar year (Freidel, Schele and Parker 1993: 34, 78, 85-87, 155-156).

Maya ritual symbolism is part of an adaptive regional system that for millennia has changed in response to population density, new ideas, and variations in climate (Folan et al. 1983; Folan, Josserand, and Hopkins 1983; Gunn, Folan, and Robichaux 1994; Hodell, Curtis, and Brenner 1995). The local tropical forest ecosystem is precariously balanced between a limestone subsoil and a difficult climate. The limestone lets rainwater escape through cracks to the sea while the climate imposes periodic droughts, floods, and wind damage.

Maya traditions are open to change, but they also represent an awareness of the fragility of local ecosystems, an awareness built on centuries of experience with change and experimentation. During the 1980s and 1990s, new practices and technologies have been introduced in a manner that has circumvented the traditional mechanisms for testing the new and has subverted the traditional social mechanisms for prevention of over-use. There have been many pressures for uncritical adoption of the "modern" and rejection of past ways. Opportunities for short-term profits, buying on credit, and loans have combined forces with the disrespect and discrimination often shown to traditional Maya persons.

Recurrent fieldwork in the peninsula since 1985 has made clear that social pressures combine with economic ones to overwhelm the old culturally embedded mechanisms for protecting scarce community resources. Until the last fifteen years, the forest replenished the soil of agricultural fields in sustainable twenty-year cycles of traditional Maya agriculture, including the slashing and burning (swidden) of small patches that regrow within the forest. The patches are multicropped, maintaining substantial biodiversity and mimicking the complexity of the forest (Terán and Rasmussen 1995). The forest also provided materials for house construction, furniture, baskets, twine, and medicine, as well as being a place where wild fruits, seeds, and roots were collected and wild birds and animals were hunted (Folan, Fletcher, and Kintz 1979).

The destruction of this local sustainable system of forest use is necessary, according to the local government agents promoting modernization. When I asked why, they patiently explained that it was not efficient because it did not produce enough per acre, and then they cited impressive statistics for hybrid corn and rice grown with modern equipment. It did not occur to me then to ask if these statistics were based on rain-dependent fields (rather than irrigated ones), on similar soils to these, and a similar climate. Neither did it occur to the villagers to ask these questions. The development agents also said that swidden destroys new forest every year, whereas the large 247–494 acre (100–200 hectare) plots being bulldozed for monocropping would be permanent, so that the rest of the forest would not need to be cut for swidden, but would be protected by a government agency for "ecology." These agents found unbelievable the information I tried to give them concerning new evidence that indigenous swidden is sustainable and cyclical, that monocropping in the tropics has produced ecological disasters, and that heavy machinery can damage soils with high clay content, such as those in the Edzná Valley.

Some of the modernizing Maya elders have struggled repeatedly to find ways to control the modernization process, to adapt it to the Plumed Serpent. A few have tried to integrate new technologies and knowledge with the system they inherited from generations of ancestors, who had passed down to them the lessons learned during centuries of experience. However, the recent forces of modernization have often imposed either-or choices on the village, while the authority of the elders has been undermined by schools, television, and the disrespect of outsiders.

Elders complained to me frequently about their inability to control their own grown children's use of the forest. They recalled wistfully the control their parents exercised over them when they were young. They now understand that that control was wise—restraining the short-term greed of youth for the future well-being of the grandchildren, who will need the same land and forest to provide for their children. Elders also complained that the community itself was less able to control those families who over-used the water supplies for their cattle, endangering the gardens and fields of the poor.

Some of my "New Age" students in the United States have idealized indigenous knowledge and believe it to be the infallible result of mysterious vision. Popular interests in shamanism and the exotic have been growing rapidly as many people become weary of and frightened by news of health hazards and environmental disasters connected with industrial processes. It is easy to romanticize and mystify the knowledge of indigenous peoples as an escape from the complexities of industrial civilization. It is also easy to believe that the scientists can find some cure to fix whatever ecological disaster results from unwise use of new technologies for short-term profits. Daniel Botkin (1990) has examined the various myths and images of nature that have directed research and policy in the West, focusing attention away from the very information that is most necessary to building a sustainable relationship with nature. Both modern science and indigenous practices are fallible, as we know from Love Canal and Chernobyl as well as from the abandoned cities of the Anasazi and the Maya Collapse of the ninth century. However, by combining the two, it may yet be possible to save the natural systems needed to support human life and the biodiversity required to minimize the risks our children will face. Maybe we can even save some "wilderness areas" and "flagship species" for aesthetic and ethical reasons, even if not absolutely required for our own species' survival.

A survey of the archeological and historical literature as well as long-term research with the elders of Pich have resulted in understandings that the living knowledge of this community is not a matter of clairvoyance but rather results from continuing experience and experimentation. This local knowledge is passed on in dreams and visions, ritual symbolism, stories, and proverbs. It is not foolproof, but neither is it opposed to new knowledge, new techniques. It does not have the power to specify the details of the DNA of a particular species as does Western science; however, it has accumulated holistic information concerning the behavior of local systems over time.

In Pich, the traditional approach to change is not to experiment with only a few isolated variables but to incorporate the new within an awareness of system, context, interrelationship, and long-term processes. Individuals are trained in this perspective by their elders, by daily practices, and by rituals. They are made aware of connections between humans and nature, between generations, between sexes (Faust, forthcoming). These understandings were once supported by traditional sanctions, which had the authority of custom and a legitimacy based on shared values. Those sanctions have been replaced by a system of national laws that protect individual rights to exploit resources rather than upholding long-term community needs and public goods.

It has become increasingly difficult for indigenous people like those of Pich to flee from industrial modernization. Government programs, national laws, poverty, oppression, and prejudice all have combined to pressure the younger villagers to discard the knowledge of their elders. The children learn in school to reject any identification with their own stigmatized culture in order not to be discriminated against or laughed at. They do not wish to become apprentices to their elders. They want to become rock stars and businessmen. They dream of making a fortune in the city. In another generation much of what the modern world could learn from communities like Pich will be lost—a great deal is being lost with every death of an elder who has not found anyone to listen (Martínez 1995).

The elders' knowledge has been defined by the outside authorities as backwards, ignorant, the cause of their poverty. It was, in fact, an adaptive system, open to the new, while respecting the fragility of the local environment. The traditional way provided human beings with challenges, with opportunities for creativity and problem-solving and gave them enormous emotional satisfactions. However, there has been both a pull—the attractiveness of the new—and a push—the external forces of national government, markets, the power of status differences, the fear of being ridiculed. Now there are only fragments left of that integrated way of life. I have attempted to piece together what that way of life was like, how it became fragmented and weakened, and how the people of Pich view the process of modernization that they have been experiencing. Forty years ago the paved road came, then the drilled well, electricity, and finally (in the past ten years) tractors, bulldozers, chainsaws, and television. Some Pichuleños now see modernity as a trap in which they have lost much of what made life worth living. Others value the new conveniences and opportunities. Some look around them and see their forest dying, their cornfields drying up. However, they also see electric light bulbs, a telephone, a medical clinic, a school, and water spigots in house yards.

Unfortunately, the first ripples of desertification are difficult to distinguish from normal variations of weather. It is hard to tell what is happening. No one is certain, in the village or the government agency for ecology, if the weather is changing. Gradual change in yearly averages is hard to see when there is normally much variation within and between years. But in Pich a few of the elders are afraid. There have always been bad years and occasional droughts, but the last few years seem different. Doubts abound; some have concluded that the end is near, but others still hope and want to be part of the larger world they see on television.

Like environmental damage, cultural destruction is hard to define. When does change become destructive? Pichuleños are losing much of their cultural heritage as well as the resources upon which their ancestors depended. The children cannot understand Maya language, their parents can understand but not speak it, and their grandparents hardly ever use it except with each other, in private. Television and schools have largely replaced the storytelling of the Elders. Pichuleños in the 1990s numbered 1,400—less than half of what they did fifteen years ago. People have migrated to Cancún, Mérida and Campeche looking for work, after cutting nearly all of the valuable tropical hardwoods in their forest commons of more than 160,000 acres (65,000 hectares). There are a few deer left, but they are "hard to find." Logging was banned for a few years by the Mexican environmental protection agency[2] but was allowed to resume in 1995 and 1996, with cutting of *guayacán (Tabebuia guayacan)* and *chakah (Bursera simaruba)*. An abandoned *ejido* (common land for agricultural use) in the center of the forestry commons is being requested by forty applicants, who hope the government will put in a road. This will provide access to increased hunting of the now scarce deer, wild turkey, and wild pigs as well as encourage cutting of forest for pasture and agriculture. It may be too late to salvage the forest of Pich and the way of life that both used and protected that forest. It may take twenty to forty years for the transplanted cedars of the reforestation project to grow to a usable size. It is also possible that large areas of the forest may never re-grow without massive human intervention. Grasses may take over, or scrub forest, or thorn bushes, or desert.

The environmental protection agency is attempting to regulate the logging it has again permitted, but supervision is difficult. Tropical cedar has been replanted in a few areas, but the young trees are growing very slowly. Hundreds of acres of savanna, wetlands, and forest were clear cut for rice plantations in the Edzná Valley. These no longer support commercial crops and are being used for cattle ranching. When the pastures no longer can support cattle, they are used for goats and sheep, which may further degrade soils, vegetation, and the potential for new crops.

Rural development agents often discount the traditional knowledge of Maya communities. This knowledge could potentially contribute to the design of more culturally and environmentally appropriate policies for rural development. Government agents (including teachers, doctors, cultural advisers, agricultural development experts, and malaria squads) are all admonished to treat the villagers with respect and to learn about local ways. However, in 1985–86 the purpose of this advice was generally understood to be more efficient change in the direction planned by the experts. Consultation, friendship, and learning about local ways was done in order to more smoothly introduce the new, modern, "better" ways planned by the government. These ways were adaptations of modern agricultural techniques developed in more temperate northern areas. Little attention was paid to developing scientific research on tropical ecosystems, including processes of nutrient recycling in soils, the interaction of insect and plant communities, processes of desertification. Available literature documenting problems with modernization projects and recommending alternative technologies was discounted as "idealist" by one agricultural extension agent with whom I talked. Biologists working at the Centro de Investigaciones Forestales del Trópico Húmedo had despaired of stopping the bulldozing operations of the Secretaría de la Reforma Agraria.

Discussions of Maya traditions and processes of change have often resulted in reflections concerning the underlying assumptions and consequences of modern industrial civilization. Present-day global processes of ecological destruction are the context in which development agents convince Maya villagers of the benefits of herbicides, tractor cultivation, insecticides, chemical fertilizers, forest clearing for cattle pasture, and monoculture (Sonnenfield 1992:29–52). Yet, Maya cosmology and traditional practices are based on three thousand years of experience with resource use in a difficult and fragile tropical environment, in a system that (during its peak centuries) maintained populations estimated by some archeologists as over 460 individuals per square mile in its southern central lowlands, a density similar to that of Java and China (Clark and Haswell 1964) —"among the most densely populated regions of the pre-industrial world" (Culbert and Rice 1990:26). There is considerable controversy among archeologists concerning these very high estimates, which are based on surveys of housemounds. In many tropical regions widely separated agricultural plots with simple houses are typically abandoned after two or three years of use, which could greatly increase the number of housemounds per family unit, reducing the population estimates based on those mounds. In some of the Maya area, however, research on relic terraces, raised fields with canals, and other structures associated with intensive land use have indicated intensive production while research on canoe trade indicates the capacity to transport food supplies over considerable distances. Climate shifts appear strongly correlated both with the abandonment of some sites and with population declines, information without providing needed assistance. They requested the return of anthropological information to their communities, the publication in Maya and Spanish of their own oral traditions, and our assistance in getting Mayan language and history taught in the schools as well as in negotiating better market terms for their products. They did not ask for firearms, but Paul Sullivan has reported isolated incidents of such requests to anthropologists beginning with the Carnegie expeditions of the 1920s and 1930s (Sullivan 1989). Most of the Maya elders (like many others in Mexico who remember the Mexican Revolution) appear to be determined to find peaceful solutions. "Political action is beautiful." Unstated but implied is, "Violence is ugly."

NOTES

1. Mesoamerica is a cultural area that includes the Valley of Mexico and areas east and west to the oceans, and south into Honduras. The term refers both to the ancient and the contemporary indigenous cultures of this area, which produced the ancient cities of Calakmul, Cerros, Chichén Itzá, Copán, Lamanai, La Venta, Monte Albán, Palenque, Tenochtitlán, Teotihuacán, Tikal, etc. It was first defined by Kirchoff (1968).

2. The agency with the responsibility for environmental protection in Mexico has changed three times in the past eleven years. It was the Secretaría de Desarrollo Urbano y Ecología; then it became the Secretaría de Desarrollo, Ecología y Solidaridad; now it is Secretaría del Medio Ambiente, Recursos Naturales y Pesca.

including those of the famous Maya Collapse of the ninth century (Folan et al. 1983; Gunn, Folan, and Robichaux 1994).

In this book I describe both ancient and recent Maya technologies, their fit with the local ecosystem, the environmental knowledge on which they are based, and the supporting ritual symbolism of Maya culture. The symbolism once structured both the protection of communally owned resources and the work involved in providing the human community with water, food, medicines, and materials for the construction of homes and furnishings. Now it whispers a nearly inaudible protest against the modern forces of destruction. While documenting the potential of traditional Maya techniques for long-term resource management, I am also reporting a Maya village collapse of the twentieth century, as Pich faces the end of its timber resources, the loss of its bees, the invasion of its soils by Johnson grass, the disappearance of game animals, and flood damage related to the destruction of ancient drainage canals by bulldozers clearing for mechanized agriculture. It is the paradox of the global situation that those native traditions that can help us envision a new road for the survival of our species are disappearing just as we realize we can learn something from them about how to live lightly on the earth.

The cultural reflections based on this fieldwork in Campeche Maya culture have grown in two directions. In seeking to understand the history of their struggles, I have learned to see the industrial world's ecological crisis from a different perspective. This is not only a book about a Maya community but one of reflections concerning the relationship between human beings and the natural world—reflections formed in conversations with traditional Maya concerning the world they see on television and in which they struggle. They say they are "*luchando para defendernos*" (fighting to defend ourselves). They are fighting economically and politically to defend their interests, their cultural identity, and the resources they need, not only to bring up their children but to pass on to these children when they are grown, in order that they, in turn, will be able to bring up the grandchildren, who will need the same resources for the great-grandchildren. Unlike other rural populations in Mexico, including related Maya groups in Chiapas (Gossen 1994), the Maya of the Peninsula have not recently turned to military organization in order to defend themselves.

There are, however, memories of the relative independence of the Territory of Quintana Roo after the Caste War of 1847–1849. In July 1995, Dr. John Sosa of the State University of New York at Cortland brought twelve representatives from the heart of the Quintana Roo area of former Maya rebellion to the Third International Congress of Mayanists in Chetumal. They presented their own individual messages to the Congress through their own bilingual interpreter. They explained to us the circumstances which had convinced their ancestors to fight with guns and then explained to us the hardships that they are now suffering. In typical Maya style, they left us to draw our own conclusions. They also politely suggested that Maya scholars have been remiss by indigenous standards of reciprocity, having accepted gifts of hospitality and

Mexican Rural
Development and the
Plumed Serpent

1

Fieldwork:
Navigating Friendships in the Dark

An aged blue bus crawled over axle-breaking speed bumps, rounded a corner and lurched to rest underneath a Pepsi-Cola sign in the village of Pich, Campeche. From the innards of the "blue cow" emerged a sudden bustle of Maya faces, cloth-wrapped bundles, upside-down chickens, a squealing net full of piglets, and an American anthropologist. As I stepped down from the bus, a huge Mercedes diesel truck roared past, loaded with logs from the village's communal lands, its "commons."[1] The paved road ends in Pich (see Figure 1.1 for a map locating the state of Campeche in southeastern Mexico). Two miles beyond, in the *monte* (brush or forest), was the refugee camp I would be denied permission to study. It would be in Pich that I would remain as a ship-wrecked stranger—navigating between the submerged reefs of cross-cultural misunderstandings, negotiating friendships out of the flotsam of contingency and mutual aid.

We have managed after a fashion, the people of Pich and I, to learn from each other and to take care of each other, and ultimately to care for each other, as well. We dream about each other, remember each other over the years, and feel an intense attachment; we cry each time I make it back "home." Part of the very special feelings we have for each other have grown out of the difficulties. We have had to struggle hard to understand each other. I was trained for the struggle; they were not. I have been financially and professionally rewarded for what I have learned from them—eventually writing a Ph.D. dissertation and a book on the subject. They have been rewarded only by the presents I bring back to them and the information they have received from me about the outside world. I have made arrangements for eye glasses for two elders and physical therapy for handicapped children, have talked unofficially with government officials in the city of Campeche about water problems and have given a soil testing kit to one community leader. I have given a blender and other gifts to my adopted family and a fan and screens to the Presbyterian Church for its guest rooms, one of which I sometimes occupy. I have also paid the going rates

Figure 1.1
Map of Modern Mexico with Enlargement of the State of Campeche

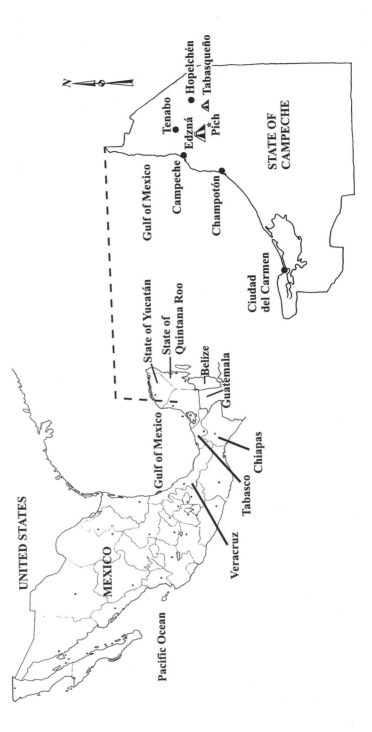

for room and board, established by school teachers and other visiting government agents. I have donated a Spanish-language book on rural medicine to the clinic and deposited a copy of my dissertation in the village archives. I bring toys, school supplies, and clothes for children of the families I know best. Despite my gifts and payments, it has not been an equal exchange; however, half of the royalties I receive from this book go to the community elders to help them preserve and teach the traditional knowledge. I also hope that what I write will someday help shape policies that will include traditional Maya elders in the planning of rural development. There are days when the processes of modernization seem to be inexorably pushing us all toward an environmental Armageddon, despite anything we can learn from either ecologists or native peoples concerning living in harmony with "the Plumed Serpent," the forces of nature upon which we depend. But we must keep trying, as the original peoples of the Americas have kept trying despite colonization. It is to my grandchildren and those of Pich that I now dedicate this *ilbal*, an instrument to see with, a book that preserves our "reading" of what we have seen, a record of our struggles to understand so that our grandchildren's children may also eat deer and marvel at hummingbirds (see Hunt 1977; D. Tedlock 1985:26).

FIRST IMPRESSIONS, SUMMER OF 1985

I began the study of Pich thinking it was a non-traditional, modernizing village. It is described in local government documents as "mestizo," indicating that it belongs to the dominant national culture. Yet I was to discover that its Maya roots are deep, but so is the shame that the community has learned—a shame that reflects a felt need to hide their Maya identity from outsiders and even among themselves. The old traditions emerged only gradually, as my new neighbors and friends gradually learned to trust that I really valued the old ways and wanted to learn about them.

If I had known what to look for, I could easily have seen evidence of Maya heritage during a quick walk around the village. Archeological evidence of a Late Classic Maya community and of sixteenth-century Spanish colonial occupation is mixed with twentieth-century basketball courts, street lights, political slogans from national elections, and Pepsi-Cola signs (see Figure 1.2 for a map of archeological sites and modern roads in Campeche). But what I saw my first day, as I stepped down from the "blue cow," was an assortment of roofs—thatched, corrugated metal, asbestos, and treated cardboard. The houses are separated from one another by walls of stone or bushes, usually slightly higher than Maya eye-level, a little more than five feet. Electric wires cross over the tops of the walls from house yard to house yard, as black pipes burrow under them—rising inside the yards with spigots for heads. Television antennas search the air waves over a few two-story houses in the center of the village, while several large lumber trucks rest below, beside the houses, in the shade.

Figure 1.2
**Map of Area Around Pich, Showing Historical
and Archeological Sites**

Source: Adapted from Map of Campeche made by INAH, Campeche, one made by the Campeche office
of Agrarian Reform, and one in S. G. Morley, *The Ancient Maya* (Stanford, CA: Stanford University
Press, 1964), Plate 19, the last used by permission of Stanford Univesity Press.

Coming into town, I had been reassured to see on the first major corner a small general store with a sign indicating "telephone." Looking around the village center, I saw a children's playground; but it was empty. I had arrived at bath time, which follows the siesta dictated by the extreme heat and humidity of tropical afternoons.

The community's priest had selected for me a family "of respect," which had two rooms they could rent. The family consisted of parents, two children, and grandparents, who were about to move to the city of Campeche. The rooms contained two small tables, chairs, nails for hanging clothes, a coffee table, and a bench. Two wardrobes were full and locked. The rent was 7,500 pesos per month (US$30 calculated at 250 pesos to the U.S. dollar in 1985). I asked about a bed, "Didn't you bring a hammock?" was the shocked response. The grandmother graciously offered to lend me hers—this night she would sleep with the children, in their hammock. Tomorrow I would go back to Campeche for my trunks and buy my own hammock. This was my first field lesson concerning cultural differences in what an individual should be responsible for and what others can be expected to provide.

The next cultural misunderstanding came over the evening meal. I was offered coffee, crackers, and cheese: but I had been waiting for tortillas and finally asked for them. Everyone was greatly amused and relieved that I would indeed eat tortillas; the local priest from Spain did not like them, so they assumed I would not like them since I was a foreigner like him. I later discovered that they could not distinguish between our two foreign accents and thought that my nation, the United States, was a part of his. They also believed for a long time that we were brother and sister, but I did not know that then.

After supper, I was shown how to get into and out of a Yucatec hammock, which I practiced amid howls of laughter. Then the enamel-ware chamber pot was introduced, the trip to the back garden not being advisable after dark. They explained to me with straight faces that the chamber pot is called *el radio* because it broadcasts the news of what is being done—loudly! We all burst into laughter. The conversation continued, but I was having to work harder and harder to keep my fatigue from showing. Finally, the grandmother shooed everyone else out of the room and lit a candle *"para acompañarle en la oscuridad, tan lejos de su casa"* (to keep you company, in the dark, so far from your home).

After everyone retired, I began to notice large black things with wings fluttering slowly, now and then, around the ceiling. Too tired to get up or even call anyone, I lay there reasoning with myself that if these bats bit people, someone would have warned me. At breakfast I finally asked if the bats bit. After some discussion concerning what I meant, everyone began to laugh. The creatures I had seen were not bats at all but large black moths, moths that announce the coming of the rains. Since this is an agricultural village dependent on rainfall to feed the community, the return of the moths is an anxiously awaited event, one greeted with great joy. My apprehension concerning them contrasted so strongly with Maya feelings for these harbingers of the blessed rains that the difference provoked a mood of hilarity. This was my first lesson concerning the intimacy of Maya relationships with the local ecosystem.

Refreshed by a good night's sleep, I took a closer look at my new surroundings. "My" house was somewhat more prestigious than the average in that it was larger, had four rooms and square corners, rather than the rounded ones of the more typical, one-room Maya houses (see Figures 1.3 and 1.4; Wilk 1984; Wilk and Ashmore 1988). It was near the center of town, adding to its prestige. The two front rooms each had one door and one window opening onto the street. These were normally left open except at night or when no one was home. Each front room was connected by a door to a back room; each of which had an outside door to the back yard.

The house was constructed of uncut stones and concrete. My front room had a tile floor, my back one a concrete one. Roofing over the front rooms of the house was a deeply corrugated asbestos fiber, but over the back rooms the roofing was cardboard, waterproofed with a tar-like substance. These new types of roofing are thought by many villagers to be superior to the traditional thatch in that they do not harbor insects or snakes—and they "look modern." However, everyone agrees that the houses with thatched roofs are much more comfortable on hot days.[2] This was my first lesson in the ambivalence of the community concerning modernization.

Both front rooms had chairs, benches, and wardrobes, all arranged along the walls. Normally they both would have had family altars and photographs as well, but these had been removed from my room and stored in the wardrobes. At night, hammocks were normally stretched across the front rooms in a zigzag fashion for family members. The back rooms functioned as guest bedrooms, storage rooms, and dining rooms during inclement weather. The back room on the parents' side also had become a kitchen, since the new stove could not be properly protected in the traditional, three-sided kitchen shelter behind the house. The back rooms each had one door and one window facing the double house yards, divided by a cement-block wall, that became a pole fence farther into the yard. Just outside the backdoor were two cement *pilas*, square water tanks a little more than a yard high and square, covered with metal roofing. Spigots were turned on early in the morning and the water was saved for the rest of the day; the village system was usually out of water by noon during the dry season.

Beyond the grandmother's *pila* was the original communal kitchen—a rustic, three-sided, roofed enclosure with a large table, benches, a hearth, and a storage area for firewood and for lime to soak corn. The grandmother normally cooked there, when she was home. My rent payments eventually helped buy her a new gas cooking stove, which was moved into her back room. However, gas is expensive and in 1986 the grandparents were still collecting *leña*, deadwood from the forest, saving the cookstove for special occasions.

Figure 1.3
Plan of a Traditional Maya House

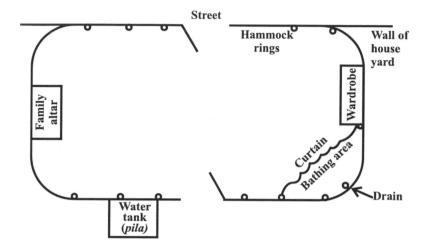

Figure 1.4
Plan of My First Home in Pich

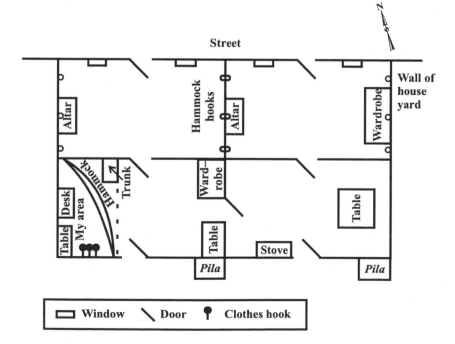

By 1992, age had weakened the grandparents and the grandchildren had grown bigger. Men of the family who ate often in the house had begun delivering piles of *leña* from their work in the forest. Sometimes they worked digging up stones and loading them on trucks; other times they worked on their traditional corn-fields; and there were days when they were hired to repair fences or do other jobs for the *ricos*, the relatively rich men in the village who owned private land with cattle pastures.

In 1985–1986, two of the sons-in-law of my host family were the workers of Don Milo, one of the wealthy *patrones*, who were sponsors, landlords, and bosses of their own relatives and neighbors. Unlike the typical *patrones* in other regions of Mexico, these *ricos* are members of the community and work alongside those they hire. My entire adopted family always spoke well of Don Milo and his family, comparing them favorably with the other *patrones* who "would not give a man the day off to go to his father's funeral!" They appreciated the opportunity to work for him for wages, even though it interfered at times with the planting and care of their own crops. They also enjoyed the fiestas he sponsored on holidays and the loans he made available during crises. Don Milo had died by the time I returned in 1990, but his sons had taken over the family lands, and by 1992 his half-brother had come back to the village and bought land for a private ranch of his own.

FAMILY, FRIENDS, AND NEIGHBORS

In November, after I had had the grandparents' rooms to myself for several months, the grandfather's job as a night watchman on a construction site ended and he and his wife returned home. This, at any rate, was the reason I was given. I suspect that their return may have been at least partly precipitated by tensions between their son's family and me. The initial period of careful, mutual politeness was clearly over. We had had some major disagreements over the use of my camera (the only one in the village) and over my contacts with other families. We were clearly having problems adjusting our mutual expectations. We shared somewhat veiled expressions of relief that Don Pablo and Doña María were coming home.

Don Pablo and Doña María's arrival required major adjustments in my living arrangements, of course. What had been my living room became our living room, as well as their bedroom. What had been my bedroom became divided. I was given about a third of the space, screened off with feed sacks on a wooden frame. This gave me a private area in which to hang my hammock at night; a place under one end of the hammock for my chair and table, for writing field notes; and one under the other end for my two trunks. In the remaining two-thirds of the room, the new gas stove was moved under the back window and a small table and chairs provided a place for us to eat, one or two at a time. We often ate in the outdoor kitchen, particularly when there were many visitors.

Once the grandparents returned, the house was always full of people. Besides their son's family in the adjoining rooms, three daughters with their husbands and children lived in the village. The adult children, the grand-children, and assorted other relatives often joined us for meals. One of the grandparents' nephews and an adult grandson found work in Pich during the six-month dry season and moved in with us, as their parents lived elsewhere. We all took turns using the concrete-block bath house and the "squatting" area. Evenings became more social than they had previously been, as the entire extended family gathered to visit (see Figure 1.5 for a kinship chart of the family).

The return of the grandparents provided me with new understandings of traditional, extended family life and the changes that were affecting it. I learned that all the women of childbearing age were using family planning methods supplied by the local government clinic. For young women, the desired number of children had become two or three. The grandmothers agreed, because of the lack of land and the expense of education. Alcohol abuse among the men was said to be increasing with each generation. In one family I knew well, among the grandfathers and their brothers, only two out of eleven had had serious alcohol problems; of their sons and sons-in-law, four out of ten were said to be problem drinkers; of those grandsons who had reached their late teens or early twenties, six out of twelve had a similar reputation. Before the paved road came, problems with alcohol were said to have been very rare because there were "not enough pennies to buy it."

Despite my own discomfort with the drinking behavior of some of the men, I greatly enjoyed becoming a fuller participant in the extended family. The grandparents were also very astute consultants, discretely assisting my bumbling efforts without injuring my ego, which had grown more sensitive than usual under fieldwork conditions. I greatly appreciated their help. However, the lack of both privacy and quiet for writing field notes became increasingly burdensome.

COMMUNITY DIVISIONS

My living arrangements were probably typical of those of the top third of Pichuleños but definitely inferior to those of the top five extended families—the *ricos*—who had televisions, tape-recorders, trucks, refrigerators, blenders, and other modern conveniences bought with the money they had made by cutting and selling the tropical hardwoods in the approximately 143,000 acres of communally owned forest lands. The traditional ethic had been that anyone in the community could take wood from public lands. But this wood had been

Figure 1.5
Kinship Chart for Adopted Family for 1986

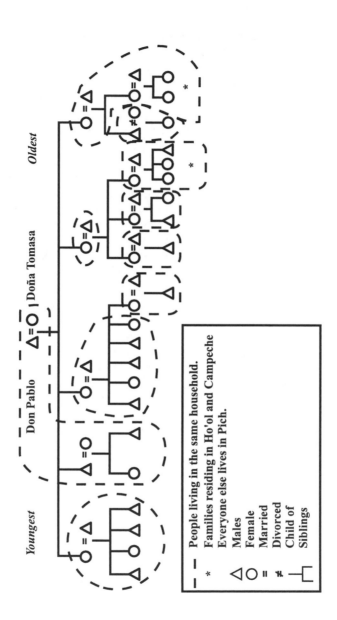

Note: In 1986 there were 5 children, 23 grandchildren and 10 great-grandchildren.

for personal use, not for a market. When the paved highway came twenty years before (in the 1960s), there was an expanding market for the logs.

The conversion of communal resources to private wealth had resulted in a new division within the community. Resentments were initially hidden because the entrepreneurs paid cash wages to their neighbors and relatives to cut and transport logs from the communal lands and to tend beehives, plant orchards, and build fences for cattle pastures on their newly acquired parcels of private land. These were new opportunities to earn money and were less dangerous than working as a *chiclero,* which some of the men had done earlier. *Chiclero* work involved gathering the tree sap originally used for commercial chewing gum manufacture. The men were taken by plane to distant areas of high forest, where they were left for months to gather *chicle.* Grandfather had been a *chiclero* and had been badly injured in a fall from a tall *chicle-zapote* tree, after which he was unable to do hard manual labor. He now repairs hammocks to earn cash.

Others with whom I talked in 1985–1986 were less dependent on and more critical of the rich *patrones*, explaining the debt-for-alcohol process whereby a man's social drinking creates a need for cash and a dependency on wage labor, which then takes time away from his own independent farming. Another perspective on the situation, explained to me by several of the men, was that the weather had become more unpredictable and their own crops often failed, making it more important to earn money to buy food. Some of the elders opined that the weather had changed because too much forest had been cut, whereas others said that these were the excuses of drunkards who simply wanted cash to buy more alcohol. Perhaps the stress caused by weather change had resulted in an increase in drinking, in the use of alcohol as an emotional anesthetic. For some, alcohol had become a *vicio* (an addiction) creating a constant need for cash.

Eventually I moved to one of the guest rooms behind the Presbyterian Church, where I had some privacy and quiet. I continued contact with my original family, who were Catholic. I cooked my own meals on my Coleman stove most of the time, but I visited my "grandparents," Doña María and Don Pablo, nearly every evening for hot chocolate or coffee and cookies. We would visit socially until it was time for bed, when I would return home using my big flashlight. I also hired Rosaura, the nineteen-year-old granddaughter of the family as my "assistant." She was unmarried and studying in the adult education program in order to finish elementary school. Years before she had left school because she could not see well enough to read, but a government program had recently provided her with glasses. Rosaura helped with laundry, cleaning, marketing, and—most importantly—accompanied me into the fields with her young siblings and cousins so that I could study farming techniques once the agricultural season began. Without such company, it would have been considered most scandalous for me to go out in the fields with the men!

The various churches were the focus of the major social divisions within the community. My search for housing had created a situation where I could maintain good relationships simultaneously with the two major religious groups. After I moved into my new quarters in March, I began attending Presbyterian services, but I continued to attend Mass both in Pich and occasionally in the hamlets, accompanying the parish priest from Spain on some of his rounds in his pickup truck, taking pictures and talking to him about Spain, Catholicism, Mexico, and the Maya. I sometimes attended the women's meetings and prayer groups of the Presbyterians, as well as their adult Sunday school. I knew the village Pentecostalists less well, but I did attend four services of one of their churches and accompanied them on a picnic in the woods.

The Catholics were involved in farming, cattle ranching, beekeeping, and lumbering. They included the five families of *ricos* and the poor who worked for them, as well as some independent farmers, store owners, and others. The Presbyterians and the Pentecostalists tended to be less involved in traditional agriculture and more involved in commercial activities that were independent of the "*ricos*." Presbyterians were the leaders in the mechanization of agriculture on communal land. The founder of the Presbyterian church also established the first and only village pharmacy in his livingroom; this carried many commercial medicines not available in the government-supplied clinic. These medicines were "prescribed" to customers on the basis of advice from a daughter who was a nurse in Mérida. A widowed daughter managed the large store with the telephone and had learned to help customers make long-distance calls—a tricky business in this part of the world. Another Presbyterian family started a successful bakery. Presbyterians were also in the forefront in sending their children to middle school, high school, and technical schools. The Pentecostalists were heavily involved in commerce: owners of small stores and truckers of factory-made items. Both groups of Protestants were less involved than the Catholics in traditional forms of food production and health care, although a few of them would still call on the *h-men* (traditional Maya ritual expert) to treat a sickness that the doctor could not cure or to end a prolonged drought.

I was unaware of the activities of the *h-men* until February, when I was asked to accompany the grandmother, mother, and daughter of "my family" to seek medical advice concerning the daughter (Faust, forthcoming). Previous efforts to obtain a cure from the modern medical clinics provided by the government had failed. The local *h-men*, Don Pedro, held healing ceremonies and rain ceremonies, made predictions concerning the future, counseled families, settled disputes, and prescribed herbal treatments for various illnesses. After our initial introduction in February, I visited him about once a week, observing his curing techniques and talking to him about Maya traditions and ceremonies. He was very interested in my recording the old ways, having become concerned that they might be largely lost before the next generation realized their importance and began to appreciate them.

My interaction with him eventually included his treating me for some lingering problems with digestion, which had followed a month-long bout with paratyphoid. The paratyphoid had been treated with pharmaceuticals prescribed by city doctors. Don Pedro scolded me for not having come back to be treated by him. He blamed my continuing discomforts on the "strong medicines" that had been given to me. His treatment of these lingering problems included head-to-foot massage with pressure from binding with cloths. The binding pressure lasted approximately one minute in each place, beginning with a cloth placed horizontally around my head, just above my eyes. Then my shoulders were bound, my hips, my knees, and my feet. Then I was given an abdominal massage to replace my *tip'te* (which I believe to be a pulsating part of the intestines) beneath the *cirio* (belly button). It was explained to me that the *tip'te* is a very important organ, which often is dislodged from its proper place by the contractions of diarrhea or childbirth. This dislodgment results in symptoms like mine, which will disappear when the *tip'te* is put back where it belongs. The treatment was successful. After that I went to him with stress-related problems (sleeplessness, tension headaches, diarrhea, and gas) following a very frightening interrogation by immigration officials which followed my repeated request for permission to do research in the Guatemalan refugee camp. Don Pedro prescribed a liquid medicine to be swallowed at bed time for these symptoms; however, in 1986 I felt an insurmountable emotional resistance to taking the medication he had prepared for me. It was one thing to study these ideas as the folklore of another culture; it was another matter to swallow them. I lied to him, telling him that I had taken it and was better, because I could not bear to admit that I did not trust his knowledge that much! In 1992, however, I happily swallowed a medicine he made for me to cure a severe attack of dysentery accompanied by a fever. I feared this might be the beginnings of cholera, which was epidemic in Campeche that summer (and for which the vaccine I had taken was said to be only fifty percent effective). It never even occurred to me to go first to the village clinic or to the doctors in the city, although I am sure I would have eventually gone to them had I not recovered quickly.

GAINING TRUST AND LEARNING TO TRUST

Generally trust came slowly on both sides of this fieldwork experience, but there were some sudden changes. Village trust of me had reached a low point after immigration officials took me off the bus in the center of town the first week in December 1985. My son's Christmas visit came only a few weeks later. His presence seemed to reassure most people that I was a regular person and not a spy. I had shown them all pictures of my son and other family members, but pictures are not quite the same as a personal visit. My son played baseball with the men and boys, shot off firecrackers with them in the plaza, and became very popular at piñata parties because of his great height. They found it difficult to believe that a boy who was five feet, eight inches tall was only thirteen years old.

I gained even more credibility in the eyes of Pichuleños when I brought three of my students to the field with me in 1990, training them to write down the kinds of information I had collected. However, Pichuleños sometimes told my students, in response to their questions, "Doña Betty already knows that. She already wrote it down." They were sharing in the responsibility of teaching my students what did and did not still need to be done.

The students stayed with me in the guest rooms of the Presbyterian Church; however, I did not attempt to cook for them and myself. I brought them "home" to Doña María for meals. And I took one who suffers from a chronic back problem to Don Pedro for twice-weekly massages, which gave the student great relief.

While Doña María and Don Pablo helped me and my students in many ways, I also learned a great deal from other elders in the community. Collectively, over the years, the elders have seen a lot of changes and had time to reflect on them. Two of the elders I interviewed were modernizers, two were quite traditional; others were in between. One was reputed to be the richest man in town; another was said to be the most traditional. Although their grandparents had considered themselves equals, according to village oral history, these two men were seen as belonging to different classes in 1985. Maya ideology of equality can mask considerable economic differences, but in the case of Pich the differentiation appears to have gone beyond the point where it can be masked by ideology.

I interviewed Don Ramón, often mentioned as the most powerful person in the village. He made his initial profits in lumbering and invested some of them in a large herd of cattle and in private land, as other early lumber entrepreneurs did also. He then diversified his investments by adding a bus service, picking up and dropping off passengers at all the villages and hamlets during a daily round-trip, which left the village at 5:30 A.M. and delivered passengers to Campeche by 7:45. It left the city for its return trip at 2:00 P.M., arriving at the village by 4:30. His profits on the bus service were somewhat reduced in 1982, when the village added a communally owned bus system, although by 1985 the newly arrived Guatemalan refugees provided plenty of passengers for both. By the summer of 1992, there were five buses carrying people from Pich to Campeche and back. Don Ramón's original bus had a reduced clientele owing to an accident the year before. It also was competing with the communal bus, a new bus owned by the Cherres', and one bus each from two settlements of Guatemala refugees (Quetzal Edzná and its extension, Los Laureles).

I also interviewed the *patrón* of my family, Don Milo. Although a successful village entrepreneur, most of his money had come from agriculture, not lumbering, so he was not usually counted among the "*ricos*." He and his family often invited me for family celebrations, to which they also invited the Catholic priest, my family, and other families of their workers. I was very sad to discover, when I returned with my students in the summer of 1990, that this *patrón* had died. His adult sons were trying to fill his role in the community, and one of them was then acting mayor, while the elected mayor was out of town (a common response of local mayors to wide-spread protest provoked by an unpopular decision).

Another interviewee, Don Genaro, the founder of the local Presbyterian church, was not one of the original lumber entrepreneurs either, but had been strongly upwardly mobile as a tailor, store owner, and farmer. He was considered one of the important elders of the village (although not one of the "*ricos*") and had helped sponsor the man who was elected mayor in December 1985. He had founded the church after hearing a Presbyterian missionary preach in Campeche, back in the 1950s. Since this was before the paved road and the trucks, he organized local men to construct a landing strip so the missionaries could fly into the village to teach this "new religion."

I also interviewed Don Pablo and Doña Benita, the parents of the wife of Don Milo, my family's *patrón*. Other wives had been too busy with grandchildren and cooking to be interviewed. It may also be that my personal connections with this family were stronger, I had previously become acquainted with Doña Benita while I was attending family novenas for the Virgin, Mass, and fiestas for the saints.

Don Pablo had made a great deal of money lumbering, according to village talk. He had bought private land and cattle and turned them over to his son. His daughter-in-law had recently left the village, taking the grandchildren to Campeche and his son would not listen to him. Despite his success, both he and his wife were sad and commented at some length on how life has become worse with modernization.

Don Pablo and Doña Benita's comments contrasted sharply with those of Don Tacho, who was probably the most determinedly traditional farmer in the village (despite owning a television set). He was also suspicious of all organized religion and did not attend any church. He was not a wealthy man by modern standards, but he served a term as mayor and was widely respected. He was the only person I knew who still kept native bees in hollow logs behind his house, something once done by everyone. He was very happy with the independence and financial security that traditional farming had provided for him and his immediate family and was continuing to provide for his married sons and grandchildren. He had to keep lecturing his sons to keep them from being tempted by the false illusions of modernization and alcohol, but he was succeeding. He had bought a small herd of cattle, of which he was quite proud.

The vast majority of my data came from conversations with village elders, with the *h-men*, and with my adopted family. These people were willing to accept the burden of teaching me in greater depth than the other villagers. They were willing to spend more time sharing their accumulated knowledge and their perceptions of the meaning of the changes they have experienced. They told me these things in part because, "Our own children won't listen to us any more. But someday they may realize they are making a mistake and then they will need to know these things our parents taught us. It is good that you write it down so it doesn't get lost." Others thought that what I was doing was a waste of time. Some found my presence in the village irritating; some were angry that I did not bring presents for them or take photographs of their children, when I did so for others. There are probably some who still think of me as a spy or as a crazy *gringa*. More than anything else I have done, I suspect it was bringing my students with me that has finally given me validity, a recognizable social status, that of "teacher." "Anthropologist" was incomprehensible to them, try as I might to explain what the term means and what it was that I write and why. They now tell visitors that I am writing their history and that I am a teacher.

Those who are regularly involved in bringing outside information into a traditional community are often referred to as "culture brokers." Among these, I interviewed a traditional midwife who had been trained in a government program (Faust 1988), the owner of a store that is the primary competition for Don Genaro's, and the village healer who traveled frequently and was from Mayapán, Yucatán. In addition to these people, I had regular conversations with the owner of another store in the village market where I often went for soft drinks, with the woman who ran the *puesto* (a kitchen with a few stools in front where simple meals could be purchased) next to his store, with the village clerk, and with all the people in my extended family who lived in the village. I spent several days in the homes of one married daughter and one married granddaughter, who lived in Campeche and Ho'ol respectively. I kept field notes of many of these conversations and a daily field journal of observations.

Beyond these sources, some of my understanding of the community came through friendships with government employees living in Pich. One of the Maya agricultural experts from Mérida became a friend, as did several of the teachers with the national government's Cultural Mission. They sometimes teased me about visiting the *h-men*, although several of these formally educated government experts spoke Maya as a childhood language. The priest also teased me about talking to the "witchdoctor," although he knew it was important "for collecting folklore." One of the sons of a store owner was getting his Master's degree in Sociology in Mérida. All of these various culture brokers shared with me their perceptions and analyses of the traditions and recent changes in Maya villages, as did many professionals in Campeche who had worked in Maya villages for various government agencies. I, in turn, shared some of my general perceptions and puzzlements with them (although I did not discuss specifics about individual families). By talking with these culture brokers in the village and the city, I informally gathered information from a "vertical slice" of Campeche society, following Laura Nader's recommendations to study "up the power structure" as well as down it. City friends included a group of medical doctors who published their own poetry journal, a journalist, a couple of politicians, a restaurant owner who had been born in a Maya village, a hotel owner from an old city family, a pediatrician of Maya descent, a woman painter from Uruguay, a woman social worker, and the director and staff of the university's research center, the Centro de Investigaciones Históricas y Sociales. The Spanish priest, who lived in Bonfil and gave Mass in Pich, was another source of assistance in understanding the village. Each of these people had his or her own points of view concerning Maya culture, the culture of Campeche, the local processes of modernization, the local effects of international politics, and other topics.

While discussions with all of these people benefited my understanding of Pich, an invitation from the sixth-grade teachers to accompany the class to Uxmal provided an experience that greatly clarified my understanding of the relations between Maya identity and the dominant society.

LESSONS FROM THE SIXTH GRADERS' VISIT TO UXMAL

It was the Day of the Child in Mexico, and the sixth-graders were graduating that month, June 1986. Their teachers had arranged a field trip to the archeological site of Uxmal, a magnificent ruined city originally built by the students' ancestors during the Late Classic/Early Postclassic period of Maya civilization (A.D. 900–1200).

After a full day at the ruins, the children patiently lined up and waited to see the evening spectacle, "The Sound and Light Show at Uxmal." I watched in fury as Mexican tourists of status and education pushed in front of them. Today's urbane adult visitors seemed to view themselves as the heirs of Spanish conquerors that should not have to wait in line behind "uncivilized" native children in order to view the ruins of ancient Maya civilization—behind children who are the heirs of the same Maya who built the city.

When I objected to the tourists' pushing, one of the men graciously invited me, a white foreigner, to join the elite adults at the entrance. As politely as I could manage, I said, "The children were here first, let them go first." I was ignored, equally politely—as though I had just been flatulent in public!

Earlier that day, the manager of a hotel near the ruins had been reluctant to allow the Maya children to swim in either of his two pools during off season. I had insisted on speaking with him when the clerk initially refused my request. The manager did not allow me to talk to him in his office, but rather from the telephone on the registration counter of the hotel. I offered to pay "a consideration," if he would allow the children the privilege of swimming, pleading that it was Children's Day, arguing that the hotel allowed other non-guests to swim for a fee, insisting that these children's ancestors had built the ruins that attracted the foreign and Mexican tourists who stayed in this hotel. Eventually I lost all sense of my place as a foreigner, a guest of the country, and threatened to bring this situation of "racial prejudice" to the attention of the governor of Campeche and the local office of tourism. The manager's reply was a shocked denial that anything he did had to do with racial prejudice. That, he insisted, was a typical problem in the United States, not here in Mexico. Here, he continued, the problem was one of not being civilized. Peasants were simply not civilized. Clearly not, because they lived in the country! I stood there aghast. Since my own mother grew up on a family farm in Oklahoma and my grandmother was born in a log cabin, I found this reasoning rather offensive. So I said nothing.

The manager continued in a more patient tone, explaining his reasons for denying access to the pool, to wit: (1) these children of course would not know how to swim; (2) they certainly would not have bathing suits; (3) they are dirty and would make the pool dirty; and (4) they would make noise and disturb people. Clearly, according to him, I had failed to comprehend the local situation. I informed him that I had already lived in the village with these children for nearly a year. I was sure that they would not make noise and were very clean, as all Maya villagers bathe at least once a day. Many of the children already knew how to swim. As for the question of bathing suits, many had them and those who did not had brought clean clothes in which to swim. All had come prepared since I had offered to pay the fee so that they could swim. I promised that I personally would help their teachers supervise them, making sure that those who did not know how to swim would stay in the shallow end of the pool. While I continued arguing with the manager on the hotel's telephone, the teachers had the children sitting on the steps leading to the front door of the hotel. None of us gave any indication that we would leave the hotel any time soon, and in fact we had nothing to do until dark when the "Sound and Light Show" in the archeological site would begin.

We were finally given permission to enter the pool, and the offer of money to make up for the inconvenience was rejected. Our stay in the water was a deliciously refreshing break from the humid heat of mid-afternoon in the tropics. I tipped the janitor generously for the extra work he would have cleaning the two changing rooms and the bathrooms used. I also had helped the teachers supervise the children in these rooms and knew there was very little extra work. In final triumph we left as we had come, quietly. All the children enjoyed the pool experience very much.

There was little doubt that I was seen by the hotel manager as an intruder, an "Ugly American," disrespectful of the local ways of doing things, ignorant of proper behavior, of what was frequently described to me as "our situation" by apologetic local elites, who insisted that the Maya have to be treated this way because, according to them, they are "not civilized."

My sense of personal outrage over my perceptions of social injustice clearly had overcome my professional commitment to cultural relativism and noninterference. This was not an isolated incident. I was very much concerned that my actions might be interpreted as violating the Mexican government's prohibitions concerning foreigners involving themselves in Mexican politics. I also recognized throughout the year that my concern as to the villagers' welfare was shared by many government officials. Nevertheless, I was continually frightened that whatever statements I made or actions I took on behalf of the village and its people would be interpreted as meddling.

On two levels I found it imperative to run the risks involved, despite my fears. On a personal level, I could not deny my support to those whose lives I shared. On a professional level, I owed the Pichuleños a debt. They had freely given me information for my fieldwork, and I had an obligation to help them in return. Not to contribute to their efforts to "defend ourselves" (*defendernos*) was to set myself apart from the "collective enterprise of survival" (see Farriss 1984), to announce that I did not personally consider myself in solidarity with them. They saw active involvement as necessary to participation in the community, and they connected it with communal sharing of information.

After our return from Uxmal, news of my telephone argument with the hotel manager quickly flowed through the village. Resentment softened among some of the other school teachers, who had repeatedly taken me to task in local stores, the park, and other public places over such things as American race relations, the Vietnam War, United States interference in Nicaragua, the "stealing" of one-half of Mexico's national territory by "your country," the martyrdom of the Heroic Children (*Niños Héroes*) who defended Chapultepec in the Mexican-American War, and so forth. They had previously sent village children to my home with the assignment of asking me to make them a map showing the parts of the United States that had been "stolen from Mexico."

After the incident with the school children at the hotel swimming pool, I was increasingly seen by villagers as an ally. I was asked repeatedly to intercede for them with government officials. I had to inform them repeatedly that since I was from somewhere else I could not directly represent them in any visit to the political authorities in Campeche, but I would do whatever I could to help in unofficial ways. During this period, I was aware that people were increasingly open to me, anxious to tell me more about their struggles with the world outside, beyond the village. My last three months were spent torn between listening, writing as much as I could as quickly as possible, and trying to help without overstepping my bounds as a foreigner. Some of the city elite welcomed, helped, encouraged, and respected my efforts on behalf of the village. Others of the city elite told me in no uncertain terms to mind my own business.

My understanding of the villagers of Pich and theirs of me evolved through a number of phases: initial curiosity and efforts to please, testing limits of generosity, fear, worries about being taken advantage of, frustration with cross-cultural communication, suspicions of manipulation, guarded expressions of anger, sudden insights that cleared up fears, worries about possible betrayals of trust, moments of intense closeness and affection, doubts whether one's feelings were reciprocated, the increased trust following the trip to Uxmal, a last month of awkwardness and anxiety concerning my impending departure, and the final days of grief for the separation from intimate relationships built painfully and slowly over sixteen months.

I have returned to Pich many times since then: I came for a triumphant one-day visit in April 1989, when I delivered a copy of my dissertation to the village archives. I came for the month of August 1990 with three of my students; for six weeks in the summer of 1992 to record the *h-men*'s knowledge of herbal medicines; for the month of August 1993 with one student; and spent several days in December 1993. Since September of 1994 (when I began a research position in Mérida), I have made eleven visits of four-to-five days each. Each time I have come back, we have discovered new layers of misunderstanding, reviewed past misconceptions, recalled nostalgically the first days of our relationship, laughed at each other and ourselves as we grow old, marveled at the growth of children, grieved for those who have gone *más allá del sol* (beyond the sun), and shared our fears and our hopes about industrial progress and modernization.

The hope of Pichuleños is that modernization will allow them to escape the repression and exploitation they have suffered as Maya, as a colonized people. Their fears are similar to those of some of our biologists and ecologists: that modern, industrial civilization is hurting human families, climate, agriculture, and forests. The elders have an additional fear: their adult children and grandchildren will give up Maya identity in order to escape poverty. The motivation of younger generations is somewhat similar to that of many Okies and Arkies in the 1930s who fled rural poverty for the Golden West, disowning their roots. The consequences for the Maya, however, are far more serious. The world is losing an oral tradition in which is encoded some of the knowledge of an ancient, pre-Columbian civilization, long thought to have been destroyed completely by the sixteenth-century Spanish Conquest.

COMMUNICATION, DISCRIMINATION, AND PROGRESS

It is curious that the same elite who treat the Maya with disdain celebrate the triumphs of Aztec civilization and its contributions to Mexican national culture in their parades and school performances. Part of the difference in attitude stems from early portrayals of Maya civilization as having ended in the ninth century and of later Maya as degenerates (see Wilk 1984). Recent research has made clear the strong continuities in ritual practices and symbols (Hunt 1977; Bricker 1981; D. Tedlock 1985; Love 1986; Gossen 1986a, 1986b; Earle

1986–1987; Faust 1988a; Hanks and Rice 1990; Freidel, Schele, and Parker 1993); agricultural practices (G.D. Jones 1977, 1982; Pohl and Feldman 1982; Faust 1988a); water management (Faust 1988a; Faust and Morales López 1993); and political organization (Jones 1982; Farriss 1984; Restall 1995).

One of the greatest tragedies in the Campechano elite's disdain for living Maya culture is adoption of their attitude by many persons of Maya descent. The young adults have been to school and learned not to listen to the elders. However, it is not just school teachers who discourage Maya children from learning Maya traditions. There is a political context that one encounters on entering the city or areas frequented by travelers. How the Maya are taught by the dominant culture to deny their identity became particularly clear to me during the visit to Uxmal. Public discourse and public behavior patterns made clear that being Maya is being not quite human and certainly is not being civilized. Under these circumstances many Maya stop identifying as Maya, and the larger Mexican society loses access to the wisdom of centuries stored in their oral traditions.

The problems of discrimination I encountered with the village children on their trip to Uxmal were evident during my later visits as well. Incidents of the same type have frequently been reported to me by village friends, who complain bitterly about the devaluation they suffer both outside the village and in interactions with some of the government experts sent to the village to help them modernize their agriculture and cattle ranching and to enforce measures to protect the forest and the wildlife. The irony of this "aid" is not lost on Maya elders, who know that the modernization of agriculture is what destroys the homes of deer, peccary, and turkeys. The Maya's recent lumbering practices can be improved; but, relative to the clear-cutting done in U.S. national parks, their practices have a minor impact. They have been doing select cutting of large tropical hardwoods; they could do more replanting. The practice of dragging logs to the logging road leaves deep scars in vegetation and soil. The logging roads themselves result in erosion of fragile, shallow soils. However, it is the federal government that sends in bulldozers to clear hundreds of acres of tropical forest for subsidized cattle raising and rice farming projects. Traditional hunting provided protein for families and was sustainable until outsiders came in with high-powered rifles, telescopic sights, and refrigerated trucks—in order to supply tourist restaurants in Mérida and Cancún. But it is the peasant who has his nineteenth-century rifle taken away by the government agent as a punishment for hunting for meat for his family.

Poor communication and abuses of power by some of the elite are probably the major impediments to government efforts to help the Maya and Maya efforts to defend themselves in the modern market system. The differences in power and legitimacy, connected with cultural traditions and "race," result in a communication short-circuit. The Maya are caught between their own population growth (which is slowing), a fragile tropical forest ecosystem, and the forces of the market, mediated by a political system that has historically derived part of its hegemony from devaluing Maya culture and knowledge. The resulting discrimination makes it difficult for the Maya to communicate effectively with policymakers concerning the negative effects of modernization on their communities and their resources. To question any aspect of modernization is to put one's self in the category of "*indio*," which is like being referred to as a "nigger" in the Alabama of the 1950s. Those who have mastered some aspects of the modern world do not wish to jeopardize their new status by identification with a pariah category. They dissociate themselves from their own grandparents and the traditional knowledge of how to save the forest. The result is that Pich is suffering a twentieth-century collapse: ecologically, economically, politically, and socially—a process often euphemistically referred to as "adjustment" by policymakers. The men of Pich have gone from being successful farmers (who regularly sold large surpluses to the city) to successful timber workers (supplying plywood factories and export companies) to digging up, breaking up, and transporting rocks for building supplies in the city. They are having difficulty feeding their families and are losing their hopes of buying new appliances: a blender, a stove, a refrigerator, a television set. The irony is that this is not a result of provincial ignorance, but of the replacement of Maya traditional knowledge with modern technological expertise. The rice projects have failed. Deforestation, or global warming, is adversely affecting rainfall patterns. Even traditional farming is failing two years out of three. The deer and peccary are hard to find and the wild turkey survives only in the forest commons, a six-hour drive south over a rough path cleared for lumber trucks.

The continuing *desprecio* (scorn) shown by most agents of modernity toward the traditional culture deepens an existing division in the village: the split between the traditionalists and the modernizers. The traditional elders repeatedly attempt to save the wisdom of the past and to adopt only those aspects of modernity that do not jeopardize the forest, the resource base and survival insurance of the village. When their attempts are ridiculed and development agents demand all-or-nothing responses, the community splits between those who choose the old versus those who choose the new. The "refusal to change" of traditional elders is often misinterpreted as an "innate" rejection thought to be "typical" of indigenous peoples or is seen as a resentment of the sixteenth-century Conquest. James C. Scott (1985) analyzes similar mechanisms of resistance as responses to and defenses against exploitation of peasants as a class. The age-old Spanish attitude toward peasants justified their exploitation and was combined in Campeche with a colonial attitude of racial fear intensified by the "Caste War" of the mid-1800s: the *indio* has to be kept under control and is not to be listened to with respect. Therefore, the knowledge the traditional elders have concerning local ecosystems is being lost.

Living Maya elders still have a pattern of sustainable interaction with the local ecology encoded in their everyday behavior. Their traditions once provided some protection of public resources needed for survival: water, soil, plants, and game animals. The protective mechanisms have included (1) ritual symbolism and religious prohibitions that reflect local ecological knowledge; (2) political organization making elite individuals accountable for the use of local resources and for the survival of the poor; and (3) mechanisms for testing new ideas and for perpetuating adaptations that prove sustainable.

Now that roads, televisions, radios, clinics, agricultural extension programs, development workers, and schools have penetrated these villages, the traditional institutions are failing to protect the resource base. While elders predict catastrophic long-term results, a generation of young parents is determinedly exhausting the community's resources to provide their children with a chance to make it in the city. They are protected by the larger political system, which encourages the individual entrepreneur. Now that the *ejido* land-owning system is being dismantled, the process should proceed even faster. Elders who seek to preserve a resource base for the poor, lands for communal hunting, and forest homes for the sacred beings are seen as ridiculous anachronisms.

In Pich, the Campeche Maya are turning their backs on the wisdom of their elders, on this tradition that perpetuates some of the knowledge of Classic and Postclassic Maya civilization. Television, schools, and rural development are destroying what their ancestors managed to preserve through the ninth-century Collapse, the "virgin-soil epidemics" of Contact (Bianchine and Russo 1995), the horrors of the Spanish Conquest, and five centuries of colonial domination (Crosby 1972, 1986). This loss is occurring even as present-day scientists read us the daily warning signs concerning accelerating degradation of the biosphere by the industrial civilization that these village Maya are struggling to join(e.g., Ledec and Goodland 1988:8–9; Botkin 1990; Munro 1991:30–31; Groombridge 1992:xvi–xvii; U.S. National Research Council 1992:32; Gibbons 1993:1–3; Heywood 1995:12–13; Ehrlich and Ehrlich 1996:242–244).

The traditional technologies the Maya maintained into this century may very well have evolved in response to their own ecological mistakes. Today many scholars interpret the Maya Collapse as a political and economic crisis rooted in an underlying environmental catastrophe—the result of escalating population growth and ever increasing techniques of intensification in food production and water management (e.g., Lowe 1985). Others attribute it to climate change (Folan et al. 1983; Gunn, Folan, and Robichaux 1994, Hodell, Curtis and Brenner 1995). It may have been a combination such as occurred recently in the Sahel where a recurring cycle of drought encountered an ecosystem weakened by modern agricultural exploitation (Bennett 1990:443; Lees and Bates 1990:251; Bates and Plog 1991:197–198).

David Sonnenfeld concluded his research on Mexico's "Green Revolution" with a reference to the "tropical-humid sector," which includes Campeche,

> In the tropical-humid sector, accumulation has been sustained by short-term "mining" of rainforest nutrients, obtained through burning while clearing the

> forest for intensive agriculture or cattle-ranching. Workers have not been sustained as colonization efforts fail. The tropical environment has not been sustained, as tropical moist forests have been destroyed faster than they can regenerate or are replanted. Cattle have destroyed vegetation and soils. Rain has washed away soils. (Sonnenfeld 1992:47)

He ends his evaluation of rural development throughout Mexico with a question,

> What is the possibility of the Mexican environment recovering from destruction?. . . Perhaps the fundamental question is whether Mexico's agricultural development strategy is reformable or if agriculture there must be reestablished on an entirely new basis. (Sonnenfeld 1992:47)

NOTES

1. The land of the village is divided in three categories, two of which are usually referred to as "the *ejido.*" The first of these is the official *ejido,* which is a legally granted area for agricultural use by the joint legal owners, the *ejiditarios,* who are limited in number and can give their position to only one heir. These owners have the legal authority to make decisions concerning the use of the common lands and they elect a *comisario* to represent them in dealings with government agents. The second is another type of communal land, the *ampliacion forestal,* a forest commons which legally is for the exclusive use of the *ejiditarios* but comes under the supervision of a government agency which can approve contracts with commercial loggers. The third type is privately owned land. Beyond the village there is also national land.

2. Air spaces in the thatch insulate and the light color reflects heat. The thatched roofs are constructed with vents under the peaks, which also permit a continuous flow of air as the hottest air rises and escapes. These would be my guesses as to why they are cooler. The fact that they are cooler is considered obvious by everyone.

Maya Cultural Heritage

Doña María gives water to her pig in a simple, hand-carved stone bowl that her father found in his cornfield. It is a little more than an inch thick and ten inches in diameter at the top. She considers it indestructible and therefore suitable to use for the pig, but its practicality does not overcome a sentimental connection with the Ancient Ones. The pig will eventually be "sacrificed" to celebrate a life-crisis ritual (wedding, baptism, or funeral) or a holiday visit by relatives or friends. Despite its destiny as food, the pig is treated with affection and respect. Despite the bowl's use to water the pig, it is also treated with affection and respect. It was rescued from the mud, carefully cleaned, and proudly presented for me to photograph—as a prized family possession. I was also asked to photograph the family in front of their new refrigerator—whose principal use is to store cold Coca-Cola and other soft drinks for sale to the neighbors and distribution to guests on special occasions.

Children are given general guidelines to follow concerning how to deal with ancient things, but learn to understand the connections with the past fully only as adults. Old potsherds can be played with, even used as slingshot ammunition; but you do not make noise in the woods or approach the ancient underground storage chambers (*chultunes*)[1] at noon, the sun's sacred hour. Because some of today's children have not learned respect, it has been necessary to seal up the entrances to the sacred cave in Pich, which is under the church and the elementary school.

Legend has it that the passages of the cave extend to the nearby archeological site of Edzná; to the port city of Campeche; and perhaps even to Uxmal, a major Maya city farther north. The cave is associated with spiritual forces and ancient times. Powerful spirits live there. During the War of the *Cruzob* (the "Caste War" of the 1840s) and the *Cristero* Rebellion (1920s), Pichuleños hid their saints in it to protect them from outsiders. Three green crosses are also said to have mysteriously appeared in the cave. They cannot be removed because they grow miraculously heavy whenever anyone attempts to move them. However, copies have been placed in the church, where they serve, collectively, as the patron saint of the community and its lands. It is rumored that there is a miraculous image of the Virgin in the cave, taken from the church and hidden very far down there during one of the wars; but she is less well remembered. When people have gone looking for her beyond the crosses, their torches and candles have blown out.

Today there is no sculptured image of the Virgin in the church, only a picture. A new statue of Saint Isidro, brought from Spain by the priest, joins the replicas of the three green crosses and an old wooden crucifix. A modernizing *Hermano* (friar)[2] is said to have stolen other old wooden saints from the church and sold them to art collectors. He is also credited with selling a "gold" bell that used to hang in the facade of the church. The bell had a beautiful sound that could be heard even in the farthest cornfields of the community.

The facade and nave of the church have been described by the Instituto Nacional de Antropología e Historia (INAH) as being in seventeenth-century style. The chancel may be older, perhaps having served as an open chapel, like the one at Dzibilchaltún (Folan 1970). The chancel is attached to the west wall of the roofless ruins of a Franciscan friary,[3] whose defensive, fortlike walls tower over the church. These structures have been stylistically dated by INAH to the sixteenth century. The church has been burned and rebuilt twice, according to community oral history. The friary serves no present-day purpose and thus has not been rebuilt. On cloudy nights, bats and ghosts are seen around its crumbling walls. On such nights, grandparents sometimes retell the stories they heard as children: stories of young women of Pich who were held prisoner in that friary, where they were sexually used by the friars and priests, their babies buried in the courtyard at night. The grandparents say that the reason they know this to be true is not only that their parents told them but also that they themselves saw the bones of babies, found in the 1940s by a man who decided to plant an orchard in part of the abandoned courtyard.

The old friary, the church, and many village sidewalks were constructed of cut stone taken from a large mound overlooking the village. From a distance, this mound appears to be just an arm of the limestone ridge that rises sharply to the south of the church and school, and I had lived in the village for months before anyone mentioned to me that it was a *montículo* (mound) with cut stones. I then asked my assistant, Rosaura, to take me to the top. She pointed out the white edges of cut stones that could be glimpsed here and there beneath branches and leaves. On the top of the mound was a government-constructed water tank, made out of stones and cement. Many of the stones in the tank were cut, like those I had been shown. Today, next to the water tank, the antenna for the village's cable television stands sentinel, an outpost of industrial civilization. All the cut stones have disappeared from the surface of the mound, only the ones used to construct the water tank are still visible. Friends tell me in confidence that someone has taken the rest of the stones to sell in Campeche, even though everyone knows that the law now prohibits such activities.

From certain places on the mound, one can look down over the village. On the far side (northeast) of the plaza is the *aguada*, an ancient Maya reservoir shaded with giant *pich* trees (*Enterolobium cyclocarpum*), for which the village is named. On the near side, at the base of the ridge that supports the mound is the church, whose east-west nave runs perpendicular to the north-south axis of the friary, to which it is attached on its eastern (chancel) end. The central plaza slopes steeply from the church to the *aguada* in wide, shade-speckled concrete terraces ending in benches that surround islands of different trees: slender, arching palms; spreading *flamboyanes* (*Delonix regia*) with their "flaming" orange blossoms; and the quieter beauty of the pink and white *flor de mayo* (*Plumeria rubra*). There are a number of ancient Maya archeological sites near Pich, including (1) the ruined city of Edzná (Matheny et al. 1983; G. F. Andrews 1969), (2) a small site called Tabasqueño (Morales López and Sumner-Faust 1986), and (3) the ancient city of Kampech (or Ah Kin Pech), which lies underneath Campeche.

The village of Pich is built on an ancient Maya settlement that dates at least to Late Classic times, and possibly even to the Preclassic. Surface shards found near the village center indicate Late Classic occupancy.[4] There are also a few mounds containing cut stones, a stone-lined reservoir with canal and wells, and ancient Maya stones incorporated in present-day construction. The large size of the old church and its attached ruined friary suggest that the area was densely inhabited by the Maya during the early years of the colony. The church and the friary were probably built very early in the seventeenth century with the labor of Maya converts and then used to further missionary work in this frontier area. There are no known resources other than "heathen souls" that would have attracted a Spanish presence to this region.

A LIVING, BUT HIDDEN, MAYA HERITAGE

In Pich today, Maya identity is often hidden from outsiders because of the treatment the Maya repeatedly suffer at the hands of Mexican elites. Maya language and culture are seen as making one vulnerable to discrimination—politically and economically—thereby endangering one's ability to *"defenderse"* (defend one's self and family). Consequently, villagers usually identify themselves to outsiders as *pobres* (poor people), *campesinos* (peasants), or *mexicanos* (Mexicans) rather than Maya. In public, Spanish is spoken nearly exclusively. A local variant of the Yucatec Mayan language is normally only spoken, even in private, by the grandparent generation. The *h-men* uses Mayan at home with his own family as well as for ritual prayers, for invoking Maya spiritual beings, and for consultations with his older patients.

The *h-men* and nearly all of the grandparents are fully bilingual and use Spanish in public in order to avoid possible ridicule and stigma.

Heirs of autonomous pre-Columbian metropolises, today's indigenous villages struggle under the control of Mexico's dominant culture. The Maya have an enduring culture, adapting to conquest, colonization, and new technologies while maintaining their own values and cultural identity. The term *Maya identity* as used here does not imply either homogeneity or stasis. Maya culture is continually adapting to historical circumstances and changing technologies as well as to the different ecosystems of the Maya area.

Research in archeology by K. V. Flannery (1976) and in ethnohistory by M. León-Portilla (1988) indicates that the social structure and religious practices of Mesoamerican villages formed the basis of urban Mesoamerican civilization. Therefore, the dismantling of city-states, empires and trade routes during colonial times need not be interpreted as entailing the loss of Maya cultural knowledge, the essentials of which were preserved in the villages.

Following the Conquest, these villages were the only form of social organization that retained some freedom from Spanish control and a significant connection with the pre-Columbian past. The complex technologies that supported the cities were lost, but in many areas those that served the needs of simple villages were retained. Conquest, colonization, and integration into the nations of Belize, El Salvador, Guatemala, Honduras and Mexico have strongly affected Maya culture in more recent centuries. A surprising continuity has been maintained; a continuity not recognized in the scholarly literature until recent decades, but now receiving increasing attention in ethnographic and historical research (Gossen 1986a:1–8; 1994; Kintz 1990:133–148; Freidel, Schele, and Parker 1993:11–14).

THE CAMPECHE VARIANT OF MAYA CULTURE

There are many variants of living Maya culture, generally categorized as either highland or lowland. The highlands are found in parts of Chiapas and western Guatemala. The lowlands are also divided into two parts: the drier northern area in Mexico's Yucatán (the region best known archeologically for its Postclassic cities) and the wetter southern area, which includes southern Campeche, eastern Chiapas, and the Petén of Guatemala (the region best known archeologically for its Classic cities). The village of Pich is located on the southern boundary of the northern area. To the south is a scattering of new hamlets and unpaved roads. Farther south, beyond the Valley of Edzná, in the high forest near the Guatemalan border, archaeologists are investigating the Classic Maya metropolis known as Calakmul.

Today's Pichuleños insist that the southern Campeche version of the Maya language has always been distinct—that it has differed in recognizable ways from the Yucatec Maya spoken in other parts of the peninsula. Pichuleños also describe their traditions as being different from those of the Maya to the east and the north (in the modern states of Yucatán and Quintana Roo).

The cultural values of the Maya underlie their various adaptations to different political and natural environments. These values are encoded in a symbolic system, that, in Pich, is quite open and loosely organized—when contrasted with the more closed and tightly organized systems described by J. Sosa (1986) for Yalcobá in the state of Yucatán and G. Gossen (1984) for San Juan Chamula in Chiapas.[5] These differences may result from different patterns of Spanish domination. The sparse population southeast of Campeche may have attracted less agricultural development and forced labor in the early years of colonialism than the northern area of Yucatán. Low population density may have resulted from greater problems with post-Conquest diseases since heavier rainfall and deeper soils form propitious habitat for disease-bearing mosquitoes.

The city of Campeche surrounds a port and was the commercial center for the western half of the peninsula until the end of the nineteenth century, when two other ports were built close to the rapidly growing henequen zone and the city of Mérida: first Sisal and later Progreso. Until the twentieth century, the principle export of Campeche was dyewood (*Haematoxylum campechianum*), hauled by draft animals and floated down canals for export to cloth manufacturers in Amsterdam, Barcelona, the Hague, Hamburg, Liverpool, New Orleans and New York (Vadillo López 1994:114–117). This region relied less heavily on exploitation of indigenous labor than did the sugar cane, cattle, and (later) henequen haciendas around Mérida, Valladolid, and some northern areas of Campeche, which were more densely populated. Dyewood exporters periodically registered official complaints concerning continual desertion by Maya workers, despite the relatively high wages they were paid and despite the device of loaning them money and then expecting them to work off the debt (Vadillo López 1994:69–82; Contreras Sánchez 1990:42–45). The implied resistance by Campeche-Maya workers is particularly impressive because cutting dyewood did not even compete with traditional agriculture; dyewood grows in damp areas which become inaccessible during the rainy season, when Maya farmers need to be home tending subsistence crops.

THE COLONIAL POPULATION

The natural ports of Campeche (Kampech) and Champotón (Chak'anputun) were part of the Putún-Acalán trade network during the sixteenth century (Scholes and Roys 1968; Villagutierre Soto-Mayor 1983; G. D. Jones 1982). Spanish colonists also profitted from coastal and ocean fishing, which did not depend on the physical control of large numbers of Maya villagers. Indeed. it appears to have been more cost-effective for Spanish colonists in Campeche to trade with interior Maya villagers for dyewood by offering merchandise on credit rather than trying to force them and their families to live on haciendas. In addition, except for the port city, southwestern Campeche was less healthy than the north. Tropical diseases introduced by African slaves brought to work on sugar plantations near the coast included amebic dysentery, hookworm, and malaria. These multiplied and became endemic in the tropical wetland environment of southwestern Campeche and Tabasco (Crosby 1972). The impact of these diseases drastically reduced the population, directly killing many and weakening the resistance of others to epidemics such as small pox and influenza, thereby reducing the population in those areas by ninety percent or more (Crosby 1972; Villaguetierre 1983; Scholes and Roys 1968; J. E. S. Thompson 1970). Clendinnen estimates that, for the Peninsula as a whole (most of which is drier and therefore freer of the wetland endemic diseases), the population at the time of the first smallpox epidemic was 800,000 and that at the end of the Conquest was only 250,000 (Clendinnen 1987:36). She also cautions that there are many different estimates of both the pre-Columbian and early colonial populations, due to difficulties in interpreting the historical accounts and the tribute lists.

Serious efforts to control the independent Maya villages inland from Champotón and Campeche did not get under way until the seventeenth century, when the remaining population began to grow. In 1604–1605 the Franciscan friars of Campeche established the Forest Missions (*Misiones de Montaña*) to serve the remaining scattered Maya settlements in this southwestern Gulf Coast area (Scholes and Roys 1968:251–290). Pich is not included under its present name in the list of Forest Missions, but the nearby abandoned site of Ca'uich is. Both the friary in Pich and the church in Ca'uich are sixteenth-century in style, indicating that the friary in Pich was probably part of this early chain of Forest Missions. Pich appears in the 1815 census as San Diego de Pich, the *cabecera* (administrtive center) of the surrounding region, a title it still holds. The total population of the region administered by Pich was reported in one place in this census as slightly over 2,000 and the population of the town of Pich to be 689 (Dumond and Dumond 1982:201; see Table 2.1). There is another reference to Pich in the census of 1815, which gives the total population as 2,601 (Table 2.2). It seems reasonable to assume that the latter figure refers to the total administrative unit, not just the town itself (Dumond and Dumond 1982:327), but there is no explanation of the earlier reference to "just over 2,000" for what appears to be the same large unit. It may be an error in the hand-copying of the colonial documents.

A TRADITION OF PEACE

The interior Campeche Maya were pulled into the economic, political, and religious life of the colony more gradually and in a less coercive manner than the northern Maya, who were conquered by the Montejos (father and son) in a long and bloody campaign during the sixteenth century. The Montejos formed an early alliance with the Maya of southern Campeche, who assisted them in some stages of the Conquest. The interior villages of Campeche, initially approached by the relatively peaceful Franciscans of the seventeenth century, had heard the stories of rebellion and defeat from fleeing northern Maya, and may have also remembered the defeats at the coastal cities of Campeche and Champotón in the early 1500s. Whatever their motives, the interior Campeche Maya in the seventeenth century began their involvement with European colonists primarily through negotiations with the Franciscans, who had considerably modified their behavior after the disciplining of their Bishop, Diego de Landa, in the 1560s and 1570s (Clendinnen 1987:112–128). Since that time, they have developed (1) expertise in negotiation for favorable terms; (2) patterns for avoidance of outsiders considered to be untrustworthy; and (3) flight to the forest to escape unacceptable treatment (Scholes and Roys 1968; Villagutierre 1983; Aranda 1985).

When the rebel *Cruzob* Maya from the east reached Campeche in 1847, many of the local Maya fled to their caves and forests. To this day they refer to the rebel Maya as "Indians who came burning the churches." When the rebels

Table 2.1.
Population of the Village of Pich in 1815

Caste (*sic.*)	Males	Females
Spanish and Mestizos	66	67
Indians (Maya)	205	240
Negroes and Mulattos	56	55

Source: 1815 Census of Campeche, in Dumond and Dumond 1982, p. 201.

Table 2.2.
Population of the District of Pich in 1815

Caste (*sic.*)	Males	Females
Spaniards and Mestizos	95	86
Indians (Maya)	1,047	1,150
Negroes and Mulattos	107	116

Source: From the 1815 Census of Campeche, in Dumond and Dumond, 1982, p. 201.

Note: The district appears to have included the towns of Tixmucuy, Bolonchén Ca'uich, Ca'uich, and Pich, as well as a number of ranchos in the area.

left, many local communities quickly signed truces with the Mexican troops who came through after them. The Campeche Maya today often describe their more eastern cousins of Yucatán and Quintana Roo as less peaceful, less intelligent, and less "civilized." The latter, in turn, characterize the Campeche Maya as cowards and traitors, and say that they are no longer really Maya at all. Whatever labels we use for their behavior patterns, the "peaceful" Maya of the interior of Campeche served initially as a buffer between the colonizing whites in Campeche and Mérida and the independent Maya forces to the south with headquarters at Lake Itzá in the Guatemalan Petén, until these were finally conquered in the late eighteenth century. In the late nineteenth and early twentieth century, there were peaceful but relatively independent Maya communities in the central and southern interior of the state that were in communication and trade with each other and those of Belize and Quintana Roo. These maintained some separation from the rebel headquarters of the *Cruzo'ob* Maya at Chan Santa Cruz (now Felipe Carrillo Puerto) and allied communities which continued in open defiance of the Mexican government until their military defeat in 1901 (D. E. Dummond 1977:103–138), after which they have only gradually become involved in government programs. The area between Pich and Quintana Roo appears empty on maps but according to oral tradition has always been inhabited by communities of Maya "living under the tropical canopy" (cf. Kintz 1990), away from control by the authorities in the cities, trading with both the *Cruzo'ob* and the "peaceful" Campeche-Maya .

Over the centuries since the Conquest, waves of outsiders periodically arrived looking for slaves, converts, dyewood, *chicle* (sap for chewing gum), tropical hardwoods, and labor for sugar and rice plantations. Even before the European Conquest, this was an area where outsiders arrived, bringing trade goods and politico-religious symbols from the Valley of Mexico. Peace and commerce have both evolved as strong cultural values; the city of Campeche is seen by local villagers as a center of trade, a place to buy and sell. The benefits and dangers of new technologies, tools, and manufactured goods continue to be considered and tested. They are not rejected for being foreign. Nonconfrontive strategies are preferred in political interactions with the dominant outsiders. Here, there is no general rejection of the new, although there is an intense aversion to being treated with disrespect.

There is a strong tendency to combine the new with the old, reminiscent of the pattern of "imbrication" in time sequences noted by Barbara Tedlock (1982) among the highland Maya: as one period of time ends it is understood to overlap and be partially integrated with the period which follows.[6] Thus, it is understood that the afternoon of one day is a preparation for and thus in a sense belongs to the day that will follow it, just as the final days of rainy season are mixed with the first days of the dry season; there is no clear boundary. Similarly, Pichuleños orient their new tractors to the path of the sun while planting the Sacred Corn. The traditionalists try to weave together the new and the old, attempting to improve production while following the environmental ethics that structure their interaction with the tropical forest. Many of the younger adults, however, are not interested in this task, preferring to simply adopt the new and forget the old, pursuing individual incorporation into the national, urban culture. They mine local resources to help their children struggle for acceptance and opportunities in the city. They are not concerned about preserving the forest. Those who wish to remain, including most of the elders, have two challenges: (1) to maintain an indigenous identity within a national one; and (2) to use *ejido* resources within a national and international economy, without destroying the resources that they perceive as belonging to future generations. Their efforts have largely failed in the face of government and market support for deforestation. That failure has been partly due to a general attitude of openness to change, and partly to lack of information about the long-term consequences of agricultural modernization in a tropical environment.

THE PRESENT-DAY POPULATION

The population of the village is experiencing considerable fluctuation. The 1981 census by the state government reported more than 3,000 inhabitants. When I arrived in 1985, the local medical clinic was completing a survey that indicated the population had fallen by nearly a half—to 1,564. By 1992, many of the young people had migrated to the city or to Chilam Balam, a new *ejido* to the south created by government bulldozers and credits for growing rice. The migration was also encouraged by internal pressures. Logging has been declining since the late 1970s and was stopped by a government agency in 1991, in order to protect the few remaining young trees. With a new federal government in power in 1995, the agency yielded to Pichuleños requests and logging was allowed to resume. Rising prices have made it worthwhile to haul the only remaining valuable hardwood, *guayacán (Tabebuia guayacan)*, from the most remote corner of the forest commons. Once the road is cleared, cutting of the softer *chakah (Bursera simaruba)* for plywood is also *rentable* (worth the costs in fuel, tires, and repairs to the trucks). While they are cutting these species, they check for tropical cedars (*Cedrela odorata*) that are legal size for cutting, taking any they find.

In the summer of 1992, I was not doing research on the village as a whole but collecting medicinal plants with the *h-men* and recording his knowledge about them. People told me, however, that there were now empty houses in Pich and that there were probably only 1,500 people in town on major holidays. Most of the adolescents I had known in 1985–1986 had migrated to the city or to Chilam Balam. They had gone because they were now married and raising children and so needed to go where they could earn money. A new group is now planning to start a community in the abandoned *ejido* of San Juan Cantemó, in the center of the *Ampliación Forestal* (the forest commons).

According to the 1981 census, the population of 3,000 had occupied 310 houses, eighty percent with one room, fifteen percent with two, five percent with three. This is a densely packed population, averaging a little less than 7.75 persons per room. Most homes were clustered in the center of town, distributed over thirty blocks (Figure 2.1). These categories of information were not collected in the 1985 survey. However, my search to find a house to rent revealed only four to be vacant. According to village talk, there had recently been a tendency for young couples to move into their own homes, rather than residing with either his parents (traditionally preferred) or hers. This trend could account for the scarcity of vacant houses despite the halving of the population. In 1995, young adults began to return from the cities. The national economic crisis reduced construction and other urban employment. Young men again planted corn with their fathers and grand-fathers, only to have their crops destroyed by hurricanes Opal and Roxanne. In 1997, many have planted three different times, waiting for the rains, watching the young corn die in the sun.

THE *EJIDO* LAND

During the period of study (1985–1996), the village held 69,560 hectares, or 171,813 acres (calculated at 2.47 acres to the hectare), as a type of "commons," under the national *ejido* system of Mexico, a form of collective land ownership with individual usufruct rights, based on indigenous customs. The term refers both to a village with such rights and to the land itself. Individuals have the right continuously to use plots in which they have invested labor. However, they may not sell, give or will them to anyone not a member of the community. The community ultimately has the right to make decisions concerning uses that have long-term consequences as well as to collect fees from individuals who cut lumber or take other resources from the *ejido*.

Mexico's agrarian reform was planned during the Mexican Revolution (begun in 1910). The original *ejido* grant (2,500 hectares) to Pich (see Figure 2.2) was given by President Alvaro Obregón in 1923. The Lázaro Cárdenas reforms of the 1930s eventually resulted in the addition of a forest commons (see Figure 2.3) of 64,400 additional hectares.[7] Another addition by President José López Portillo in 1980, added 2,660 hectares to the agricultural *ejido* lands, annexed from the former Hacienda of Solbul.

In the summer of 1992, most villagers were unaware of the changes in the Agrarian Reform Law making possible conversion of *ejido* lands to private property. By 1994, however, there were major conflicts over the possibility, resulting in a candidate for local mayor running on the platform of the Partido de la Revolución Democrática (PRD) rather than the traditional, dominant Partido Revolucionario Institucional (PRI). In 1996, against the wishes of the PRD supporters, the community decided to divide the agricultural *ejido* lands (5,000 hectares) and the government began the process of surveying in order to delineate the individual plots.

Figure 2.1
The Village of Pich

1. Baseball field
2. Basketball court
3. Catholic Church
4. Market
5. Plaza
6. Presbyterian Church
7. School
8. Store with telephone
9. Village Offices
10. Water pump
11. Women's Sewing Center

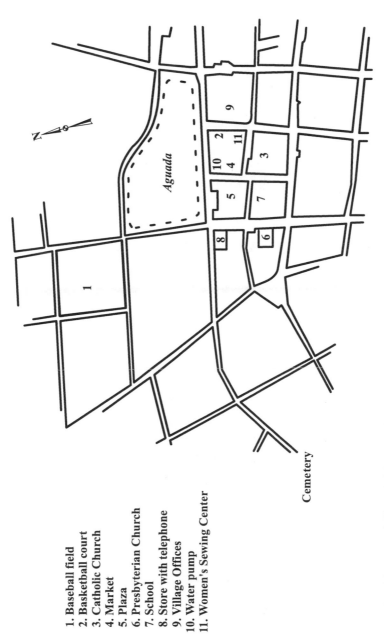

Source: Adapted from Map of Village of Pich, Campeche Municipal Office, 1981.

Figure 2.2
The *Ejido* of Pich

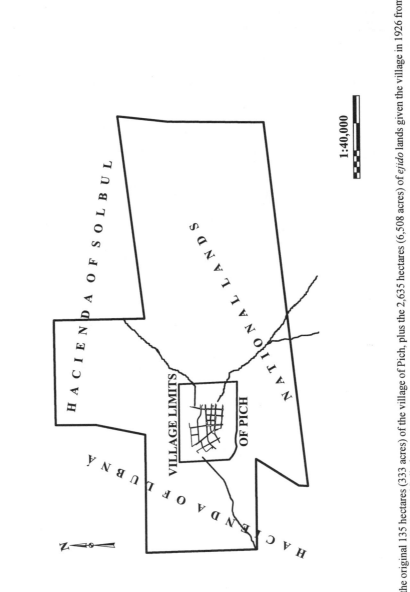

1:40,000

Note: This map shows the original 135 hectares (333 acres) of the village of Pich, plus the 2,635 hectares (6,508 acres) of *ejido* lands given the village in 1926 from national lands and the haciendas of Lubná and Solbul.

Figure 2.3
The Forest Commons of Pich

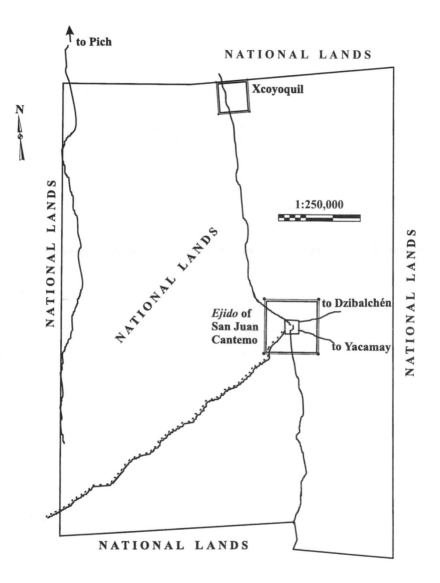

Note: This map shows the original 64,000 hectares (159,068 acres) of the forest commons of Pich, given the village in 1940 from national lands.

   Unlike the agricultural *ejido* lands, the forest commons cannot be divided into individual plots. It was originally given in connection with the gathering of *chicle* as a major source of family income. Later, tropical hardwoods were cut for railroad ties and lumber. The designation of *ejido forestal* entitled the village to more land per person than is the case with strictly agricultural *ejidos*, recognizing the community's economic dependence on forest products. However, even in the government survey of 1981, it was clear that although the majority of village income no longer came from lumbering—less than six percent—this was the major source of income for more than eighteen percent of the economically active men in the village. Although less than four percent were working with cattle, they brought in more than sixty-seven percent of total village income. This is an indication of the increasing separation of the *ricos* from other villagers, complained about vehemently by the poor majority in 1985–1986. In 1981 the most common occupation was still agriculturist (which included keeping bees and producing crops but not raising cattle), employing sixty-seven percent of the labor force while producing only twenty-seven percent of the income (combining the numbers for honey, wax, corn, and beans). Approximately nine percent of the labor force was employed in unspecified "service and industry." (See Tables 2.3, 2.4, and 2.5.)

   In 1986, I took notes concerning the number of businesses in the village, the number of adults working in each averaged two. There were seven village stores, three mills for grinding corn (two of which were also simple tortilla factories), four carpentry shops, three bakeries, and the village diner. One person served as the village policeman and another as the village clerk. Most of these people also farmed, and the clerk had a very large beekeeping operation and a large, irrigated orchard of fruit trees. The elected village officials received compensation from the government for their work, but the clerk received only small fees from those registering marriages, divorces, births, and

Table 2.3.
Occupations of Pichuleños in 1981

Occupation	Number	Percent
Agriculture	365	67.4
Cattle raising	20	3.6
Industry	8	1.4
Services	40	7.8
Woodcutters	100	18.4
Day laborers	8	1.4

Source: Figures from the Municipal Census de Pich, 1981, p. 18.

Note: No criteria accompany the figures in the census.

deaths. Individual patients paid the three young women who had been trained to give shots when needed. Two government-trained midwives were beginning to replace the traditional ones (see Faust 1988b). When their services were needed, two respected prayer makers received small amounts of cash. Three men were paid to clean the streets, the public market area, the plaza,

Table 2.4.
Value of Production for Market of Pich in 1981

Type of Production	Value of Production: (in Thousands of Pesos)	Percentage
Agriculture'		
Corn	327.6	2.61
Beans	756.0	6.03
Cattle raising		
(700 heads)	8,400.0	67.05
Beekeeping		
Honey	2,240.0	17.88
Wax	126.0	1.00
Lumbering	677.9	5.43
TOTAL	12,527.5	100.00

Source: Census de Pich 1981, p. 15.

Note: Information in this table is does not include production consumed within the village.

Table 2.5.
Harvest Records for Pich, 1980–1986

Year	Land Planted	Harvest Weight
1980	50 ha.	60 kgs/ha. sorghum
1981	100 ha.	1,100 kgs/ha. maize
1982	180 ha.	1,500 kgs/ha. maize
1983	130 ha.	950 kgs/ha. maize
1984*	100 ha. (40)**	950 kgs/ha. maize
1985*	30 ha.	0
1986*	61 ha.	0

Source: Figures were provided by the Campeche Office of the Agrarian Reform.

* These are the years of conflict with the government, resolved finally in 1986, when credits were finally available, but government-supplied inputs were late in arriving for planting season.

** Only 40 hectares were harvested

playgrounds, and the area of government offices. By 1994 there were two, because there was less money to pay them. In 1986 a number of men still worked for wealthier ones making traditional milpas or fencing pasture for them. Most men did some masonry, and several made the majority of their income from this work. By 1992, many men had to go to Campeche for work and only a few were employed on the private ranches of the rich people. The saw mill that used to employ several workers has closed; a home for those elderly whose children will not care for them has been built on the same foundation. Some trucks that previously hauled lumber to Campeche now carry raw limestone rock to the city for sale as building material or water to cattle or cattle to market. A few men are still hired as truck drivers, but most owners drive their own trucks as part of their cattle ranching activities. Beekeeping was a major source of income until 1996, when a combination of drought, disease, and "Africanization" drastically reduced the number of occupied beehives. The African "killer bees," which began to arrive in the early 1990s, crossbred with the local commercial bees, producing a mixed race. The new bees produce more honey but are difficult to handle and swarm off to the woods under conditions that the other bees tolerated.

Pich is still, in 1996, at the end of the paved road from Campeche. Now, in addition to the trucks, five buses make a round-trip to the city every day, picking up people in various villages all along the route. Each bus employs a driver and a ticket collector. Some men earn extra money making charcoal or digging up stones for building or shoveling the calcareous sand used in homemade cement. Women still contribute to the household economy through raising vegetables, fruits, and domestic animals in their house yards. They also make clothing on sewing machines (some treadle, others electric) for their neighbors, relatives, and themselves. They cook food and sell it or give it to neighbors and relatives, obligating them to reciprocate. They are sometimes paid to do laundry or cooking for wealthier neighbors. Older women help younger ones with child care and receive food in appreciation. Some women work in the village stores, tortilla factories, and corn mills; a few are the actual owners.

Some corn and beans are sold, but most are used within families—as are most of the chickens, turkeys, and pigs. Deer, wild pigs, and other game are usually eaten at home—but may be sold to a wealthier family, a local school teacher; or to people from the cities (of Mérida and Campeche and even Cancún). Income figures for agricultural production are very misleading because they give no indication of the amount produced for local consumption, only what is sold to the outside market through government intermediaries and reported to government census takers. Many villagers fear the census takers and do not report what they sell privately to friends and relatives at home or in other villages. They often claim to have lost part or all of their harvests in order not to have to repay money given by the government at planting time to purchase seeds and fertilizers. The harvest figures given throughout this chapter are from government censuses and thus should be interpreted with caution.

EJIDITARIOS

The term *ejido* refers not only to the village land, but also to the group which has official rights to use the land. The maximum number of these *ejiditarios* is set by the federal government, in accord with the quantity and quality of the *ejido*'s land. New members are voted in by the existing members whenever a place becomes vacant. The number of *ejiditarios* in Pich is 216, plus 2 women who represent the women of the community. *Ejido* members meet to make joint decisions concerning use of the land and expenditure of fees collected from lumber trucks. The trucking of *ejido* lumber over the past 30 years created a class of village *"ricos,"* wealthy extended families who have invested their profits in private lands and cattle. The men in Pich who do not belong to the *ejido* can still farm *ejido* land, cut wood, and raise bees. Many younger men joined a new *ejido* group, Chilam Balam, that formed in 1983 to apply for land farther south, in the middle of the Edzná Valley, as part of a government program for rice production. By 1986, they were building houses on the land and harvesting rice, waiting for the promised electricity, water system, school, and clinic. However, the rice program was abandoned by the government, and by 1992 most of these young men had returned to Pich or gone to the cities looking for jobs.

POWER AND POLITICS

Even relatively well-off villagers view themselves as at a disadvantage when dealing individually with the government and the wealthier people in the city. They complain of getting no response from the government when they argue for better prices for their products, cheaper credit from government banks, more legal control over their land, or better access to markets and transportation. Everyone wants a chance, like the people in the city have gotten. Pichuleños want a factory to process something, jobs, individual control of plots of land, but community control of public goods. Many want a way they can get ahead together, as a community. Others think that is hopeless; there are too many divisions. On the one hand, they do not know exactly how the government might help them, but they are convinced that "the government should do it." On the other hand, when the government oversteps its bounds and threatens the rights of communities, they react.

In Tenabo, forty-four miles to the north, the 1985 election of local officials was protested for months. Armed troops were sent in to reinstall disliked politicians, who had had the backing of the dominant national party, the PRI. Protesters went to the state capital to demonstrate, where I talked with a number of them. There was no mention in the media, which is widely believed to be controlled by the dominant political party. According to later rumors in Pich, the Tenabo officials sponsored by the PRI were kept in office despite protests, but other concessions (gifts of new public facilities) were made by the state government. People in Pich wondered whether or not they ought to "defend themselves" like the citizens of Tenabo. One of the respected older men of the community speculated, "Maybe being peaceful is stupid; it just gets you stepped on." By 1994, Pichuleños were divided in two factions, one supporting the PRI, the other the PRD. When the PRI announced victory for its candidate, there were angry protests and someone padlocked the door to the *Ayuntamiento* (the office for village authorities).

A pragmatic approach to power is evident in discussions of the political process. Peace is strongly preferred, but it has its limits. During the summer drought of 1986, there was a rebellion in Pich against the village president. Approximately one hundred men attempted to take the door off the jail cell to free a companion. This kind of collective social action is considered legitimate, even though physical violence in personal conflicts is generally condemned. There is a strong sense that group and community rights are above individual rights and violence in their preservation has a degree of legitimacy not extended to individuals with private grievances. This tradition may stem from pre-Hispanic Maya concepts of the *cah*, the community as a collective, geo-political unit, with locally chosen officials. The *cah* functioned at least from 1557 to 1851, the period covered by notarial documents under Spanish rule. This indigenous political structure has been analyzed by M. B. Restall (1995) on the basis of more than a thousand legal documents written in the Yucatec Mayan language from more than a hundred different villages across the penin-sula. In 1994 Pichuleños used the term *Pich cah* in campaign speeches in support of one of the political candidates for mayor.

In Pich, some of the older women told me that they have been talking about political strategies for influencing the government, being heard as women—for the children, for the future, for the whole community. They complain that the men are too divisive, competing with one another as individuals, helping only their brothers and friends. I asked about elections and was informed that it is neither possible nor necessary to affect the outcome of elections by voting—the PRI always wins. The thing to do is to find ways to bring pressure in the community, gain visibility, make sure the right questions are voiced, and make the arguments that move people to see what will be best for the children, "who *are* our future." If the community is united, it can make a powerful appeal to the government. If it is united with other communities, together they can influ-ence the government.

A younger woman asked the older ones if they were not afraid of political work and if it did not take a lot of time. One replied, "Yes, but it is beautiful work. When your children are grown you will have more time for it." "Yes," agreed another, her face glowing, "political action is beautiful." Older women feel they represent the whole community and the future of the grandchildren. They are a potent, often hidden, force in village politics. They have ample knowledge, time, and informal networks. They have always influenced their husbands' political actions. In 1986, they were beginning to form their own political groups and to speak out in public on their own issues. By 1992, more than two hundred women had organized a political demonstration for a visit of the candidate for governor. The men tried to convince the candidate that the women were drunk, but he listened to them. In Pich, there is an understanding that one can speak out, address grievances, and ask for what is needed to "defend the village from poverty." A threat to people's abilities to take care of their basic needs is seen as equivalent to physical attack, as is an attack on political rights. Defense is needed and defense is seen as legitimately based in collective action. There is fear that those with strong connections to political power (the PRI, which has been the ruling party for more than sixty years) in the city of Campeche and the state government can have those who speak for the community's poor thrown in jail on the basis of false accusations that will be believed by judges, who are friends of these powerful city *patrones*.

There is some confidence that in Pich, unlike Guatemala, one can organize politically without being "disappeared." This is a point Pichuleños often made in conversations comparing the two countries. It is also something they repeatedly tried to teach the Guatemalan refugees in the nearby camp. "Here, you do not have to put up with those abuses. You can say no and they cannot make you give them your daughter" was the advice given by the women of Pich to refugee women who were complaining about the sexual advances by some of the Mexican guards in charge of security in the camps.

ELECTIONS

Participation in national and regional election campaigns is seen both as a way of forming personal alliances and of attempting to gain a *patrón* who will look favorably on the village's petitions. Pichuleños enjoy the diversion of listening to political candidates for elections. When a right-wing party (Partido de Acción Nacional [PAN]) candidate came to campaign in Pich, I was told by several of the elected officials of Pich to go and listen, "because what they say is the truth. If you really want to know what goes on here, listen to them; they know. What they say is right." I went and listened to the criticisms of the dominant party, which were broadcast with loud speakers. Few people gathered to listen in any observable way. They sat on the edges of the plaza in small groups, appearing to ignore the speakers. A few of the braver young men went up afterwards for some of the literature being offered. After the candidate left, people who had been around corners, in the doorways, and in the shadows, came out. They had heard. Some went home, a few stayed and talked.

The discussion in the plaza involved only about fifteen people. Later, on informal occasions, in homes and stores, on street corners, small groups of relatives and friends made comments. I was told to listen and understand—but not to write down names. By then I was trusted as a friend, a part of a family. I was quietly cautioned that the government has "ears." To summarize these quiet, hidden conversations in groups of trusted friends, their answer as to how they would vote was no, they would not vote for the PAN candidate, "because the PRI has all the power. These people say the truth when they talk about how the PRI cheats us, but we have to go with the PRI because they have the power."

When the PRI candidate came to town, the local political leaders made a special dinner to celebrate, with venison dishes and rum cokes. Everyone in town was invited and expected to attend. The speeches were well attended, although people expressed great skepticism and cynicism after the candidate left, always in private, in family groups. Those to whom I was close enough to be trusted with this kind of talk represented both poor and well-to-do and all religious persuasions.

On voting day, in November 1985, the women of Pich gave their ballots to their husbands to mark, except for one woman whose husband was out of town. My adopted sister, who knew I would be there to photograph, cast her own ballot and laughingly asked me to photograph her, "the first woman in Pich to vote." No one took voting very seriously. Knowing that their names would be checked off a list, they referred to voting as an "obligation" to the PRI. They did so despite the *corridos* they sing about how López Portillo sold Mexico to please his mistress. But over the following months, criticisms of the corruption of the PRI grew stronger with each rise in the prices and devaluation of the peso. Yet there was the memory of the Revolution (from 1910 through the 1920s) and the end of "slavery" on the haciendas, the memory of the Cárdenas reforms, the visible reminders of government assistance—the street lights, the paved streets, the clinic, the school. And, there was the hope for new projects and facilities that the powerful PRI might give, and was promising to give. Hence, the PRI carried Campeche easily in the 1987 elections, but the 1997 ones have proven more difficult. The daughter of a well-liked former governor of Campeche has nearly became the new governor, running on the PRD ticket. The results of the election are still being contested.

FEARS AND HOPES

Existing literature concerning contemporary processes of change indicates both the need and the potential benefit of including the Maya in development planning. The Maya of Pich regularly combine both traditional and modern technologies in prenatal and obstetric care (Faust 1988b). Mechanisms for including the Maya in the planning and administration of ecotourism have been proposed by the author (Faust 1991).[8] Biosphere reserves in Quintana Roo (Sian Ka'an) and Campeche (Calakmul) are already serving ecotourists and local populations while protecting endangered species (Sian Ka'an 1988; Jones and Wersch 1989). For the protected area of Río Lagartos, the author and John Sinton (Faust and Sinton 1991) have documented the social and political consequences of lack of communication between park administrators and various groups of local users. If such problems could be solved, water management and food production could be improved through creative combinations of indigenous and Euroamerican systems.

Many government planners and administrators assume that Maya "superstitions" should be replaced by modern ways, "for their own good, whether they like it or not." The Maya are frequently referred to as "childish" and "ignorant," hence in need of supervision, guidance, and discipline by their "superiors," the local "civilized" elite. The viewpoints of some villagers reflect those of the development agents. However, there are other perceptions in the village. Those villagers who have become *ricos* through involvements with outsiders are perceived by many as betraying the community and joining the exploiters—even as they are admired by many of the young for their wealth and their knowledge of the outside world.

Some of the traditional elders look beyond individual successes to the effects of the new ways on the welfare of the community and its resource base. These elders are also concerned about their own decline in power relative to that of newly wealthy, younger men. The younger men often ascribe the concerns of the elderly (particularly those who are poorer because they did not participate in the trucking of lumber) to envy. Even the wealthy elderly, however, sometimes lament that their children pay no attention to them any more. One told me he was just waiting to die, there in front of his television set. Most of the poorer villagers, both young and old, believe that the wealthy families have been led by this "modernization" to more and more exploitative behavior. Such concerns are often misunderstood and interpreted by outsiders as evidence of blind antagonism toward modernization. This interpretation is common among development agents, whose perspectives tend to be short-term (focused on quarterly reports and politically determined agency goals), and whose understanding of Maya communication style is minimal.

While living standards did improve by conventional standards in the 1960s, 1970s, and even the early 1980s, social status in the village became increasingly linked to the cash economy. The majority of village families became dependent on the rich for wage work. This trend occurred despite the availability of land for individual use through the *ejido* system. Selling crops depends on having both transportation and connections with buyers in the city (or bureaucratic arrangements with government agents, who are believed often to offer less than the market price). For one man to grow a crop substantially larger than needed to feed his family requires either hiring additional workers or buying modern agricultural aids, both of which require cash or involvement in government programs. For a person to make appropriate decisions concerning loans or government credits requires the ability to predict changes in interest rates and inflation, both of which have been growing rapidly. Trusting the advice of government agents may well threaten one's children with hunger and malnutrition. Agents are frequently transferred and cannot be held accountable for their advice. By 1992, a new credit policy had been established for seeds, fertilizers and herbicides, one understood in Pich not to involve interest payments. No new loans can be given, however, until the old ones are paid. Interest is still charged for loans to purchase equipment such as tractors.

Alternatives to crop production as a means for earning additional cash have been tried by Pichuleños, but many have been found to be destructive of the local environment. Cutting the large tropical hardwoods that provide shade for their own seedlings and other species is reducing biodiversity. Clearance of large tracts of forest for cattle pasture may be adversely affecting local rainfall patterns, in combination with global warming (Schlesinger 1991; Gunn 1994a, 1994b; Gunn, Folan, and Robichaux 1994; Gunn and Folan 1996). Commercial beekeeping with imported bees has caused near extinction of the native stingless bees formerly kept in each house yard. Over-cutting of fronds killed the majority of the *guano* (*Sabal yapa*) palm trees in easy reach of the village, although a couple of farmers have planted some groves. Over-tapping killed many *chicle-zapote* (*Manilkara zapota*) trees, thereby decreasing the local supply of fruit as well as the source of resin to sell to manufacturers of chewing gum. Use of village water for irrigating commercial orchards and for watering cattle is straining the system and has decreased the supply for human use during the dry season. As a result of such experiences with economic "development" during the last thirty years, the poor majority is increasingly apprehensive about the destruction of their forest resource base and their *aguada* water supply, and about their growing dependence on cash wages from the minority that has become relatively wealthy. There is still enthusiasm, however, for the new *ejido* within the *Ampliación Forestal*. If only the government would build a road, then those resources could be available to the poor; they could be turned into money and the problem would temporarily be solved.

In Pich, there are still many fears of being manipulated by outsiders; but, at the same time, the road, the many radios, a few televisions, and the schools have provided more information about opportunities outside the village. More than 80 percent of persons over the age of six are somewhat "literate" (Censo de Pich 1981:4–5). Most of the parental generation attended at least the first three grades of primary school, which was offered in the village when they were children. The village now has its own middle school and adolescents can travel 15 kilometers by bus to the local high school.[9]

The poor increasingly attempt to keep their children in school through high school. The rich try to send their children to a university, in Campeche or Mérida. Even after graduation, many of these children return home on week-ends, maintaining family ties. Some contribute to modernization efforts in the village. One is a school teacher. Another is organizing a local group of Alcoholics Anonymous. A third is a veterinarian and gives advice to friends and relatives on his weekend visits. Many bring gifts and cash to their families in the village. Periodically some of these emigrants lose their city jobs and return to their village kin for shelter and food. This system is a form of economically balanced reciprocity that functions as an insurance policy for both city and country cousins.

The village primary and middle schools and the regional high school are major avenues to employment outside the village as well as valuable sources of knowledge concerning the outside world. From the perspective of the Maya elders, however, the schools have a serious disadvantage. The teachers often teach village children to question traditional knowledge and to value the status hierarchy and competitive individualism of the larger Mexican system. Adolescents often lose respect for their elders, with resulting family conflicts and discipline problems. Undesirable behaviors include glue sniffing, problem drinking, adolescent pregnancies, thefts, and fist fights. Failure to fulfill family obligations is more widespread. Community oral history and traditional knowledge about the environment are disappearing, and the loss of information concerning earlier attempts to use new technologies in this particular habitat is particularly critical to the future management of community resources.

Most families visit relatives in Campeche periodically. Almost all families have at least one extended family member residing in the city, someone who often returns to the village for fiestas and family occasions. Many older adults report having rejected traditional knowledge during adolescence or their early twenties and are somewhat tolerant of their adolescent children's adoption of the attitudes of their school teachers and city cousins toward indigenous cultural knowledge and values. "They will understand when they have lived more," is a commonly expressed response, although there is much worry that the old ways are in fact being lost.

THE VIEWS OF DIFFERENT GENERATIONS

Many of the young and the middle-aged are preoccupied with the daily struggle to secure survival needs and status, but some of the elderly have time to reflect on the processes of change. Although the young find many aspects of the new to be attractive, the elders see the process of modernization as disruptive. Many of them view the larger, national system as irrational, destructive, ignorant of local realities, disrespectful of villagers, immoral, and very powerful.

Many modern things are very much appreciated (such as radios and electricity), but the whole of life is somehow getting worse. "You can't depend on anyone anymore." The oral tradition alerts them to some of the dangers. This tradition contains symbolically stored, historical lessons, rooted in the local ecosystem and in local political history. Stories of arbitrary cruelty and despotic control by hacienda owners are ubiquitous, as are stories about sexual abuse of village women by priests, friars, and medical doctors. Deception by outsiders is a common complaint, especially concerning the prices paid for Maya products and labor and charged for products sold to them.

Present differences in power and wealth within the village are understood by the elders within the context of history. Rich and powerful neighbors once manipulated the elders into debt slavery on haciendas. Individual wealth today is, in fact, quickly converted into ownership of adjacent private lands, which reinforces the elders' fear of a return to the hacienda system. The willingness of young villagers to go into debt in order to buy consumer goods increases their need for cash and thus their willingness to work for the local rich for cash wages. "Now we have new needs," they say. It was through a similar process that the parents and grandparents of today's elders became *esclavos* (slaves).

Recent division of neighboring *ejido* lands has combined with the North American Free Trade Agreement to make it possible for international cotton growers to use lands for export agriculture which were previously used by local people to feed their families. Some of these lands were divided into individual plots in 1995. Then, "the company came and offered a good price to lease the land and many people signed." Even *ejidos* which had not divided their land decided to rent parts of it. Pichuleños are impressed by the large, new John Deere tractors and associated machinery but they told me, "people from your country are leasing 15,000 hectares (38,050 acres) to plant cotton, but we said no. We are afraid that the sprays will kill the bees." I thought, "and the birds and the butterflies and the iguanas and the boas," remembering well the Pacific Coast of Guatemala in the 1970s.

In 1986 I had been told that Mexico's politicians (principally former President López Portillo) had sold the country into debt slavery to the United States. It was only a matter of time before foreigners and their local favorites would again own the land of Mexico and use the labor of the poor to grow crops for export. (I was told this as part of an explanation as to why they had initially been afraid of me. They thought I was coming down to obtain information that would be used to set up this new national hacienda.) This situation was seen as a recurrence of the situation under Porfirio Díaz (before the Mexican Revolution), when henequen was grown in Yucatán for U.S. businesses. The Maya still refer to this period as "the time of slavery." Debts were manipulated so that poor people lost their access to land and were kept in virtual slavery on the henequen plantations (Joseph 1986).

Some of the village elders can look back on their own experiences as children of peons on sugarcane and cattle haciendas. Others recall the stories their parents told them. They remember the changes that followed the Revolution, enabling them as young men to become *chicleros* (gatherers of the resin used in chewing gum), lumberjacks, laborers, and farmers with crops to sell.

My research was guided by elders willing to accept the burden of teaching me some of their accumulated knowledge and their perceptions of the changes they have experienced. They have told me these things in part because "our own children won't listen to us any more. But someday they may realize they are making a mistake and then they will need to know these things our parents taught us. It is good that you write it down so it doesn't get lost."

Village elders are not categorically opposed to the new; they are, however, concerned about the loss of the past—the rejection of the knowledge collected by the ancestors through generations of living. They see ways in which new technologies could be combined with the wisdom of old ways, allowing the community to guard itself against new forms of enslavement, while getting richer, as a "family," and without destroying the forests. They grieve over the loss of the *chicle-zapotes*, the *guano* palms, the tropical cedars, and the native bees. They are concerned about the scarcity of deer and wild turkey because hunting is not a sport, but the source of animal protein for the family diet. As the elders worry, the grandchildren watch their parents cut down the forest to send them to school—destroying the local resources in the hope of providing a child with enough education to survive in the larger system.

The local *h-men* says that the foreign, mechanized practices being introduced by the government will eventually bring about the end of this cycle of time, corresponding to the world we know. The primordial serpent of Maya creation will rise from the sea to preside over the end of this world and the beginning of the next sun, or cycle of time. The elders often shake their heads and say that for them it does not matter so much; they have lived. But they are concerned for their grandchildren. And the grandchildren are concerned for themselves. Some of them see what is happening. In 1986 eight-year-old Domingo Jesús asked me to take a picture of him on a pile of logs of tropical cedar, which were about to be trucked to Campeche for sale. He said he wanted the picture for when he grew up, "So I can remember the woods and what happened to them . . . how they disappeared." He was seeing the future far more clearly than I then suspected. In 1992, before he had finished elementary school,[10] the logging was ended and a long process of cedar reforestation had been begun by the government agency charged with the protection of forests. If the reforestation efforts are successful, Domingo Jesús may be able to cut tropical cedar by the time he is thirty-five or forty. By 1995, rich Pichuleños succeeded in pressuring the government to allow logging of a small patch of *guayacán* in the south, along with the remaining *chakah* used in plywood. These will soon be gone and no reforestation projects exist for either of these species or dyewood or mahogany.

NOTES

1. In Maya, plural nouns do not end in *s* but rather in *o'ob;* however, in the spoken Spanish of Pichuleños, Maya loan words are given Spanish plurals, thus ending in *s* or *es*.

2. *Hermano* can be either a friar or a monk or a member of a Protestant church. In this context it probably refers to a friar, certainly not to a Protestant.

3. The Franciscans were friars and thus, technically, their home would be a friary

not a monastery. However, normal Spanish usage refers to the homes of monks, frairs, and nuns as *conventos*.

4. Abel Morales López of the Centro de Investigaciones Históricos y Sociales (Universidad del Sureste, Campeche, Mexico) analyzed the ceramic shards from the surface of the aguada banks as dating from the Late Classic, indicating the village has existed since at least A.D. 1000. The nearby Maya city of Edzná has been dated stylistically to the Preclassic, A.D. 200 or earlier.

5. Manning Nash (1967) reported great interest in new technologies and an openness to change in a community in the highlands of Guatemala. Investigation of the colonial history of that community could supply critical information to test this hypothesis concerning Maya openness to change and previous experiences with outsiders.

6. B. Tedlock's (1982) use of the term "imbrication" in her analysis of Mesoamerican time periods builds on previous work by Claude Levi-Strauss (1966:22), who referred to *"bricolage"* as the construction of something new from pieces, as done by a *bricoleur*, a handyman. According to Levi-Strauss, this is the process by which indigenous peoples build complex cosmological systems with concrete symbolic references to local species of fauna and flora, as well as to other aspects of their environment.

7. The documents kept by the *comisariado ejidal* (the elected head of the *ejido* organization) include applications made to President Cárdenas for this augmentation of the *ejido*, and local oral tradition credits Cárdenas with the land grants. According to the village documents, however, the grant was officially issued after he left office, by President Ávila in 1940.

8. The model was developed for the "Ruta Maya," an international system of protected areas being planned for the ecotourism trade by the governments of Mexico, Belize, Guatemala, Honduras, and El Salvador (Garrett 1989).

9. In 1985, twenty-seven out of twenty-nine graduates of the elementary school continued their education in one of the regional *secundarias* (middle schools, including seventh through ninth grades), and by 1994 there was a *secundaria* in Pich. The *preparatoria* (last three years of high school) has been available in Bonfil since the early 1980s.

10. In rural Mexican communities it is common for children to not finish elementary school until they are thirteen or fourteen, or even older. Illness, lack of money for books, and the need to help at home can all set back educational progress. Students are not, however, simply passed to the next grade without mastering the material, as they are in many areas in the United States. In Mexico, children are held back until they can pass their examinations. They do not graduate from sixth grade without knowing how to read, write, and do arithmetic at a standard level.

Past Transformations of Maya Technology

For centuries after the Conquest, deep inside the dense tropical forest of the south central area of the Yucatán peninsula, some Maya communities hid from the church and government authorities who were determined to change them. They were protected not only by dense forest but also by European fears of malaria and other tropical diseases. These conservative hamlets preserved aspects of their culture compatible with a base of slash-and-burn agriculture and hunting. They accepted and taught outsiders, marrying descendants of Africans and Europeans. Although racially mixed, they maintained Maya identity and cultural orientation. In between these communities and the northern and coastal centers of domination were communities like Pich, politically controlled by those centers but in communication with the hidden hamlets (Kintz 1990). These communities have gradually been abandoned over the past twenty to thirty years, as people were attracted to the electricity, running water, schools and clinics provided in the larger settlements connected by paved roads to the cities. However, the heirs of those who lived in the hidden hamlets, still tell the stories, providing an umbilical cord to the past. Thus border communities like Pich have been able to maintain many aspects of Maya practical and environmental knowledge, while complying commercially and politically with the demands of powerful Hispanic elites in the major cities of the peninsula.

THE ECOLOGICAL BASE

The Campeche area has special conditions to which traditional Maya technologies were adapted: very distinct wet and dry seasons, a limestone topography that offers few sources of groundwater during the dry season, and frequent patches of acidic bottomland soils of high clay content. These become seasonal, shallow lakes or swamps (*bajos*) when the rains come (see Figure 3.1).

Figure 3.1
***Bajo* Formation in the Yucatán Peninsula**

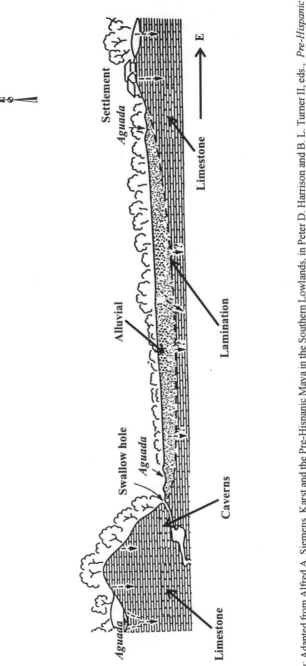

Source: Adapted from Alfred A. Siemens, Karst and the Pre-Hispanic Maya in the Southern Lowlands, in Peter D. Harrison and B. L. Turner II, eds., *Pre-Hispanic Maya Agriculture* (Albuquerque: University of New Mexico Press, 1978), p. 135, Figure 6.10, by permission of the University of New Mexico Press.

Some *bajos* that form at the foot of limestone ridges are deep enough to hold water throughout the year. Both these ponds and the reservoirs built by the ancient Maya are locally referred to as *aguadas*. Both depend on the yearly rains to replenish water lost to evaporation and human use. Clay bottomland is typical of much of the southern lowlands, occupied by Classic Maya regional states, whereas limestone outcroppings are more typical of the northern Yucatán area.

In this tropical universe, there are two zenith passages of the sun, in May and in August, bracketing the most critical part of the year when steady rains from the east are needed for the growing crops. Wind damage and flooding are common from August through November, due to hurricane acitivity in the Gulf and the Caribbean. The dry season begins in December and by March lack of water and rising temperatures cause severe stress. During 1983, archeologists investigating the hydraulic system of the Edzná site found that

> March, April and May . . . [is] the period of maximum moisture stress for both plants and animals in the Valley. Temperatures soar to 40 degrees C (104 degrees F) in April and as high as 47 degrees (116 degrees F) in May. During these hot months the open ground is parched. Leaves that have fallen from many of the deciduous trees protect the trees from excessive water and temperature stress; animals seek shade near the few remaining water sources. (Matheny et al. 1983:1)

The humidity and the temperature both rise in May and June. Rain clouds arrive on an easterly wind from the Caribbean. As clouds rise over the eastern sides of hills and ridges, they cool and rain is released, sometimes over large areas and sometimes over small ones. Variation in wind speed and direction as well as in cloud height interact with small variations in altitude to create unpredictable variations in rainfall. One village may receive several weeks of good rainfall, while its neighbor suffers a drought and loses its crops. The following year the situation could easily be reversed. Farmers in Pich reported in 1986 that they were averaging only two good years out of three, and that every twenty or thirty years there is a very severe drought with an accompanying invasion of locusts and rats—which may last two to three years. Such events were the subject of concern in colonial texts written in Maya language but with European letters, the *Chilam Balam*. These texts were written by Maya town scribes and hidden from ecclesiastical and colonial authorities; they include references to pre-colonial events and appear to be copies or reconstructions of previous records kept in hieroglyphs. Their reports of recurrent shifts in weather suggest that variations may be due to recurring cycles in wind currents and temperature (Folan, Josserand, and Hopkins 1983; Folan and Hyde 1985, Gunn, Folan, and Robichaux 1994; Gunn and Folan 1996).

The peninsula's eroding limestone base (known as karst) combines with climatic conditions to create an environment in which techniques of water drainage, collection, and conservation are critical. Water does not travel across the surface in streams and rivers—rather it seeps into cracks in the limestone base and travels underground to the sea. The underground water level varies greatly over short distances, depending on variations in this karst topography. In some places erosion has produced a concavity in a strata which resists seepage. Rainwater seeps through the more pervious, higher strata, forming pools in these natural pockets, perched higher than the major drainage system. These formations are referred to as perched water pockets (Gates and Folan 1986). In other places, water that has been flowing at one level in a natural channel in the rock will be forced higher by the structure of the karst. As a result, it may be necessary to drill more than 400 feet to reach water, only a short distance away from a well 10 feet deep (see Figure 3.2). Problems of water conservation are exacerbated by the high temperatures that increase evaporation rates. Ray Matheny and his colleagues describe experiments with evaporation during the three coolest months of the rainy season, October through December. Even during these months when evaporation is at its lowest, there was one thirty-four-day period when it was measured at 12 inches, while precipitation was only 3 inches (Matheny et al. 1983:14–18)!

THE PUZZLE OF MAYA HISTORY

The Maya cultural adaptation to the local environment was based on very complex technological systems long before European contact. It has been a generation since the first population estimates from Tikal and Dzibilchaltún indicated dense populations, overturning previous impressions that the archeological remains of large buildings constituted ceremonial centers in a sparsely populated jungle area. Data are now available from Copán, Seibal, Uaxactún, Tayasal, Santa Rita, Sayil, Komchén, Calakmul, and other sites, where the center and the periphery have been surveyed for house mounds.

It is clear that Maya science and technology sustained sophisticated regional states, with population densities estimated by some archeologists at 180 persons per square kilometer in the central southern lowlands, which include large areas of swamp. According to T. P. Culbert and D. S. Rice (1990:26), "This figure would place Maya lowland densities in the range of those in areas such as Java and China [Clark and Haswell 1964]—that is among the most densely populated regions of the preindustrial world." Many have expressed serious doubts concerning these estimates, since the present-day swidden agriculture can only support between twenty-five and fifty persons per square kilometer, in years of normal rainfall.

The author's ethnographic findings may clarify some aspects of the problem. In both Pich, Campeche, and Sahcabá, Yucatán, small groups of related families customarily made *milpa* together, living in *rancherías* (groups of rustic households) near reliable sources of domestic water during the entire agricultural season. At the beginning of November, they would return to their

Figure 3.2
Yucatán Karst with Subterranean Caverns

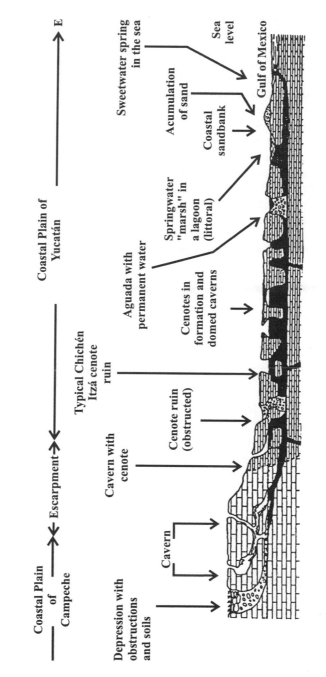

Source: Redrawn from Alfred A. Siemens, Karst and the Pre-Hispanic Maya in the Southern Lowlands, in Peter D. Harrison and B. L. Turner II, eds., *Pre-Hispanic Maya Agriculture* (Albuquerque: University of New Mexico Press, 1978), p. 118, Figure 6.1, by permission of the University of New Mexico Press.

village homes with their initial harvest, using the new corn to prepare the ritual foods and beverages for the souls of deceased family members, who return to visit the living during these days. Later the family would return periodically to the *rancherías* to harvest the rest of the crops, as needed. Each family group (patrilineage) had rights to two or three *rancherías* that were used cyclically, located near the swidden fields of the men. Even today an abandoned swidden field is considered to belong to the man who originally cleared it; his own relative must ask permission to use the field in the event that he does not when the trees are tall enough to be cut again. No ethnographic documentation has yet been found confirming the construction of house platforms on swidden *ranchería* sites; however, such sites are always near reliable sources of domestic water and many are in areas where flooding is a repeated problem during the agricultural season. A house platform would have been a good investment under these circumstances.

Oral history interviews may yet disclose memory of such platforms in *rancherías* early in this century. However, colonial punishments for establishing households outside supervised communities may have eradicated such a practice. A pole-and-thatch construction with dirt floor could have been overlooked as a family home and interpreted as a rain shelter or storage facility for farmers, thereby escaping notice by colonial administrators. A problem with the ethnographic record is that the first ethnographers in the Maya lowlands began research after public schools, health services, and other conveniences had been provided by the government. According to interviews, these conveniences have resulted in families' unwillingness to relocate from May to November. Men search for land closer to the village so they can return home at night, and those who must settle for land further away go with a few other men, living under primitive conditions for a week or two for each of the different tasks of the agricultural season, returning home between them. The men know how to cook and wash clothes. They can take care of themselves out there alone, but they do not like it. Elders fondly recall family life in the *rancherías* during *milpa* season, before the new conveniences in the towns.

Careful analysis of middens and housemounds may be able to clarify whether many pre-Columbian sites were used for family homes only during swidden season. A custom of lineage rights to cyclically used *rancherías* would have given incentive to invest in house platforms. Since swidden fields in this area are generally used for two years, with a traditional fallow period of fifteen to twenty years, each head of a nuclear family could be expected to build or maintain three platforms for use during agricultural seasons during his lifetime, as well as one in the community center for use during the rest of the year. Dividing a population estimate of 180 persons per square kilometer by four house platforms per family, gives forty-five persons per square kilometer. This is within the limits for *milpa* agriculture, but only under ideal climatic conditions, and in areas with good soils and drainage (see Harrison 1977:479). Archeological evidence for intensive use of land (terraces, drained fields, ridged fields, and canals) close to major cities or canal routes may indicate not only the provisioning of full-time specialists who did not plant their own swidden fields, but also the storage of basic grains for famine relief following the extreme climatic events relatively common to the peninsula: drought, fires, flooding, and wind damage.

Drought damage to crops is often exacerbated by associated invasions of stored grains by rodents and insects. Present-day swidden farmers try to protect grains by storing them in unoccupied houses within the village. This practice may be very old and would be another source of error in population figures based on housemounds, a factor recognized by some but not all archeologists doing population estimates. There is also the problem of climate shifts (Folan et al. 1983; Gunn, Folan, and Robichaux 1995). These periodically required movement of populations to previously abandoned or uninhabited sites, where new houses would have to be built (Gunn and Folan 1996), resulting in more housemounds during a time when population decline is probable. Careful laboratory dating combined with stratigraphy of Maya household ceramics may indicate the proportion of houses occupied in each area during particular climatic periods (see Meggers 1996 concerning similar conditions in the Amazon). Analysis of middens and ancient pollens may indicate which residential areas were occupied only seasonally and cyclically for swidden.

An argument for larger population estimates has been made on the basis of labor requirements for the construction of the ceremonial centers, roads, canals and water reservoirs. Refuting this are recent estimates by E. M. Abrams concerning the relatively low labor requirements for construction of Classic period Maya ceremonial architecture at Copán. A total population for the city-state of 25,000, with 20 percent conscripted as household heads, provides enough corvée labor for ceremonial building such that each man only would have needed to work for the state during two months of the non-agricultural season once every fifteen to twenty years (or two or three times in his lifetime). Food to supply this labor force would also be required and Abrams suggests that it may have been supplied either by taxing farmers or requiring them to supply days of labor to state or lineage-owned farms. In summary, the analysis of the number of years of construction, the methods of construction, and the resulting labor requirements make clear that very large population estimates are not necessary to explain the impressive architecture (Abrams 1994:106-108).

Another important factor in Maya demography is the density of the urban population and its size relative to the supporting rural population. Maya urban population had many specialists but the large space around most urban housemounds indicates that food production was not restricted to the agricultural periphery. Home gardens may have produced a large proportion of the fruits, herbs, medicinal plants, and animal protein consumed by commoners, as they do today in towns such as Chunhuhub (Anderson 1995) and in the outskirts of cities (Faust, personal observations in Mérida and Campeche, in the homes of migrants from rural areas). Such customs would have reduced the amount each peasant farmer contributed to the city, another factor involved in estimating population sizes in ancient civilizations.

The engineering knowledge and administrative expertise necessary to the construction of monumental Classic architecture was doubtless provided by full-time specialists who benefitted from a highly developed writing system, capable of accurately preserving detailed information. Urban centers were not only the home of the noble rulers but also supported specialists in the arts and sciences, an administrative class with an executive bureaucracy, religious and military personnel, court entertainers and artisans, including stone masons (Weaver 1993:248). Scribes were sometimes of the nobility and were highly respected individuals, allowed to sign their works and sometimes depicted in sculpture (Weaver 1993:156, 280). The recording of astronomical cycles was connected with royal activities, with almanacs, agricultural cycles and weather prediction (Aveni 1992:43–86, 229–242; Love 1994:30–32) and probably with concerns about extreme climatic events as well, in an effort to predict and prepare for such events. Prediction of both droughts and wars are important themes in the post-Conquest *Chilam Balam* (Folan and Hyde 1985).

Archeological research during recent decades demonstrates that the Maya developed complex trade networks (see Sabloff and Rathje 1975; Matheny et al. 1983:205), systems of sophisticated water management (E. H. Thompson 1897; Matheny 1978; Matheny and Gurr 1979; Sandoval Palacios and Morales López 1982; Matheny et al. 1983; Zapata Peraza 1985, 1987, 1989; Barrera Rubio 1987; Bonor Villarejo 1987; McAnany 1990; Faust and Morales López 1993; Dominguez Carrasco 1993; Scarborough and Gallopin 1994; Fedick 1995; Scarborough 1996), and a highly resilient system of agriculture, which included great biodiversity and a variety of practices adapted to different econiches as well as intensive systems in some areas (Harrison 1978; Siemens 1978, 1989; Donkin 1979; Denevan 1982; Turner 1983; Lambert, Siemens, and Aranson 1984; Gómez-Pompa 1987; Gómez-Pompa et al. 1982; Gómez-Pompa, Flores and Sosa 1987; Gómez-Pompa et al. 1993; Atran 1993; Terán and Rasmussen 1993, 1995; Siemens, Hebda, and Heimo 1996). The Maya did all of this within a fragile, tropical ecosystem and did it without draft animals or machinery, relying on human skills and social organization.

What happened? Why do they now live by slash-and-burn agriculture in small, poor villages? In the sixteenth century, the Maya (like most of the indigenous peoples of the New World) suffered a terrible demographic collapse. There had been earlier episodes of depopulation accompanying the fall of states, particularly that of Teotihuacán (A.D. 600) and the collapse of several regional states in the Classic Maya core area (A.D. 800), which included Palenque and Tikal. While the mystery of these earlier episodes is intriguing, the demographic decline following the arrival of Europeans was far more cata-strophic. Estimates of population losses during the first century of colonization range from 75 to over 95 percent (Crosby 1972) compared to losses of approximately 65 percent over two centuries (a decline from a population estimated between 2.6 and 3.4 million to one of 1 million, A.D. 800–1000) during the Collapse of the Classic Maya (Turner 1990:310). The sixteenth-century population losses were primarily due to virgin-soil epidemics (Crosby 1972; Bianchine and Russo 1995; Settipane and Russo 1995; Naranjo 1995). New varieties of malaria, hookworm, and amebic dysentery increased human population losses both directly and through decreased resistance to epidemics of smallpox, measles, chicken pox, influenza, yellow fever, and typhus. Joseph de Acosta reported the effects of European invasion on coastal areas of the Yucatán Peninsula, "the habitation of which coasts is . . . so wasted and condemned, that of thirty parts of the people that inhabit it, there wants twenty-nine: and it is likely the rest of the Indians will in short time decay" (Acosta [1500s], in Crosby 1972:38).

Africans had centuries of previous exposure to these health hazards and thus had some immunity to them. They were brought in as slaves to work on sugarcane and cotton plantations in some areas of the lowlands. Europeans, with hegemony and less resistance, built their cities in highland areas and close to ports with sea breezes.

> Few, very few, aborigines of the New World have crossed the Atlantic to colonize in the Old World, but aborigines of Europe and Africa have crossed by the tens of millions to found nations in the regions of America where their pioneers had done the heroic work of bringing diseases to destroy or reduce the resistance of the native Americans. Indeed, the Euro- and Afro-Americans now often consider themselves to be the natives of those nations, and the Indians to be the aliens. (Crosby 1972:212–13)

The indigenous states and empires became reduced to scattered villages of ethnic minorities, dominated by a transplanted European cultural system adapting itself to a New World frontier environment. Simultaneously with the shocks from disease came drastic changes in land use, including the pasturing of herds of cattle, sheep, and horses on land once used for subsistence agriculture and wildlife. Imported domestic animals brought diseases that spread to wild animals; European weed species replaced many perennial grasses, altering processes of secondary forest succession. The distribution and population densities of many species of native flora and fauna were radically altered (Crosby 1972 and 1986). In the Yucatán Peninsula, African slaves arrived from Haiti and Veracruz, mixing with Maya populations (both on haciendas and escaping from them into the interior region where Maya hamlets maintained some independence), thus providing their descendants some immunity from the imported diseases (Fernández Repetto and Negroe Sierra 1995). Today, the Maya, mixed racially and devalued culturally, struggle to "defend" themselves within structures imposed on them by a dominant national culture. They attempt to find a sustainable method for managing their resources, while exploring the advantages of increasing involvement in the global economy to meet the needs of a growing population.

ANCIENT TECHNOLOGICAL TRANSFORMATIONS

The prevailing paradigm in Maya studies until recently was swidden agriculture, low population densities, ceremonial centers, and priest-astronomers concerned primarily with cycles of time. Swidden agriculture combined with a tropical lowland environment was seen as incompatible with state-level political organization. The intellectual and artistic achievements of the Maya Classic were thus seen as very special—produced by a small elite residing in centers of ceremonial activity, living off the collection of tribute from swidden farmers, doomed to failure in an unfriendly environment.

Ellsworth Huntington (1915) and others were convinced that humid tropical climates severely limited civilizations and the Maya collapse was evidence of such limitations, despite the 1841 and 1843 publications of Stephens and Catherwood with descriptions and illustrations of the complex architecture and sculpture of the many different Maya sites throughout a large region. In 1937, Griffith Taylor was still describing tropical environments as "zones of stagnation," arguing that the lack of seasons produced races incapable of civilization and that world peace would be achieved when "each nation realized the place in the world's 'order of precedence' for which its racial, intellectual, and economic status equips it (1937:468, as quoted in Bodley 1994:416). John Bodley describes such arguments concerning the effects of tropical climate as examples of racism, used to legitimize economic exploitation of the labor and lands of others (Bodley 1994:415, 416, 420).

Some of the early assertions may have been based on observations of colonial attempts to enforce temperate-zone work habits on native populations in tropical areas. Hartmut Brendt has reported research that clarifies the effects of tropical climate: *both* humidity and temperature increase the difficulties of dissipating the body heat generated by physical exertion. Rising body heat creates physiological stress, which results in a condition commonly known as heat exhaustion; repeated exposures to this condition cause ever *more serious* reactions rather than the acclimatization responses found in high altitudes (Brendt 1979).

The present-day Mayas protect themselves from the risk of such reactions by doing work in their fields early in the day, when the heat is less. They rise long before dawn and walk to their fields under the stars. William Folan (1986) has suggested that stars and moonlight may have provided orientation points as well as sufficient light for walking the reflecting, white limestone roads constructed by the pre-Columbian Maya. These roads connected cities with each other and with secondary administrative centers and supporting villages. Use of stars as navigation aids by long-distance traders on these roads may have contributed to the early development of astronomy in Maya civilization.

Scheduling of activity is an important Maya adaptation to the local climate. The afternoon nap, seen by vacationing tourists as an example of local indolence, is another adaptation to heat stress. Tourists are rarely up and out between four and nine A.M. when the Mayas are doing their first five hours of work. The Mayas also coordinate the rhythm of their movements with the degree of heat, moving more slowly during the hours of greatest heat, more rapidly during the cooler hours. By one or two P.M., men return home from their fields for dinner and rest (*siesta*), after which all family members bathe, put on clean clothing, and socialize outdoors, escaping from the still hot houses into the cool, as night brings relief from the sun's heat and the day's tasks. Eventually the houses cool off with the evening breezes and people return indoors to rock to sleep in their hammocks.

SWIDDEN PRODUCTIVITY AND POPULATION DENSITY

The contemporary Maya adaptation to the local soils and rainfall patterns is swidden agriculture. Initially their swidden system was seen by Westerners as both wasteful and destructive of the soil, which it is in overcrowded conditions. However, in areas of low population density, such as Pich, swidden fields are allowed a fallow time of seven to twenty years after being used for two or three. This permits the surrounding tropical forest to fill in the small plots with secondary growth attractive to a wide variety of wildlife, including favorite species for hunting: deer, wild pigs, and wild turkeys. The fields are used in a long rotation cycle and are multicropped. Silvia Terán and C. H. Rasmussen (1995) documented twenty-eight species and ninety-five varieties of cultivated plants in the swidden fields of Xocen, Yucatán. Their research and that of others (Gómez-Pompa 1987; Gómez-Pompa, Vázquez-Yanen, and Guevara 1972; Gómez-Pompa, Flores, and Sosa 1987; Gómez-Pompa et al. 1993; Ewell and Merrill-Sands 1987; Hernández Xolocotzi, Baltazar, and Tacher 1995) demonstrate that swidden is an efficient and relatively nondestructive adaptation—but only when enough land is available to allow for sufficient fallow time.

> The investment of labor in *milpa* activities should provide a high rate of return that declined only slightly with further investment due to slight varia- tions in quality of land. . . . Eventually, the limits of land available for *milpa* expansion are reached and further investment of labor in this kind of agri- culture is impossible. . . . alternatives are labor intensive, i.e. they result in a rate of return for each man hour of labor. Some of these more intensive alternatives, such as terracing or ridged fields would show a lower but constant rate of return as indicated in [Figure 3.3]. Others, such as continued decrease in fallow cycle, would show a stepwise decline in rate of return with decreasing productivity each time the fallow cycle was reduced to a shorter interval. A decreasing rate of return for labor investment feeds back to the decision function and might be expected to have a damping effect upon decisions to invest more labor in a particular agricultural routine, which is, of course, the essence of Boserup's "law of least effort" (1965). That modern milperos have a keen sensitivity to anticipated rate of return

and a tendency to seek non-agricultural alternatives is demonstrated by Reina's data from San Jose (1967). (Culbert 1977:517–18)

Settlement surveys of a number of Classic and Preclassic Maya sites have demonstrated that the population both in the center and in surrounding areas was too dense to have been supported by swidden alone. For Tikal, William Haviland (1969:40) estimated 39,000 in the core area and 49,000 in the extended area, with densities of 600 to 700 per square kilometer and 300, in a total area of 125 to 134 square kilometers. William Sanders's (1968) more conservative estimates of 400 per square kilometer in the core area and 200 for the periphery, are still well above the 77 per square kilometer that Harrison gives as a maximum population density for swidden (Harrison 1977:479). Kintz and Fletcher (l983:196-210) estimate the Late Classic population of Cobá at 40,000 to 60,000 in an area of 63 square kilometers, giving a minimum density of 635 per square kilometer. If we divide these numbers by four, as suggested earlier, allowing for three swidden households and one urban one per family, the numbers are still impressive (159 per square kilometer), but

Figure 3.3
Efficiency Comparison of Agricultural Systems

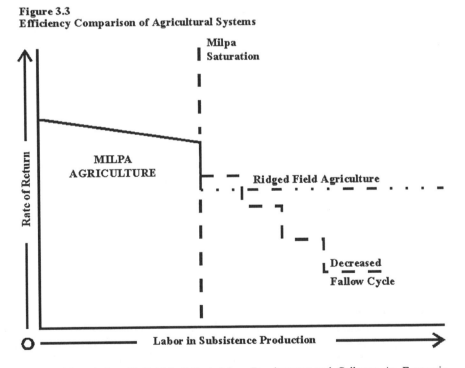

Source: Adapted from T. Patrick Culbert, Maya Development and Collapse: An Economic Perspective, in Norman Hammond, ed., *Social Process in Maya Prehistory: Essays in Honor of Sir Eric Thompson* (London: Academic Press, 1977), by permission of Academic Press, p. 518.

they are within the realm of densities supportable by major reliance on swidden with assistance from land intensive systems for the support of urban centers, corvée labor, and storage of emergency supplies. The figures become even more understandable if we also allow that more buildings (including abanadoned houses) may have been used for storage in anticipation of extreme climatic events than have been previously estimated.

EVIDENCE OF ANCIENT WATER MANAGEMENT TECHNOLOGY

Increasing evidence of the relict canals, reservoirs, drained fields, ridged fields, terraces, and check dams[1] indicates intensive, prehistoric water management in Mesoamerica. The *chinampas*, cultivated artificial islands, built by the Aztecs in shallow lakes, have been known both from modern observations and from historical documents of the Conquest (Berdan 1982:21-23), but a number of Preclassic systems of irrigation have also been documented: the Valley of Oaxaca (Flannery, Kirkby, and Williams 1967), Tehuacán (MacNeish 1972:44), San Antonio on the Hondo River in Belize (Puleston 1977), El Tigre on the Candelaria River in Campeche (Siemens and Puleston 1972), and Pulltrouser Swamp in Belize (Turner 1983). Other water management procedures provided water to cities and villages of the Maya, some of which may have also contributed to irrigation (Thompson 1897; Matheny 1978; Matheny and Gurr 1979; Sandoval Palacios and Morales López 1982; Matheny et al. 1983; Zapata Peraza 1985, 1987, 1989; Barrera Rubio 1987; Bonor Villarejo 1987; McAnany 1990; Faust and Morales López 1993; Domínguez Carrasco 1993; Scarborough and Gallopin 1994; Fedick 1995a and b). Arguments based on population density, settlement patterns, local springs, flood water, and topography have been made for irrigation agriculture at Teotihuacán (Sanders 1976).

Harrison (1978) has interpreted air photos of vegetation distribution as indicating large areas of raised fields in Quintana Roo, which were destroyed by government agricultural clearings before they could be investigated. The hydraulic system of the city of Edzná was very complex and had the capacity to provide domestic water for a population of 36,000 families, according to Matheny (1978:83). It included a grand canal, which has been documented by surface survey for 8 miles and may be longer, as well as smaller canals, reservoirs, and causeways. Drained fields may have been used for intensive cultivation (Matheny 1978:204–5).

North of Campeche, at Labná, extensive terracing and numerous *chultunes* (artificially constructed, underground water chambers) were described in 1897:

> In other places [where large reservoirs such as those at Uxmal and Xkichnook were not constructed] the people seem to have depended upon a large number of smaller reservoirs, the subterranean chambers here described. Each edifice, each terrace, even of the same structure, had one

and often more of these subterranean chambers. No one of them could hold a great quantity of water. The largest one I ever encountered held less than ten thousand gallons. Yet when these are counted by the score, as is the case in many of these groups, the aggregate amount of water supply will be found to be amply sufficient for the needs of a large number of persons. . . . We also note the significant fact that where the groups are built by the side of cenotes [limestone sink holes, with water] few, if any, of these subterranean chambers are found, while they are found by the score in groups not so favored by nature. . . . Every one of the numerous hills that surround the group [of Labná] had its crown leveled and its steep sides cut into terraces, and every terrace examined shows traces of having had one, and sometimes two, of these reservoirs. . . . A wide area around the principal structures now standing is covered with mounds and terraces, and interspersed among these are sub-terranean (*sic*) reservoirs, one at least for every mound or terrace. (Thompson 1897:7–8)

Thompson concluded from his research that the primary use of *chultunes* was for domestic water supply during the dry season, a finding confirmed by subsequent research (see Zapata Peraza 1989). They may have also been used for pot irrigation of the terraces, following Flannery, who argued (based on ethnographic analogy and archeological evidence) that pot irrigation from shallow wells enabled intensive agriculture to support a dense population in the Valley of Oaxaca by 900–600 B.C. (Flannery; Kirkby and Williams 1967:50). Kent Mathewson reported small, traditional irrigation systems in the Guatemalan highlands, still in use, apparently of pre-Hispanic origins (Mathewson 1984).

In a tropical environment with karst topography and a six-month dry season, the limiting factor for human populations may have been water, not just rainfall to produce crops but water for bathing, cooking, drinking, and irrigation of kitchen gardens and household orchards, as has been recently emphasized by V. L. Scarborough and G. G. Gallopin (1994). Other scholars (Folan et al. 1983; Folan and Hyde 1985; Gunn 1994a and b; Gunn et al. 1994; and Sabloff 1995; Folan et al. 1996) have pointed out the significance of climate shifts to the changing status of Maya city-states.

WATER MANAGEMENT IN THE VALLEY OF EDZNÁ

Pich is at the edge of the Valley of Edzná; it probably would have been part of the sustaining periphery of the metropolis of Edzná during the Preclassic, Classic, and Late Classic periods. Pich probably participated in the transformations of Maya civilization through Edzná until this center lost power to the port cities of Kampech (Campeche) and Chak'anputun (Champotón) during the Postclassic period (Gunn and Folan 1996:67–71).

Edzná was clearly a key city in Maya history, with access to the rich marine life of Campeche Bay and to forest resources inland. Its architecture shares stylistic elements with the regions of Petén, Rio Bec, Chenes, and Puuc, each of which has its own distinctive style. Its ruins are located between major sites, including Chichén Itzá, Mayapán, and Uxmal in the north, Palenque to the southwest, and Calakmul to the south. It is close to the coastal zone that includes El Tajín, an influential coastal neighbor of the highland Classic metropolis of Teotihuacán and of the later center of Tula. Southwest of Edzná are the sites of Chontalapa and Acalán, home of the Postclassic Putún sailors (Scholes and Roys 1968), and La Venta, home of the Preclassic Olmec; to the northwest is Jaina Island, famous for its figurines. To the northeast is the ancient Yucatecan city of Dzibilchaltún (well populated from the Middle Preclassic through the Late Classic). Farther east lies Isla Mujeres, named in 1517 by the Spanish conquerors for the idols of Maya goddesses worshiped there (Gómara [orig. 1553?], in Wagner 1942:41).[2] Beyond Isla Mujeres lies Postclassic Tulúm, with its diving gods, and the pilgrimage and trade center of Cozumel Island, where the Spanish found a shrine of Ix Chel, goddess of the moon, childbirth, love, medicine, weaving, and water, who was the wife of the creator-sun god, Itzam Na, and the mother of many Maya deities.[3] Many salt works have been reported along the northern coastline and have been linked to intersite trade of both the Classic and Postclassic Maya.

The Edzná Valley's agricultural potential includes both the bottomlands of the valley floor, dotted with seasonal swamplands (*bajos*) found commonly around the southern sites,[4] and the limestone ridges on the edges of the valley, with their pockets of fertile soil. These ridges are similar to those typical of the drier northern area. The valley floor is the largest area of flat, deep soils in the peninsula.[5]

Intensive agriculture in various parts of the Maya area could have supplied export products for the coastal canoe trade around the peninsula, up the Veracruz coast, and down the Honduras one. At the time of the Spanish Conquest this trade was dominated by the Itzá, the Xiu, and the Putún (A. P. Andrews 1983). Drained fields (some of which were raised) and other intensive agricultural systems could have produced surplus foods for a network of trade involving salt, dried fish, shells, obsidian, feathers, bark, cotton, cacao, plant medicines, dried chiles, and grains.[6]

Edzná had been considered a minor site until quite recently. It was not reported in the early archeological literature (John Lloyd Stephens, Alfred P. Maudslay, Teobert Maler, and others). Although it is only thirty miles south-east of the port city of Campeche, Edzná did not become known to archeologists until January 1927, when it was reported by Nazario Quintana Bello, a state archeologist for Campeche. Sylvanus Morley then visited the site with others from the Carnegie Institution. Seventeen carved monuments were reported, three bearing Long Count dates, in the style of the Classic southern sites of Tikal and Uaxactún. (Morley 1927). The site was revisited in 1936 as part of a survey of the region by the Carnegie Institution. Harry Pollock described it as having elements of both northern and southern architectural styles, including Río Bec and Chenes from the south and Puuc from the north (Pollock 1980). In 1958 and 1962, the Mexican archeologist Pavón directed consolidation and reconstruction of the largest building (Cinco Pisos, Five Stories, named for its five stories of rooms, an unusual construction in the Maya area). Mapping done by G. F. Andrews (1969:246–275) indicated that the site was larger and more complex than previously realized.

Ray Matheny et al (1983) did investigations of the settlement pattern and the hydraulic system that indicated the importance of Edzná for understanding Maya water-management technology. In the urban area surveyed, the settlement pattern is very dense. The grand canal and related water works imply large-scale engineering and regional planning. Small sites in the southern end of the Edzná Valley also have relict water management systems (Sandoval Palacios and Morales López 1982). These sites seem likely to have been part of the sustaining agricultural periphery of the urban center of Edzná. The obsidian sourcing attests to participation of the Edzná valley in a regional trade system that involved the salt works in northern Yucatán, cacao groves in Belize and Tabasco, the obsidian of Guatemala, and some elite artifacts from the Valley of Mexico, which traveled through the canoe networks of Putún traders along the southern coast of the Gulf of Mexico, around the peninsula and down to Honduras (Figure 3.4). Analysis of pollen from Edzná indicates that cotton, either in bulk or as woven cloth, may also have been traded in these networks, some of which continued into the early colonial period (A. F. Chase and P. M. Rice 1985:5–6; G. D. Jones 1982).

THE CONTEXT OF MAYA HISTORY

Ceramic cross-dating with radiocarbon dates at Dzibilnocac indicates the Middle Preclassic (ca. 600 B.C.) as a period of substantial population and building construction: both ceramic and architectural evidence indicate that Edzná was continuously occupied from the Preclassic until the Late Classic period (Matheny 1978:199). Glyphs for A.D. 810 make Stela 9 the latest according to G. F. Andrews (1969:125); however, Matheny considers a date of A.D. 731 from Stela 2 more reliable (Matheny et al. 1983:8).[7]

Various theories have been presented to explain the loss of power, influence, and population of a large number of Late Classic sites in the southern area, in or near the Petén of Guatemala. Although this Collapse did not extend to all of the Yucatán, it apparently affected Edzná (Matheny et al. 1983:8). It is possible the environmental factors (such as soil exhaustion or climate change) that affected the Petén area also affected Edzná. It is also possible that political and/or trade connections with the collapsing southern centers had negative effects on the power of Edzná relative to neighboring competitors along the Gulf Coast.[8]

Archeological literature of the region indicates that after the Collapse, power in the peninsula first moved north to Chichén Itzá and Uxmal, later to

Figure 3.4
Edzná Trade Network Traced Through Obsidian

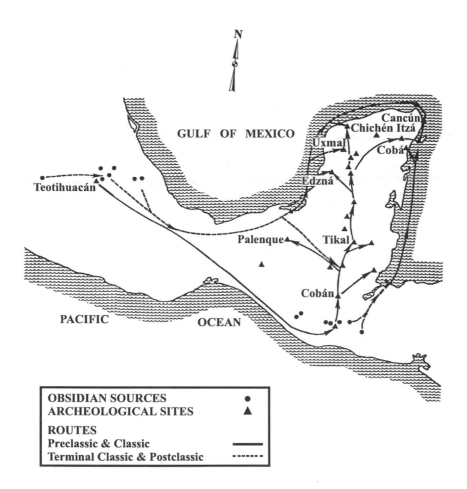

Source: Adapted from Ray T. Matheny et al., *Investigations at Edzná, Campeche, México*, Vol. 1, Part 1: *The Hydraulic System* (Provo, Utah: Brigham University Press, 1983), p. 205, Figure 169, by permission of Brigham Young University Press.

Mayapán, and finally to Maní (when the League of Mayapán broke apart). Cozumel Island (east of Cancún) and Itzamkanac (southwestern Campeche, see Scholes and Roys 1968) were important centers for the Chontal Putún of Acalán, who were described by the first Spanish explorers as expert canoe traders. The port cities of Campeche and Champotón may have functioned as important centers for the Puuc, Itzá, and Putún (Acalán) trade networks, all of which entered northern Yucatán through this Campeche coastal zone, coming from areas to the west.

Little archeological literature is available concerning the technologies of the Postclassic Maya in the western Gulf Coast region, including the inland Edzná Valley. There are considerable controversies over stylistic variations in architecture and ceramics throughout the peninsula between the end of the Classic period and the arrival of the Spanish. Chronological variations in architecture and pottery suggesting sudden abandonment of many sites after the Late Classic are contradicted by the historical documents concerning dense populations when the Spanish arrived in the sixteenth century. At Champotón, for example, although ceramic evidence implies termination in the Middle Postclassic, Spanish records describe dense occupation and excellent military organization in 1519. This contradiction calls into question previous analyses indicating large gaps both between the Terminal Classic and the Middle Postclassic and between the latter and contact with Europeans. Joseph Ball (1985:241–242) suggests that the ceramic style recognized by archeologists as Terminal Classic may have lasted well into the Middle Postclassic and that Middle Postclassic (from the Mayapán sequence) actually lasted much longer, into the full Protohistoric period, in some areas.

The ceramic tradition in the Campeche area differs from that of Champotón. The Campeche tradition has roots in the early Late Classic (A.D. 550–700) and evolves through the Postclassic (a Silho group [X], Fine Orange) (Ball 1977, 1979). Both Champotón and Campeche were densely populated urban ports when the Spanish first came. Extrapolating from the cases of Campeche and Champotón, it is easy to question whether Edzná was actually abandoned at the end of the Classic period. It is possible that architectural and ceramic styles were conserved through the Postclassic and that the site was not abandoned until the Spanish conquest, although erection of stelae ceased there as it did at Cobá, Lamanai, and other sites recently found to have been inhabited throughout the Postclassic (Folan, Kintz, and Fletcher 1983; Robles 1990).

In the Yucatán Peninsula during the Late Classic (A.D. 800–1000), the growing Puuc sphere of influence was resisted by the political sphere of Cobá. Later (A.D. 1000–1200), the Itzá were able to extend from the southern Gulf area over the politically disintegrating northwest. They pushed back the northern and western borders of the Cobá area more than had the Puuc (Andrews and Robles 1985:62–71). The Itzá network of trade and politics collapsed in the early 1200s, to be replaced later by the Putún sailors based in the Acalán-

Tixchel area, who were described by the early Spanish explorers.

Warfare was common during the Postclassic centuries, as were trade and communication with the wider Mesoamerican culture area. The Puuc and the Itzá introduced new cultural traits, including bows and arrows; defensive sites with moats, walls, and palisades; new forms of political organization; and a new art style (Chase and Chase 1985:7). While some archeologists interpret these changes as evidence of conquest by invaders from the Valley of Mexico, others have concluded that there was not sufficient replacement of local material culture to indicate incorporation of the Yucatec Maya in a foreign empire: "There are no vastly superior states elsewhere in Mesoamerica in this time period. . . . The syncretic disjunctions found in the record point to mutual acculturation between lowlanders and outsiders, the breakdown of cultural insularity on the peninsula and the incorporation of the surviving Maya into a pan-Mesoamerican elite culture" (Freidel 1985:296).

During these times, throughout the Mesoamerican area, migration itself was probably a "general means of legitimating elite authority" (Freidel 1985:300). Within the Yucatán Peninsula, the new groups seeking to extend their economic and political networks were "at most Mexicanized or 'internationalized' Maya rather than newcomers to the peninsula" (Freidel 1985:302).

FROM DRAINED FIELDS TO TERRACES?

An agricultural technology associated with the "internationalized" Postclassic Maya culture is rainfall-dependent terracing. This technique is applicable to most ridges and hills, since it is not dependent on access to streams or rivers. Dry terracing not only reduces erosion but also slows runoff, conserving water in the ground and thus maintaining moisture between periods of infrequent rain. This technique will clearly improve agricultural productivity, particularly in areas of low rainfall.

According to Robert Drennan's analysis, the dry terracing typical of the Postclassic in Oaxaca and the Valley of Mexico was more land intensive and labor intensive than the previous systems of stream irrigation such as those at Tehuacán and Teotihuacán (Drennan 1988). The increased intensification required more dispersed residence patterns than those of earlier periods. Drennan compares this northern Postclassic pattern to the southern Classic Maya pattern of relatively dispersed settlement connected with labor-intensive drained fields. These were built in swampy areas by cutting drainage canals and piling the soil removed on the narrow strips between the canals. Drennan includes in his list of intensive agricultural systems requiring continual attention from the farmer both the drained fields (some of which are raised) and the *chinampa* system found in the lakes of the Valley of Mexico. He does so on the basis of both the analysis done by Sanders and his colleagues of their own data and the sixteenth-century observations of Pedro Armillas,

[who] found that nearly the entire lakebed had apparently been covered with garden plots arranged within units of a large grid defined by major canals. In some areas of unusually good preservation it could be seen that each grid unit contained a set of *chinampa* fields that completely surrounded a single house. This suggested a general pattern in which each housemound was surrounded by the land cultivated by its members. Our own surveys . . . indicated that this isolated household pattern was very common throughout the old *chinampa* district of Lake Chalco Xochimilco, although small multi-household settlements were also present. (Sanders, Parsons, and Santley 1979:163–171)

The *chinampa* system, the drained field system, and dry terracing all have households dispersed among agricultural fields, in contrast with both the earlier piedmont canal systems and swidden agriculture which are associated with nucleated settlements (Drennan 1988:287). Swidden fields require little care, minimizing the number of days that farmers have to be physically present, and families prefer to live in nucleated villages. In Pich, however, I have found that the elders fondly recall living in small *rancherías* near their swidden fields during the entire agricultural season. These are minimal nucleated settlements, generally of three to five families. Even today, small groups of men stay there for periods of a few weeks each during planting, early and late weeding, doubling of the corn, and harvest. The corn stalks are doubled over after the corn has ripened, to protect the vulnerable tops of the ears from birds and insects, while the corn dries on the stalk.[9] Harvest of the earliest varieties of fresh corn begins in August; since there is no danger of frost, the dried corn can be havested as needed, generally between November and January. From January thorough April, the men return periodically to hunt and to cut and burn forest in preparation for planting activities, generally in groups of three or more. The work can be done alone, but most men prefer to work in small groups because of the dangers of snakebite, wild cats (jaguars and mountain lions), heat stroke, dehydration, and getting lost. The latter is a common danger because there are no outstanding features on the horizon and the forest is dense and tall. There are no rivers and sources of water are few and far apart. (In Pich, two cases are known of men who went out to make *milpa* alone and were never seen again.) Although the causes are different, the social patterns are similar to those required in the canal system described by Drennan:

> The labor involved in canal irrigation systems is not focused for each household on its own fields. Indeed, it is widely dispersed along the length and possibly the breadth of a canal system. Altogether apart from the construction and maintenance, the operation of such systems in the Mexican highlands today requires frequent coordinated trips by several individuals to widely spaced nodes in the canal network to route water to the fields. Since the simultaneous participation of several people is required, members of different households are often involved. Neither the dispersal from the

agricultural plot of the places where such labor is performed nor the need to communicate with members of other households (both as assistants and competing water users) encourages a family to live on the land it farms. Rather, the reasons . . . for living near other households are strongly rein- forced by such labor requirements. (Drennan 1988:287)

Drennan's model provides interesting interpretations of the data concerning various residence patterns and agricultural technologies. There is still a need, however, to explain the lowland Maya shift away from *bajo* agriculture in the southern area at the end of the Classic period (Freidel 1985). Culbert's graph makes clear the advantages of ridged-field (or drained) agriculture over swidden with shortened fallow, but also the advantages of long-term swidden over ridged fields. Only in conditions of population pressure is it rational to prefer ridged-fields over swidden since the labor costs are higher unless the duration of fallow is reduced, a condition developing all over the Yucatán Peninsula. Today's Maya farmers complain that the weed invasion on "young fields" (with less than fifteen years of forest regrowth) is so bad that they are driven to buy herbicides. These require cash investment and prevent the intercropping with beans and squash that is fundamental to traditional Maya swidden. Even if herbicides are not used, however, the shortened fallow results in soils too poor to support healthy bean and squash plants. These are increasingly invaded by insect pests, in turn requiring the use of insecticides.

The adoption of lakeside occupation sites for the Postclassic Maya of the Petén was accompanied by hilltop occupations in the highland area and parts of the northern lowlands. This shift may be an indication that the Postclassic Maya were adopting agricultural technologies from Oaxaca (Flannery, Kirkby and Williams 1967) as well as from the Valley of Mexico in response to drying climate, or that they were returning to a previous technology, well-known by them to be more efficient under conditions of reduced population pressure.

While there was no collapse in the northern lowlands, individual cities lost and gained power in political struggles (Chase and Rice 1985; Sabloff and Andrews 1986). In the southern lowlands, after the Collapse, population growth centered around lakes (Rice and Rice 1984). Various explanations have been suggested, including arrival of new information from the Valley of Mexico concerning Nahuatl (or epi-Toltec) technologies for managing lakeside environments. The canals and raised fields of the southern Classic Maya sites were not repopulated, possibly because they were perceived as the locus of Yellow Fever or some other disease organism (Wilkinson 1996). If the climate had changed, it might not have been possible to maintain or rebuild these complex systems. The soils in these areas could have become deficient in some trace mineral necessary for crop production (e.g. iron, zinc). It is also possible that the raised fields of the Classic era were the property of a royal elite, whose legitimacy dissolved when the limits of escalating population growth were reached or the climate dried (or both). Cessation of slavery or tributary labor after the fall of the elite culture could have made maintenance of these fields unfeasible. All of these theories have been widely discussed in the archeological literature.

TERRACES AND WATER MANAGEMENT

Very little archeological research has been done on Postclassic technologies in Campeche. Morales López (1986:30–31) has presented evidence of walk-in wells at Kitam Xpuhil (in the Río Bec area) combined with agricultural terracing similar to structures analyzed by Ray Matheny and Deanne Gurr (1979) in nearby Chiapas. The agricultural terraces in both areas depended on rainfall, conserving both water and soil behind stone retaining walls. The terraces were sloped in such a way as to direct runoff during rainy season to the underground storage tanks. These tanks have sloping, stone-lined, circular entrances, of 8–10 yards in diameter, which are sometimes called "walk-in wells."

In areas of the northern lowlands where natural relief is minimal, the ceremonial plazas of towns and cities were sloped, directing water to underground tanks with small openings, *chultunes*. These structures have been found in association with Late Classic ceramics. Unless Ball is correct in his theory that the ceramic style simply did not change for a very long time, there is a gap in the archeological record of Maya water management in the Campeche area from the Late Classic to the sixteenth century.

ENVIRONMENT AND TECHNOLOGY IN SPANISH COLONIAL CAMPECHE

The references to water in the historical records are scanty, but occur in the earliest reports. In 1517 Francisco Hernández de Córdoba sailed westward from Cuba in search of slaves. He landed in several places, including the Bay of Campeche. His men found both Campeche (Kampech) and the neighboring city of Champotón (Chak'anputun) full of hostile Indians (see Figure 1.2 for a map). According to one report, based on interviews with eye witnesses and written perhaps by 1520, initial friendly greetings in Campeche included a tour of the town and a feast. After obtaining water for the ships, however, the visitors were given signs to leave, accompanied by threats of violence.

> By signs they told us to leave their country before they lighted the wood they had piled up and finished burning it. If not, they would make war on us and kill us. . . . We began to march along the beach until we came near a rock in the sea. The small ship and the boats went along close to the shore with casks and vessels for water. We did not dare go aboard near the town where we had landed on account of the great number of Indians who were there awaiting us, as we believed it certain that on embarking they would fight us. (Díaz del Castillo [orig. 1560s], in Wagner 1942:63)

When these same ships attempted to take on more water at Champotón, the Maya attacked and the Spanish were forced to retreat to their ships with heavy losses. This battle is well documented and has come to be known in local history books as *la Mala Pelea*, the Bad Fight.

In 1518, Juan de Grijalvla traveled up the Veracruz coast and then returned to put in at Champotón to avenge the defeat of Córdoba. The Hernán Cortés expedition passed through this way, as well, en route to Tenochtitlán, capital of the Aztecs. Archival research by France Scholes and Ralph Roys (1968) has provided convincing evidence that the Acalán lands of the Chontal Putún, referred to in the chronicles of the Cortés expedition, were in the drainage of the Candelaria River, to the southwest of Champotón. It was in this region that the ruler Paxbolonacha aided Cortés, and it was probably near the Acalán capital of Itzamkanac that the Aztec ruler Cuauhtémoc was killed by Cortés, who had taken him hostage for the return march from Tenochtitlán (Scholes and Roys 1968:112–116).

From the Cortés campaign have come the earliest Spanish descriptions of Acalán and its Putún sailors (Díaz del Castillo [orig. 1560s], in Wagner 1942:63). Scattered references in this material refer to canals, abundant crops, and canoe trade—indicating at least ditched fields, at the time of contact (Puleston 1977:451). Alfred Siemens, R. Hebda, and M. Heimo (1996) are continuing their research on raised fields in the nearby Río Candelaria area.

During a 1559 attack on a Choltí-Lacandón fortress, in Lake Miramar, Chiapas, Spanish cavalry was reportedly unable to cross deep ditches or canals around corn fields (Villagutierre 1983, orig. 1701, summarizing sixteenth-century archival materials). These features are a strong indication of irrigation agriculture. For neighboring lowland Chiapas and the central Petén, Nicholas Hellmuth (1977:423–438) has encountered references to intensive agricultural systems in the unpublished archival documents in the Archivo General de Centro America and the Archivo General de las Indias in Seville, Spain. Trade between these areas and the peninsula is well documented and would have provided communication networks for the exchange of technical information.

The archeological evidence from Edzná indicates that its canals (possibly with adjacent ridged fields) were not intensively used after the Late Classic. It is difficult to understand why this hydraulic system was abandoned, particularly considering the historical indications of dense settlements in the Campeche area and of complex intensive agricultural practices in the Valley of Mexico at the time of Spanish contact. It would seem that a population rebound sufficient to have needed intensive agriculture would have cleaned and repaired the old canal and reservoir systems at Edzná, Uxmal, and other sites. The key to this mystery may be either the exhaustion of the surrounding soils or the nuisance of mosquito infestations in the canals, which had eroded through lack of maintenance.

> The "akalches" that make Uxmal today a hot-bed of deadly fevers, are the supply basins of the ancient times; their once clear bottoms are now buried

deep in swamp ooze, and decaying vegetation masks their true outline. Wild ducks, serpents, and great frogs are now the only creatures that can live beneath the great white sheet of miasma that each night shrouds the deserted yet magnificent piles [archeological mounds] nearby. (E. H. Thompson 1897:7)

Historical references to agricultural and water management practices in the peninsula could provide substantial assistance for the interpretation of Postclassic archeological evidence. However, the historical references presently available for the Yucatán are far weaker than Peter Martyr's detailed description of irrigated fields on the island of Hispaniola in the Caribbean[10] in which he explicitly likened them to the irrigated fields of Cartegena and Murcia in Spain (Martyr [orig. 1511–1555?], in Wagner 1942:388). Perhaps continuing research in the sixteenth-century archives will discover more information concerning water management and intensive agriculture at the time of contact with Europeans. It is also possible that a new Chilam Balam will be found that describes such systems.

The demographic collapse following European contact was far more devastating than the Maya Collapse of the ninth century. The primary cause of the sixteenth-century collapse was probably "virgin-soil epidemics," those that result in very high mortality rates because of the vulnerability of a population with no previous exposure to a disease. To these were added the effects of colonial domination and the introduction of foreign technologies. Disruption of local ecosystems by exotic species of plants and animals created other difficulties for the food procurement systems of the sixteenth-century Maya. All these conditions made difficult the maintenance of complex technologies and reduced the need for them.

After the Conquest, at Maya sites where there was access to ground water through wells or cenotes, newly introduced pulleys with wheels provided more water with less human labor. Mechanical devices harnessed to draft animals and windmills provided water for orchards, cattle, haciendas, and cities. In the postconquest conditions of labor scarcity (following the severe population losses of the early decades), this Spanish hydraulic technology was particularly advantageous. The Spaniards hauled water in large wooden barrels pulled by mules to the city of Campeche from wells in nearby Chiná. Rainwater is still delivered in this manner in some areas of the city. Horse-driven or mule-driven wheels (*norias*) for extracting buckets of water from wells were constructed over old Maya wells in the city and in a number of towns and haciendas[11] throughout the State of Campeche.

Local villages that obtained their water from *aguadas* were not affected by the new Spanish water system. These *aguadas* continued in use until the last twenty to forty years, when Mexican government programs brought in deep wells, electric pumps, and piped water systems with spigots at each household. City dwellers and many modernized peasants now think of these old *aguadas* as natural ponds and have no understanding of how they were constructed or maintained.

MAYA PROCESSES OF TECHNOLOGICAL CHANGE

The technologies of water management and agricultural production utilized by the ancient Maya were diverse and fitted to the specific requirements of different ecological zones. They required different forms of socio-political organization and at times different settlement patterns. They changed in response to changing climate, new ideas brought in from other areas, local inventions, and the challenges imposed by both growing and declining populations. The Maya no doubt experienced soil erosion and deforestation as their populations grew. They learned some lessons from the Collapse and from other changes in their environment: political, economic, ecological, and meteorological. They have learned from the Conquest and the national government's previous programs and will no doubt continue to learn from new programs and from their satellite dishes, their FAX machines, and their connections to the Internet. They compare new ideas with what they know already when making decisions about "rural development," but change is certainly not new to them.

NOTES

1. Check dams are constructed in areas of natural run-off, "gullies." They trap eroded soil, allowing for its recovery, and slow the movement of water, reducing the erosion downstream. They are usually relatively small and built in a series, down the natural channel of run-off.

2. López de Gómara's account is one of several that are associated with the 1517 voyage of Francisco Hernández de Córdoba from Cuba to the Yucatán, exploring the coast past Campeche and Champotón into the area called Acalán, beyond the Laguna de Términos.

3. For reviews of the historical literature concerning the worship of Ix Chel at Cozumel see Morley 1946:181, 223, 230–231, 407–408; Scholes and Roys 1968:57.6.

4. Based on archeological evidence, Harrison (1978:247–253) and B. L. Turner (1978:178–183) have developed a model of intensive agriculture for the *bajos* of the southern area, based on relics of drained fields and canals.

5. According to Sandoval Palacios (1982:86–87), in the early 1970s the administration of Mexican President Echeverría evaluated this valley as having "the only important agricultural potential in the whole Peninsula of Yucatán." It is the only northern area with good potential for irrigation agriculture, providing the possibility of year-round cropping. It was also found to have one of the lowest indices of population in the country: 5.2 people per square kilometer. For both these reasons, it became the target of a development and colonization plan involving mechanized agriculture.

6. Evidence of such a trade network has been described by William Folan, Ellen Kintz, and Laraine Fletcher (1983) and A. P. Andrews (1983), although there is no direct evidence for trade in basic grains.

7. This may be related to a problem mentioned earlier by G. F. Andrews (1969), the disappearance of stelae listed as having been moved to the Campeche Archeological Museum.

8. Edzná may have continued to serve as a ritual center and as a residence for local population, as Cobá did after its decline (Folan, Kintz and Fletcher 1983:211–214). However, political power and new construction moved to other areas.

9. Tender corn is harvested for immediate consumption and is greatly relished, but only dried corn may be stored for use throughout the year in making tortillas, tamales, pozole, and other foods and beverages.

10. For a review of those references, see the survey done by Dennis Puleston (1977) or that by Grant Jones (1982).

11. Haciendas are landed estates, which originally had legal rights to incorporate Indians as laborers through a variety of mechanisms. Some Indian laborers were residential; others had seasonal labor obligations but were allowed to live in their home communities for the majority of the year. In the Yucatán, haciendas were much smaller and less developed than in the Valley of Mexico. The primary export of the haciendas of the peninsula during colonial times was cattle. Other exports were dyewood, honey, cochineal dye, the cloth woven by Indian women, and other tribute items made by independent Indian producers. It was not until the invention of hay-binding machinery that production of henequen twine became profitable and the henequen haciendas boomed in the north of the peninsula. This occurred in the late nineteenth and early twentieth centuries (Farriss 1984:33–39). Recent research on dyewood (*palo de tinte*, *Haematoxyulum campechianum*) indicates that it was also a major export through the port of Campeche during the eighteenth and nineteenth centuries (Contreras Sánchez 1990).

Traditional Maya home with television aerial, 1996. *Photo by Bret Diamond.*

Sixth-graders from Pich on a visit to Uxmal, 1986.

The plant-covered *aguada* of Pich, with the ruined friary and the reconstructed church in the background, 1995.

Earning a living by cutting the last of the big trees, 1996. *Photo by Miguel Medina.*

Harvesting squash seeds, 1996. *Photo by Bret Diamond.*

A *milpero* and his wife and children with a mule cart in front of their home, 1985.

Planting the old way, "as God intended," 1986.

Shopkeeper weighing the purchases of a boy shopping for his mother, 1985.

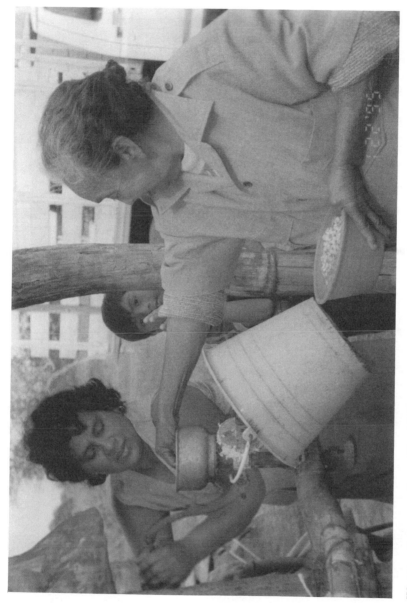

Women grinding corn for tortillas, 1995.

Woman with altar decorations in front of the altar of the Three Green Crosses of Pich, 1995.

Women and adolescent girls at a *novena* to request the help of the Virgin Mary in calling the rains, 1986.

Remains of the temple at Tabasqueño decorated with sculptures of the Rain Lords (the long-nosed *chaco'ob* on the right and left corners of the facade), the Earth Lord, and squared spirals representing mecate plantings, 1986.

H-men sacrificing a turkey in the rain-calling ceremony, 1986.

H-men and assistants preparing ritual foods for the rain-calling ceremony, 1986.

Men forming balls of corn dough and getting ready to put the flattened balls into the *tuti wah* (beneath the coconut palm fronds at the center of the photo) for the rain-calling ceremony, 1986.

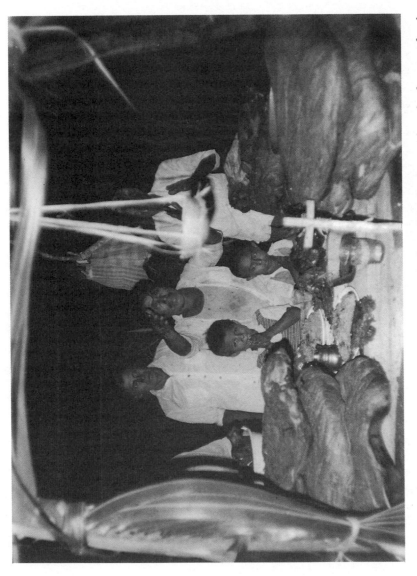

H-men presenting ritual foods to the Wind Lords, 1986. At the front of the altar is an arch made of coconut fronds (top, right, and left edges of the photo).

4

Working for Water from the Earth and the Sky

In the northern part and around the coasts of the Yucatán Peninsula, access to groundwater through natural *cenotes* (sinkholes) and caves is common. In the center, there are no natural water supplies until one reaches the east-west river systems, which branch out of Belize, Tabasco, and Guatemala. In the interior of the peninsula, artificial water-holding structures of various kinds save rainwater for the dry season. In Pich, a traditional Maya water system still exists, but is no longer used. It includes a paved *aguada* (reservoir) with wells in the bottom, a canal that brings water from the nearby hills, and two drainage channels for overflow (to prevent flooding during storms) (see Figure 4.1). The descriptions of how this system was used and maintained were recorded during my 1985–1986 field season and during the summer of 1992.

There are scattered references to similar systems in the archeological and the ethnographic literature. In addition to *aguadas*, there are sloping paved plazas that channel rainwater into *chultunes*, underground chambers with bottle-neck openings of cut stones (E. H. Thompson 1897; Zapata Peraza 1985). The linings of cut stone were sealed with a mortar made of burned limestone mixed with water and calcareous sand (*saskab*), that is locally referred to as "*concreto*" in Spanish and *bah pek'* in Mayan. These linings are also found in many *aguadas*, preventing seepage into the underlying limestone strata (Stephens 1988 [1843]:Vol. 2, 148; Sandoval Palacios and Morales López 1982:23; Domínguez and Folan 1993). Canals carry water from surrounding hills or ridges into some *aguadas*. Finally, there are shallow wells in the bottom of some reservoirs. Gates and Folan (1993) have suggested that the wells give access to circumscribed pockets of water, perched higher than the normal water table. Those small pockets could be refilled annually by rainfall seeping through the vertical cracks in their limestone roofs or by the force of water rising in enclosed channels underground (see Figure 3.2). It is also possible that the water in these wells does not come from tapping into an underground chamber but rather seeps into the well from a sponge-like stratum

Figure 4.1
Reservoir (*Aguada*) of Pich

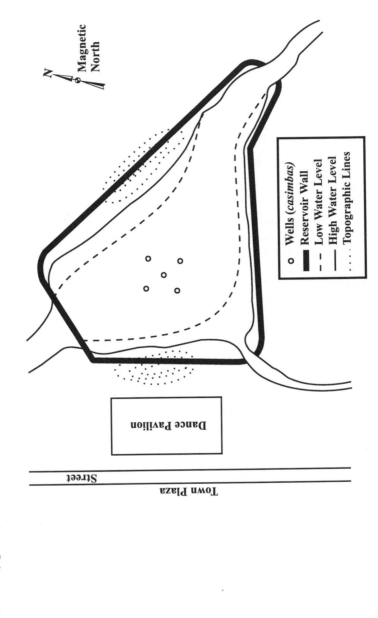

Wells (*casimbas*)
Reservoir Wall
Low Water Level
High Water Level
Topographic Lines

N
Magnetic
North

Dance Pavilion

Town Plaza
Street

Source: Original map by Abel Morales López, assisted by Michael Hoover.

of particularly soft limestone rock. However these shallow wells work, their underground water supply would be refilled by the rains during the six-month rainy season. In addition, the *chultunes* of some reservoirs and plazas would have functioned as additional storage containers for rainwater.

These water-management systems were built and used during the long centuries in which the Maya practiced various forms of intensive agriculture, only recently discovered by archeologists (see Siemens and Puleston 1972; Matheny 1978; Puleston 1978; Siemens 1978; Turner 1978, 1979, 1983; Matheny and Gurr 1979; Matheny et al. 1983; Schele and Freidel 1990; Pohl and Feldman 1992; Culbert 1996; Siemens, Hebda, and Heimo 1996).[1]

Mesoamerican water management evolved in conjunction with detailed knowledge of many aspects of the local ecological system and its seasons, together with a strong supporting ethic of collective responsibility. Nancy Farriss's (1984) finding that such an ethic was an important survival strategy for Yucatec Maya communities throughout colonial times has been given strong support by M. B. Restall's (1995) research in the colonial legal documents. Restall found references to and descriptions of the *cah*, an indigenous form of community organization in the Yucatán Peninsula. The *cah* defended communal lands and community rights in the colonial Spanish courts. I believe that this strong community organization and the ethic described by Farriss were developed through the management of rainwater reservoirs in the interior of the peninsula (Faust 1988a:167–171, 223–275). Oral histories collected in Pich indicate that forms of community management of rainwater reservoirs continued until modern water systems were installed by the national government, late in the twentieth century.

WATER MANAGEMENT IN THE ANCIENT EDZNÁ VALLEY

Pich is located on the edge of the great Valley of Edzná, which had a complex system of reservoirs and canals associated with a grand canal whose northern end was in the ceremonial center of the city of Edzná. Folan has speculated that its southern end may have flowed into the Río Champotón, linking Edzná with the Gulf of Mexico.

According to Matheny's calculations, based on contemporary ethnographic data of extended families of 12 persons and an average of 200 liters of water per family per day (for domestic uses during dry season),

> The 2-million-cubic meter-plus water storage at Edzná theoretically could support 36,000 families for about a six-month period [dry season], given the estimated consumption rates and the 0.6 percent daily water loss that has been calculated for evapotranspiration, plant transpiration, and seepage. The canals and reservoirs of Edzná, then, held sufficient water to support the needs of a populace much larger than we have reason to believe existed at the site. (Matheny 1978:204)

This amount would suggest there was sufficient water for irrigated fields.[2] With or without irrigated fields, the mapping of the site indicated that it was a well-populated city from Preclassic through at least Late Classic times. Surface surveys have located 100 public buildings, 471 housemounds, 31 canals, 84 reservoirs, and a moated fortress, as well as the great canal. Estimation of housemounds beyond the city center has not been attempted, but local knowledge of the many mounds throughout the valley and along the ridges that form its boundaries indicates they were very dense (Matheny 1978:204–5). Some of the rural population that supported the city of Edzná may have received water from its canal system. Outlying villages, however, would have needed their own water-supply system during the long dry season. It is also possible that earlier development of simple systems at the village level is what eventually provided the concepts and engineering expertise that enabled the building of the complex system associated with the city of Edzná and the surrounding valley.

Maya *aguadas* appear to be natural features of the landscape and have been so considered by most outsiders, including many explorers and archeologists who have found them around Maya archeological sites. In the middle of the nineteenth century, however, J. L. Stephens (1843:2:148) described a large *aguada* with wells at Rancho Halal (Jalal), to the north of Pich. This *aguada* was larger and had many more wells, and wells of more sophisticated construction, than those in Pich; but it apparently lacked a canal such as the one that helps replenish the system in Pich.

Stephens was told by a local resident of Rancho Halal that their *aguada* often dried up before the end of the dry season. They would then dig holes in the bottom, and water would seep in from the sides of the holes. One day while digging in the mud, a man found cut stones and upon digging around them he found:

> a square at the top, and beneath was a round well, faced with smooth stones, from twenty to twenty-five feet deep. Below the first well is another square platform, and under the latter another well of less diameter, and about the same depth. . . . upward of forty wells were discovered differing in their character and construction. (Stephens 1843:2:148)

Figure 4.2 shows a cross-section of the *aguada* and wells. Unfortunately, it neglects (as did the original Frederick Catherwood illustration) to show the two-tiered well described above, but it does illustrate the other types of "wells" (Folan, Kintz, and Fletcher 1983:47). Three appear to be not wells but bottle-shaped *chultunes*.

The description by Stephens of the process of cleaning, and the resulting abundant supply of water, is similar to the stories I was told in Pich. During the rainy season the reservoir funnels rainwater into the wells, refilling the underground pockets (or porous strata) before it accumulates in the reservoir.

Figure 4.2
Reservoir (*Aguada*), Wells, and *Chultunes* at Rancho Halal

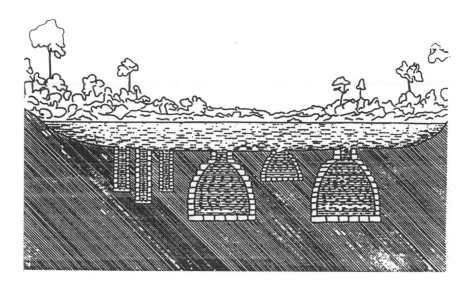

Source: William J. Folan, Ellen R. Kintz, and Larraine A. Fletcher, *Cobá: A Classic Maya Metropolis* (New York: Academic Press, 1983), p. 47, Fig. 3.16, by Permission of Academic Press and William J. Folan.

Folan has suggested that the second well and other variations in the wells may be responses to climate shifts. If the length of the dry season began to increase, it would be worth the investment of time and energy to construct additions to the water system, enabling it to supply the community longer. It is, of course, also possible that the population was growing, thereby necessitating increased water-storage facilities (P. Faust 1993).

Oral histories collected from 1985–1992 indicate that normal yearly fluctuations just result in temporary migration to relatives in neighboring villages that have more reliable wells (such as those at Bolonchen Ca'uich). These same oral histories refer to processes of village fission, where groups of young people leave to look for existing ponds (which possibly were abandoned reservoirs of former occupied settlements) near good soil, where they can begin new hamlets. It may have been easier for groups of young couples to establish such new hamlets than to enlarge by hand the relatively complex well-canal-*aguada* system. Thus, we could hypothesize that only under conditions of relative land shortage would population growth *or* a climate shift result in new additions to water-management facilities. Such population growth is well established in the Late Classic period, for a number of Maya cities (e.g., Turner 1990:310–311).

Folan, Morales López, and Sandoval Palacios have found similar *aguada* constructions in other sites in the southern part of the Valley of Edzná. The latter two reported finding *aguadas* with cut-stone linings when the forest was cleared for rice planting around Yohaltún in 1979–1980. They were found in the same general area as ancient drainage canals, which were believed to have had agricultural uses. The *aguadas* ranged from 12 or 15 feet to several dozen yards in diameter. Some crossed canals, but these apparently lacked paved bottoms (Sandoval Palacios and Morales López 1982:23).[3] Folan (1986) has information concerning another *aguada*, that of Ixkanhanó near Chuchintok.[4] The information provided him by a local informant was that the *aguada* has a stone floor with four *chultunes*. They are lined with cut stones and are only 18 feet deep. In Pich, a natural perched water table appears to be reached and refilled through shallow, simple wells between 12 and 18 feet deep. In Ixkanhanó, it is *chultunes* that collect and save rainwater. (In both Pich and Ixkanhanó, when the government drilled wells looking for water in the 1950s, they had to go down more than 450 feet to find an adequate supply.)

Naturally formed, perched water pockets like those described could provide more storage capacity for less labor input than any other water-storing mechanism available to the ancient Maya. The natural chamber only had to be located and reached with a simple well. There is no oral history concerning the origins of this water management system; however, it is said that one always knows where water is close to the surface by looking at trees, which put their roots down through rocks. One sign of water close to the surface is a very tall ceiba tree (Ceiba *pentandra*). Both iconographers of the Classic Maya and the native historians who wrote the colonial books of *Chilam Balam*, described this tree as sacred to the Maya (see Schele 1993). Given the holiness of corn, rain, and sun for Pichuleños, it would seem that the sacredness of the ceiba as well might be grounded in its usefulness. Throughout the valley, the ceiba is an indicator of water pockets close to the surface, of a good place to dig wells (Faust 1988a:213–219, 225).

In this very hot climate, the underground water pockets would not have suffered from the serious evaporation or contamination problems that beset reservoirs. Neither would they have been breeding grounds for mosquitoes. Unfortunately, natural underground formations capable of holding water in the limestone strata do not appear to have been as frequent or as large as needed. The labor-intensive *chultunes* conserve rainwater underground in much the same way, where there is no natural water pocket to be reached by a simple well.

The capacity of a simple well could also be supplemented later by a reservoir, if the population grew. The reservoir would lose less water to seepage if lined with stucco and stones. According to oral histories, the system in Pich includes the wells with access to an underground water pocket, the lined reservoir, and a canal that brings additional rainwater from the drainage system of nearby hills and ridges. It also has drainage channels to prevent flooding. The reservoir-well-and-canal complex seems likely to have been the preferred water-management system for rural villages where caves and sinkholes did not suffice for domestic water during the dry season.[5]

The development of the technology could have resulted from observations of the small, naturally occurring ponds found in parts of Campeche and Quintana Roo. These and the reservoirs are both locally referred to as *aguadas*. The natural ponds form at the foot of limestone ridges, where soil accumulates from erosion, eventually this provides a sufficiently deep base that surface water washing down the slope can make an indentation, forming a large, shallow seasonal pond (*bajo*) and later a smaller permanent one (*aguada*), in the area closest to the bottom of the slope (see Figure 4.2). As a human population settled around a pond and grew in size, it would eventually use up the accumulated water during the dry season. Digging holes in the basin floor would provide more storage and also could yield additional water from seepage into the hole. Lining such holes with cut stone would have kept them from collapsing inward during the wet season. As population grew, and with it demand for water, the holes would have been dug more deeply and, after experience, shaped more efficiently into *chultunes,* which were lined with fired clay or with stucco to prevent seepage. The Maya would have been able to cut through limestone strata with existing techniques for quarrying the limestone blocks used in construction of public buildings.[6] Once this system was developed, its rainwater holding capacity could have been increased by enlarging and deepening the original, surface pond. Lining the enlarged pond with stones in lime mortar would have prevented loss through seepage.[7] The conceptions involved in this technology could then have been applied in other areas, including those where a naturally occurring pond did not exist but where plants indicated that there was water near the surface. Where ridges or hills were nearby, a canal could have been fashioned fairly easily from the rerouted natural channel of a seasonal stream (*corriente*).

The *chultún*-and-plaza complex found in the civic centers of many of the smaller sites of the area may have developed from the reservoir-and-well complex. The plazas surrounding civic buildings were paved with stone and stucco and were sloped toward the entrances of *chultunes*. Many have stone caps, which were probably taken off during the wet season to allow the water from rooftops and plaza to enter the *chultún* and then replaced to keep the water clean during the dry season. Present-day local inhabitants report having found and entered these *chultunes*. Anthropological investigations have concluded that, in the Yucatán Peninsula, they generally were initially used for water, although some were later used as burial sites or filled with trash.

An analogous system of water management has been found in the highland Maya zone of Chiapas. Complex hillside terraces channel rain water through check dams to large walk-in wells (Matheny and Gurr 1979). These systems appear to be a highland variation of the *chultún*-and-plaza system common in Yucatán, where temples substitute for the terraced hills in directing rainwater to an underground holding tank. Logically either system could have been used as a model for the other. Without scientific excavation and dating we will not know the sequence of invention, since both areas show signs of early occupation. It is clear, however that the same hydro-logic underlies both the reservoir-well-canal system and the *chultún*-and-plaza complex.

Thompson reported in 1897 that there is usually nothing inside the plaza *chultunes* of Yucatán except what may have accidentally fallen in. He concluded that while these constructions are of little interest for those seeking tombs and other caches of valuable goods, they provide important information concerning the water systems of the ancient Maya. His call for more research on the *chultunes* as a water-management system has been largely ignored for nearly a century.

The *chultunes* of the Maya plazas, which are ubiquitous in the mounds scattered throughout the valley, were apparently not maintained after the sixteenth century, perhaps because of their ties with the Maya elite, who were replaced by Spanish colonists (although there are rumors in Pich that other villages have begun to construct *chultunes*). From colonial times until the recent drilling of wells with heavy machinery, the most common water-supply system throughout the Edzná Valley has been the rain-filled *aguada*. In many of the larger colonial homes, Spanish-style cisterns were used to collect rainwater from roofs. The remains of Spanish wells with either a mule-turned wheel for extracting water (*noria*) or a simple rope pulley for a bucket are still visible on some haciendas and in some villages. However, *aguadas* would seem to have been the major water source for most villages in the interior of Campeche.

ORAL HISTORIES OF WATER MANAGEMENT IN PICH

The *aguada* was a communally managed system according to the villagers of Pich. The rain collected in the reservoirs and was protected by prohibitions against swimming, bathing, clothes washing, or any other activity that might introduce contamination. People clearly remember that the floor of the *aguada* is constructed of stones (some blue-green ones were recalled by one elderly man) laid with stucco or plaster and that there are wells of different depths in the center. The *aguada* is about seventy-five by a hundred feet and slightly L-shaped. According to oral histories collected in the village, it has four or five wells in the bottom. The *aguada* of Pich must have been built over a high, cir-cumscribed water-retaining formation, as three or four of the wells in the *aguada* are only 9 to 12 feet deep, while the center one, which is the deepest, is only 15 to 20 feet, according to oral histories taken from people who remem-bered cleaning them. During particularly dry years, when Pichuleños ran out of water in the *aguada*, they would clean the accumulated muck from its floor in order to locate the *casimbas,* wells, which would also be full of mud and need to be cleaned. Once cleaned out, they would fill with water. People would take out buckets of water daily until the well was dry, but it would refill overnight. It was recalled, however, that in the very worst drought years this system sometimes failed. Then water was brought to the village in big barrels drawn by mules. This transport was organized by the richest family in town. Many of those who had relatives in villages with more dependable wells went there to visit until the drought ended to avoid having to buy water, if they were not *compadres* (fictive kin) or relatives of this family.

The Pichuleños have not cleaned out their *aguada* since a government piped-water system was built about thirty years ago. The government drilled approximately 100 feet away from the *aguada*, but did not find sufficient water until a depth of 480 feet. It would seem that the wells in the *aguada* access some circumscribed, perched water pocket, far above the level that supplies the government's well. However, even this new system with its deep well and large storage tank runs out of water during the dry season, by noon, if not earlier. People say this is because the cattle ranchers take too much.

Whether the *aguada* of Pich occurred naturally and was later lined to increase its water-retaining properties or whether it was dug by the ancient Maya is not clear. The banks of soil around the edge are higher than the sur-rounding land and suggest that the depression may have been constructed, or at least enlarged, by human effort. At the eastern end, a large canal still brings water from neighboring hills. It could have contributed substantially to a silting-in process, and the yearly cleaning could have produced the high banks around the *aguada*. Potsherds found on the surface of these banks have been stylistically identified as Late Classic (Morales López 1986), a period when construction was still occurring in the city of Edzná. Sandoval Palacios and Morales López (1982) have found similar constructions near Yohaltún, while doing an archeological survey before the land was bulldozed for rice planting.

According to Pichuleños, there are a number of Maya hamlets around Pich that still rely on *aguadas* for water.

In 1974 Michael Hironymous (1989) saw an *aguada* with wells in the neighboring hamlet of Dzonil. It had been recently cleaned with the help of a small bulldozer, because it had become dirty. Wells lined with cut stone were visible in the bottom, but the *aguada* itself was not lined. The people of Dzonil did not find water entering the cleaned wells, as had those of Rancho Halal. In Dzonil they were paying to have water trucked to them, as they waited for the rains to arrive and refill their cleaned *aguada*.

The *aguada* of Pich has existed since the "time of the ancient ones." Not only was the *aguada* lining constructed by the ancestors, but so was a canal that brings water from the neighboring ridges and hills, where it is known to rain more often. I was told by several people that the canal also drains water out when the *aguada* gets too full. The canal is said to go at least 3 miles into the hills in the east, although it is too overgrown to follow beyond about a half of a mile from the village. Close to the *aguada*, the canal is approximately 8 feet across on the bottom, and 12 across the top, with gently sloping sides. This large canal is said to go in the general direction of the small "canals" in the forest. In Pich, people in their late thirties recall participating as children in the communal cleaning of the reservoir and its wells. An older generation recalls participating in this activity as young adults. In addition to the practical actions taken to clean the wells and the *aguada*, villagers remember the rain-calling ceremonies that followed. Once the system was clean, the community organized the same extended family groups for symbolic actions to assure survival. The rain ceremonies began with a procession and a festival for the three green crosses, on May 1, 2, and 3. The crosses are still carried through town on May 3, but in the past, during this procession, all the men of the town fired their shotguns in unison on each of the intersections of four corners. It is said that the sound was like thunder, the smoke like dark rain clouds. In 1986 the procession for the Day of the Holy Cross was conducted by the priest from Spain, but the men no longer shot off their guns.

After the fiesta for the crosses, the nightly processions of the women began, carrying the Virgin from one home to another. Each night a novena (a ritual prayer service with candles and special foods, to which neighbors and friends are invited) was offered to her in a different home. These processions continued until it rained. In 1986 there was a drought and the processions continued well into June, even though the priest said that they should only have novenas for the Virgin during her month, the month of May.

In 1986, in addition to the procession of the green crosses and the novenas for Our Mother, I observed a traditional Maya rain-calling ceremony led by the local *h-men*. The participants asked the Lords of the Winds (*Los Dueños de los Vientos*) to bring rain to fill the *aguadas* and to water the newly planted corn. The ceremony I observed was in a neighboring community. A few private families in Pich had also sponsored such ceremonies, but there was no longer enough consensus in Pich to do the ceremony as a community. More than 300 of the 1,500 people were Protestants, approximately 200 Presbyterians and 100 Pentecostalists. Although some of these people occasionally visited the ritual expert for private healing ceremonies, they did not wish to sponsor the rain ceremony, since they publicly rejected all ritual and beliefs associated with both Catholicism and Maya traditions. To engage openly in the rain ceremony would advertise a certain contradiction in their own beliefs and expose them to ridicule and charges of hypocrisy.

SUPPLEMENTARY WATER SOURCES IN PICH

A few old wells outside of the *aguada* are known in Pich, but they have been filled in with rubble so that children would not fall in them. Three were remembered as having water that was not good for drinking, two being salty. The other was said to be bitter or bad tasting.[8] A fourth well that still functions is inside the patio of the hacienda-style house it serves and has a wall around it to prevent anyone falling in it. Although it may access a water-holding geological formation, as well as being replenished by rainwater drained from the roof, it occasionally runs dry.

Another ancient device for water management known in the village is the relic canals on the *ejido* land. These are some distance from the village, in the forested area of the *ejido*. Local farmers are aware of them, and of the great canal, the old reservoir, and the small canals around the nearby site of Edzná, where they used to hunt until the colonists from the north were settled at Bonfil. The small canals of both Pich and Edzná may once have served an ancient Maya agricultural system. I have not seen them, and they have not been used in anyone's memory, but descriptions of the ones in Pich and Matheny's research on those at Edzná indicate strong similarities with the raised-field systems reported for other parts of Campeche (Siemens and Puleston 1972), Quintana Roo (Harrison 1978), and Belize (Turner 1983).

The son of a wealthy family of the village (who is now a veterinarian in the city) reports that the "small canals" near his father's land in Pich have "hill-like rises between them, only they are little." Aerial photographs on file in the local office of the National Institute of Anthropology and History in Campeche showed a small patch of parallel lines approximately 6 kilometers east of Pich, within the *ejido* land of the village. They have the same orientation (approximately 8 to 10 degrees east of north) as the raised fields in Quintana Roo, which I determined from a map in Harrison (1977:476, Figure 3). This orientation is also the same as that of major buildings at the nearby Late Classic site of Tabasqueño (Morales López and Faust 1986) and some major structures in the main ceremonial center at Edzná (Matheny et al. 1983:17), according to compass readings. Matheny has interpreted this orientation.

the orientation of these structures is very close to true north-south since the magnetic declination in this area is between six and seven degrees to the east of true north. This also suggests that the ancient Maya relied on bearings of the North Star rather than crude magnetic compass readings when laying out the center. (Matheny et al. 1983:17)[9]

In Pich, the only remaining north-south sixteenth-century church wall is oriented approximately 8 degrees east of north, according to measurements taken by Morales López (1986) with his Brunton compass. This reading was difficult to make as the wall is rough, the stones are irregular on the surface and varying slightly in their settings. The orientation of the lines on the aerial photographs is difficult to determine because of the small size of these images. Therefore differences of 2 or 3 degrees may be measurement error. The orientation of buildings at the nearby, small Chenes site of Tabasqueño is 7 degrees east of north. The similarity of orientation suggests another reference to a widely shared Mesoamerican cosmology, such as the orientations described by Franz Tichy for Puebla where "the designs of settlements follow the same compass points as the designs in the arable land surrounding them, as well as having the same orientation as colonial churches of the 16th century" (Tichy 1981:217–245). The orientation to the North Star pointed out by Matheny et al. (1983:17) would explain the similarity in today's compass readings. An orientation of raised fields, and their associated canals, to a sacred star would be consonant with J. E. S. Thompson's (1970) and Dennis Puleston's (1977) analyses of Maya religion and the sacred aspects of both water and celestial beings.

The canals in the land near Pich have not been dated; however, the majority of the hydraulic and architectural construction at Edzná was done during the Late Preclassic, A.D. 0–200 (Matheny et al. 1983:195). There is evidence for Preclassic ridged fields in many lowland Maya areas, as well as for complex terracing on neighboring slopes (see Puleston 1978; Turner 1978, 1979, 1983; Donkin 1979; Matheny and Gurr 1979; Denevan 1982). Some of the ridges and hills in the catchment of Edzná may be relict terraces.[10]

Terracing, drainage canals, reservoirs, wells, *chultunes*, and complex combinations of these may have been devised by the ancient Maya in response to varying climatic conditions during two thousand years of occupancy (Folan et al. 1983; Gunn, Folan, and Robichaux 1994; Gunn and Folan 1996). Alternatively, all of these technologies may have been in use simultaneously, each being appropriate for a specific situation, optimizing control of water in an ecosystem in which there is danger both of flooding and of drought. The Maya population had been growing, perhaps approaching the ecosystem's carrying capacity. Except for areas around the few permanent lakes and rivers, the limiting factor was probably water, not food. In developing the Law of the Minimum, Justus von Leibig (1863) identified a variety of limiting factors that can determine carrying capacity for a specific species in a given ecosystem. An extension of that law allowed for trade (Moulton 1942; Boughey 1968), while Robert MacArthur and Joseph Connell (1966) included population dynamics and the probability of extinction of any local population over time. These biological limits, along with socio-political factors, may be important aspects of the Maya Collapse.

MAINTENANCE AND USE OF THE RESERVOIR OF PICH

The *aguada* of Pich was constructed to (1) conserve rainwater efficiently, since its artificial floor reduced seepage; (2) receive water from higher elevations, carried to it by means of a canal; and (3) have access to a perched water pocket by means of wells. The water pocket would have been refilled yearly with rainwater collected by the reservoir and canal.

When I arrived in Pich, bathing or swimming in the *aguada* was still forbidden, even though it had not been used for domestic water for twenty years. It was commonly said that the piped water system might fail, and then they would need the *aguada*. Neighboring refugees were severely scolded for washing their clothes in it. They were told to take buckets of water out and wash their clothes where the dirty water would not get back to the *aguada*.

Before I left Pich in 1986, village wisdom was vindicated: the government water system did indeed fail in the middle of a drought. However, the wall around the *aguada* had not been repaired recently and so there were places where the pigs could get in and wallow. This weakness was lamented but no one organized a work crew to fix the wall. The problem was complicated by confusion over the state of the water in the *aguada*. There were mixed opinions about how usable it was.

The problem had begun with a government development program that introduced a new kind of fish to the *aguada*. This occurred "about eight or so years ago, in the time of the governor before the last one" (each one of whom has a six-year term). The villagers were told not to eat the fish until they got big. The fish were to stay in net cages and the people were to feed them corn dough. They eventually tired of feeding these fish and let them out of their cages. The fish then ate the water plants that grew in the *aguada*, which was very unfortunate because these plants kept the water cool and fresh. Then the water was quite dirty. Someday when the fish are big, tourists might come to fish them, it was said. Others say the fish died when people stopped feeding them or have long since escaped out the canal during years of much rain. There were still a few small fish that the children surreptitiously tried to catch, but people were still afraid they would be punished for fishing and scolded the children for doing so.

In 1986 I commented to a woman in my adopted family that if someone were to bring to Pich a couple of the water plants from the *aguada* of Ho'ol, where her married daughter lives, that these plants would multiply. When I returned in 1990, the *aguada* was again covered with dense vegetation. Her experiment had succeeded; the water was clean and cool under the plants. The children are freely fishing. It is understood now that these fish are a different species than those the government brought years ago. These are the little ones, "brought by the rains."

SOCIAL ORGANIZATION RELATED TO WATER MANAGEMENT

In the old system of water management in Pich, the shallow wells in the *aguada* belonged to specific groups of extended, patrilineal families, and the deep central well belonged to the entire community. Shallow wells were considered the private property of the families that had contributed the expected man-days of labor to their construction. With ownership came responsibilities as well as rights of use: men had to contribute the necessary man-days of labor involved in cleaning in order that their families could retain exclusive rights to these wells.

The central well was said to be for "everyone," but every patrilineal extended family in town was required to provide men to clean it. The wells were cleaned only by men, who took turns in the arduous and dangerous task. One man would go down and clean, placing the muck in a bucket, which would be hauled to the surface by his fellow workers. The muck would be deposited on the surrounding banks of the *aguada* (some of which would again wash down into the *aguada* during the six-month rainy season). When one man tired of the difficult work in the well, he would be relieved by another, since working inside the well was difficult (*bien duro*).

In the less dangerous surface cleaning of the *aguada*, all family members were required to participate: men, women, children, and old people. The muck on its floor was scooped up in buckets and old gallon cans and deposited on the banks. It was an activity in which everyone could see everyone else's participation and one's contributions to the joint effort were part of one's public reputation.

No one was ever denied water who needed it to drink; however, water for bathing, washing clothes, watering house yard plants and trees, and watering animals was not nearly so generously dispensed. Reciprocity was expected. In return for the favor of using someone else's water, one was expected to give food, volunteer labor, or provide some form of compensation in the not too distant future. If the reciprocal favor was not forthcoming, any new requests for water were met more and more grudgingly with smaller and smaller amounts of water. It was possible to know how much water anyone used because the supply was in the center of the village and was guarded by a caretaker during the day. His job was not only to prevent people other than the families of those who maintained the wells from using them without permission but also to make sure that no one dirtied the water of the *aguada*. The *aguada* was encircled by a stone wall, but the gate had to be watched. The rules for protecting the *aguada* included the following: (1) children were not allowed to throw things in it or play in it; (2) no one was allowed to swim or bathe or wash clothes in it; (3) water was taken out in buckets and used in households; and (4) no dirty water was ever allowed to return to the *aguada*. During the night the *aguada* was guarded by the souls of the dead, and perhaps haunted by the *Ixtabay*, a female spirit who tempts men to follow her and abandons them in the wilderness among the jaguars, snakes, and thorns.

In the traditional system, there was accountability. Information was easily and freely available to all concerning who did his or her share of the work, and who took what amount of water. Responsibilities were overseen by the respected heads of patrilineages, who distributed and enforced work assignments. Benefits could be controlled so as to make them roughly equivalent to investments. Water was understood to be a limited good, a public good, and a serious local responsibility. Without it one could not live through a day in a tropical environment. It was a renewable resource—but only when the Lords of the Winds chose to renew it.

The Wind Lords' providence concerning water was understood to depend on both public and private morality. Cooperation, working together, and peacefulness were pleasing to the gods. Adultery was not just private behavior but a violation of the public good. It was believed to cause not private misfortune but drought and epidemics of disease. It was a community matter.

In traditional society, individuals clearly had rights. They owned property and had the right to dispose of it as they wished, within certain limits. However, individuals also had responsibilities to the public good through the mediating structure of the extended family. The collective enterprise of survival, so well described on political, social, and religious levels by Farriss (1984), was also a very practical matter on the most fundamental level: it made human life physically possible in this environment. The most critical factor for maintaining human life in this environment was not food but water, obtained, preserved, and distributed by collective action. The water-management system and the technology associated with it were conceived of as sacred because of their importance in maintaining life itself.[11]

DROUGHT IN PICH

In 1986 little rain had fallen in Pich and then the water pump broke. The village mayor attempted to install the spare pump and found that it did not fit the pipe. He called to Campeche for assistance, but it was ten days before the pump was fixed. Lack of water was at first assumed to be temporary. What was still in tanks was conserved carefully for drinking and cooking. Anyone with a large storage tank jealously guarded its water, doling it out to kin as discretely as possible.

Water-tank size generally reflects family economic status. The water system often does not function from noon until evening, so people are in the habit of filling water jugs, buckets, and other containers during the morning. Those with water tanks also fill them in the morning.

During this dry spell, people brought food and other gifts when visiting their friends and relatives who had big household tanks and had thus been able to conserve more water than others. People with large amounts of water tried to hide this fact from neighbors so that they would not have to incur anger by refusing to give it away when they wished to conserve it for their own extended family's use. People accused others of lying about how much water they had. Controversies erupted over who could use the water in the school's tank, by far the largest in town. Then one night, the school's water was stolen; the teachers threatened to leave.

Long before lack of water threatens thirst, it affects social relations and daily behavior. Corn and beans, which form the largest part of the daily diet, cannot be prepared for human consumption without ample use of water. Beans absorb twice their volume of water in cooking; corn not only absorbs water when soaked before cooking, but also must be rinsed in several changes of water in order to remove the lime in which it is soaked, before more water is added for cooking.

In addition to cooking requirements, water has great importance in bathing. It is locally believed to be absolutely essential for health to bathe at least once a day. The Maya firmly believe that human beings who do not bathe are unhealthy, get ugly skin rashes, and also stink. They are said to be rotting, like an overly ripe fruit. Clean clothing is to be put on at least once a day, after the afternoon bathing (around 4 P.M.).

During the ten days that the piped water from the government system was no longer available, people turned again to the *aguada*. However, they had learned long ago from government officials that the water in the *aguada* was a source of typhoid. Therefore, they saved the remaining safe (*potable*) water from the piped system for drinking and cooking. They attempted to use the water in the *aguada* for bathing, laundry, cleaning, and watering kitchen gardens. However, the *aguada* water was found to cause skin rashes and to wilt plants. Furthermore, the good water they had saved for drinking was rapidly being used up.

The government was held responsible for providing water. The village mayor called officials in the state capital, who promised relief. However, when water did not soon arrive, public opinion turned against the mayor rather than the state government. People insisted that as mayor he had the personal obligation to use his own trucks to provide the town with water. It was noted that he had a very large water tank in his home and trucks to bring water to his family; therefore, his lack of action was seen as a matter of selfishness—unwillingness to think about the people he was responsible for, the community.

His failure to solve the water problem quickly enough undermined his legitimacy as an authority figure. The men of the community eventually rioted over an unrelated incident. More than one hundred men repeatedly stormed the door of the jail to free a friend who had been locked up for drunken driving. When they finally brought a large lumber truck to pull the door off the jail, the mayor placed an emergency call to Campeche for police assistance. Help was not forthcoming and the jailed man was discretely released by the mayor's assistants before the truck could pull off the jail door. The government water trucks finally began to arrive the next day, and the mayor took a vacation for a few weeks, insisting that he had had plans to do so anyway. Talk of throwing him out of office subsided in a few weeks.

GOVERNMENT WATER AND VILLAGE CONCEPTS OF ACCOUNTABILITY

Although the oral traditions and the books of *Chilam Balam* provide information on patterns of periodic drought (Folan and Hyde 1985), the mechanization of agriculture seems to have worsened the situation. Since 1973 extensive deforestation and agricultural colonization with government-subsidized mechanization have been occurring rapidly throughout the Edzná Valley, as people from other parts of Mexico respond to government incentives to resettle in this area. Bulldozers strip all vegetation from large tracts of land formerly farmed in a swidden cycle. The old technique left many hectares of forest around each small cleared area of 2 to 5 hectares, which was itself planted with diverse species of plants that covered the soil, reducing soil erosion and conserving moisture. The loss of large tracts of forest is perceived by some village elders as causing a change in weather patterns that is detrimental to agricultural production. This local hypothesis is supported by the analysis of the anthropologist J. M. Sandoval Palacios (1982), the archeologist Folan (1986), and two local ecologists and a biologist working for government agencies who preferred to remain anonymous.

Low population density and the availability of national lands for settlement originally contributed to government perceptions of this area as an available frontier. Rainfall patterns, soil structure, and water scarcity have made colonization difficult. And the colonization process, in turn, may have affected the climate. Whether the current problems of drought are part of a long-term regional cycle or whether they are the result of deforestation and the beginning of a process of desertification, they are of increasing concern for the Mexican government's development of this area as an agricultural frontier zone.

AGUADA TECHNOLOGY AS AN ORGANIZING METAPHOR

The visual metaphor most clearly connected to Pich's technological adaptation to its environment is its *aguada*, the body of ground water that most younger villagers and outsiders generally consider a natural formation. It functions as a metaphor of the communication problem involved in modern attempts to understand the traditional world of Pichuleños. For most outsiders, water is a public good, an abundant natural resource. A pond is simply there to be used. For the elders of Pich, water is a symbol of discipline and order, social rules, and planning. Their "pond" is at least partially a human construction. It and its wells and canals had to be cleaned regularly and protected from contamination. The water system was maintained through a collective organization of work, with individual accountability and some division of labor.

The Maya associate reservoirs, wells, cenotes, and caves with the Virgin, Our Mother. These bodies of groundwater are thus associated with the water of the womb, released in childbirth. Water is the environment of new human life. Through women, as mothers, the continuity of the community is achieved: they produce the new generation. However, women do so through being fertilized by the "water" of men. In a parallel manner, rain is received by and replenishes the underground sources of water that give life to the community during the dry season. The rain is delivered by the Lords of the Winds, who are male. Like the *aguada* itself, the rains are not traditionally considered to be simple natural occurrences. They result from the "work" of sacred beings. Rain is water poured from gourd containers by the Rain Lords, the *Chako'ob*. The *Chako'ob* are brought across the sky by the Lords of the Winds. If these delay, then the traditional *h-men* is called to do his work of organizing a ceremony that feeds the Wind Lords and asks them to bring the rain.[12] Only men are allowed to cook these foods for the Wind Lords. The rains fill the wells. The wells themselves and all bodies of water in the ground and under the ground are associated with Our Holy Mother. Yet, wells are maintained by the activities of men, who enter them to clean them, in order that they may give life. In addition, men produce the corn that women turn into food for sustaining human life.

Thus, the social roles involved in providing food and water are strongly isomorphic with human sexual reproduction, which can then serve as a symbol for social interdependency. Gender, foods, and water are all used symbolically in the traditional healing ceremonies to promote a healthy alignment of the patient with the social and natural environment.

The above associations of water with work, life, and the sacred imply that work is an important, natural part of life and that work is sacred. These implications are corroborated both by my observations of attitudes toward work in the everyday life of people in Pich and by the conclusions of Mary Elmendorf (1976: 98–119) concerning the meaning of work in the community of Chan Kom (in the northeast of the peninsula).

Rain is not, however, seen as simply resulting from work. There are two other important considerations. Rain is tied to seasons and thus to Maya cosmology and the solar year. Rain is also tied to private morality. In order for the rains to be good for the crops, individual members of the community must exercise self-restraint in their daily, personal lives. Sexual misconduct and other failures of social responsibility can produce drought.

Illness, by contrast, can be caused by the winds. The rainy season begins with intense winds, after several months of extremely hot, humid, still weather. The beginning of the rainy season is when people, especially children, tend to develop intestinal problems, since accumulated organic debris is washed into the water supply. The other strong winds of the year bring cold, northern storms, blowing down across the Gulf of México during the fall and winter. Fall is particularly problematic due to the hurricanes that form in the Caribbean and sometimes cross the Peninsula. Both the northern storms and the hurricanes are associated with a rise in the incidence of colds, coughs, bronchitis, and flu, as most people have no sweaters, jackets, or blankets to protect them from the cold.

Agricultural activities in the absence of irrigation are even more obviously associated with the winds and the rains. Also, corn must be planted early enough that it will be sufficiently mature in the fall not to suffer greatly from the fierce winds of this season. Both agricultural and healing activities are thus associated on a practical level with the winds and the rains and the yearly seasons defined by the movement of the sun. These associations connect with the similar, cyclic dependence of the traditional village water system on the seasonal rains to refill both the underground and above-ground supplies.

A traditional rain-calling ceremony orients the community to proper social behavior as well as to Maya cosmology, which includes the sacred corn and human health. All adult men and adolescent boys are expected to participate in the work and in providing the ingredients. The ritual will not be effective if the community is not "together." Neither will it be effective if there is anyone who does not "have faith" in the ceremony. Peace and proper behavior are considered very important, and conflicts in the community make it difficult for the ceremony to have its desired effect. Immoral sexual behavior, in particular, is thought to offend the Wind Lords and prevent rain.

ATTENDING A *TUTI WAH*

Maya rain-calling ceremonies, according to descriptions I have read of those in the north and the one I observed in Campeche, are similar. In the north the ceremony is called *ch' a-chak*. In Pich it is referred to variously as *tuti wah* (a *tuti wah* is a large tortilla filled with ground squash seeds), *pan de milpa* (bread of the cornfield), or *trabajo grande* (big work). The ceremony is normally performed after planting, when the corn plant is still small and very susceptible to drought. The *tuti wah* I observed happened to be on the first full moon after summer solstice, but I have since been told that that date is not fixed; the ceremony is done when rain is needed.[13]

The ceremony begins with the ritual preparation of sacred foods, including turkey soups, turkey meat, and tortillas, and sacred drinks, including *sak-ha'* (a beverage made with honey and cooked corn that has not been soaked with lime) and rum. These activities are oriented according to the sacred directions of Maya cosmology. During the long preparation of the foods by men, there are two ritual performances, first the offering of *sak-ha'* to the Wind Lords, second a presentation of rum and drops of human blood. After these presentations the *sak-ha'* and the rum are drunk by the men who are preparing the ritual foods. Women and children attend the final ritual, the offering of the foods to the Wind Lords, after which the foods are distributed to the people by family.

Only men are permitted to prepare the food and drink. In the north of the peninsula, women are said to be excluded from the ceremony entirely, but in Pich they have always been allowed to witness the final ceremony and participate in the meal that follows. Pregnant women, however, are considered "delicate" (*delicadas*) and advised not to consume any of the food or drink because these powerful ritual substances could cause them harm.

I was invited by the *h-men,* Don Pedro, to attend and photograph a *tuti wah* ceremony he organized for Nohyaxché, one of the neighboring villages, in the Valley of Edzná. (I reciprocated his generosity with a gift of copies of the photographs taken, which he keeps on his family's altar, together with a picture of the Virgin and some important family mementos.) I had previous friendly contacts with the families in Nohyaxché and had become well acquainted with Don Pedro months before the ceremony. The village had been built within the last fifteen years by Maya colonists who had applied for and received *ejido* land in the Valley of Edzná. The colonists were originally from a Maya area to the north, referred to as *Los Chenes* (the wells), and had come looking for land to form a new *ejido*. The village was composed of four patrilineal extended families, including grandparents, married children, grandchildren, *compadres*, and some unmarried aunts and uncles—about two hundred people in all.

Don Pedro and I traveled to the hamlet on the *ejido's* bus, which leaves the village for the city at 5:30 every morning. We got off the bus about 6:15 and walked about ten minutes into the small settlement of traditional Maya homes near a large ceiba tree. I was the only woman there until the wives and children came for the final ritual, close to midnight.

Preparations had begun at dawn with the washing and cooking of the corn, one vat with corn that had been soaked in lime for the dough and one vat with corn untouched by lime for the soups and *sak-ha'*. These preparations had begun before our arrival. One of the corn-thickened soups would be left in its natural white-corn color. The other would be colored red with turkey blood and liver. The vat of white corn soaked in slaked lime had turned slightly yellow. This yellowed corn would be used for the large tortillas, prepared in stacks layered with a reddish brown paste made from ground squash seeds, and for a large corn baby with a heart made of the same paste. The *sak-ha'* was made of corn that had not been soaked in slaked lime but had been cooked for a long time to soften it. The cooked corn was ground to make a drinkable gruel sweetened with honey. Sometimes it is seasoned with chocolate and cinnamon. It is used in many Maya ceremonies performed by the *h-men*, as well as being offered by ordinary people to the spirit beings during times of danger or thanksgiving. White and yellow rum have replaced the traditional *balche'*, a fermented drink made of tree bark and honey. Incense, candles, flowers, cigarettes, and a wooden cross to accompany the ceremonial prayers had also been provided.

Shortly after our arrival, a pole was fixed horizontally to two trees in the woods. A hand mill was attached and used to grind condiments, squash seeds, and corn. The first of seven rounds of ritual drinks of yellow rum began close to 9:30 A.M. This was preceded by an offering of white rum to the Wind Lords of the four directions and the Chief Wind Lord, who is overhead. Yellow and white rum had been provided by the men of the community. The yellow rum was served individually to each participant by the *h-men*. The initial offering of *sak-ha'* to the Lords was made about noon. After the ritual invitation to the Lords, the *sak-ha'* was left in *jícaras* (a commonly used local gourd which grows on trees) for them to consume. A half-hour later the *sak-ha'* was distributed and consumed by everyone present.

After distributing the *sak-ha'*, Don Pedro performed a healing ritual that involved blood sacrifice. He sprinkled an old man suffering from rheumatism with yellow rum, using a twig of the *sip che' (Bunchosia* sp.) which had been dipped in the rum. An assistant poured a small amount of rum, from the bottle cap, on the man's head. Then Don Pedro punctured the skin of the patient's forehead and temples, around his knees, and down his shins to his ankles with a rattlesnake fang. The old man stood still in the sun, holding his arms out sideways, for about ten minutes in total silence while the blood ran down.

At mid-afternoon the tortillas and corn baby were interred in the *pib* (pit oven) and the turkeys were sacrificed by the *h-men,* after having been ritually fed *sak-ha'* and white rum and purified by the smoke of the copal incense. After being bled into *jícaras*, the turkeys were put in large pots to cook on the fire. The blood, hearts, and livers were left on the altar table. While the turkeys were cooking, the men built seven arches of coconut fronds in a line running from the altar table east to the ceremonial area. They ran a vine across the tops of the arches, from east to west, and hung three gourds full of *sak-ha'*, as gifts to the Lords of the Winds, in the exact center of the first, middle, and last arches. Slightly to the south side of each of the gourds they hung three crosses, commenting that if these crosses were placed in the center of the arches they would block the path of the rain down the cable. A larger cross stood at the back of the altar table (see Figure 4.3).

At sunset, there were important ritual prayers with extensive ceremony. The *h-men* walked through the seven arches and then walked in a small, counterclockwise circle in the middle of the ceremonial area. He used a twig of *sip che'* to fling some reserved *sak-ha'* to the four directions and overhead. He then addressed long ritual prayers to the Lords of the Winds as the sun set.

After sunset, it began to get dark rather quickly, as it always does in the tropics. The pit oven was opened in the last minutes of daylight. In the smoky darkness, the *h-men* supervised and helped with the removal of the *tuti wah* and the corn baby from the *pib*. Everyone participated except two older men, who continued attending two pots of turkey soup. After removal of the breads,

Figure 4.3
Cosmological Orientation of a Rain Ceremony

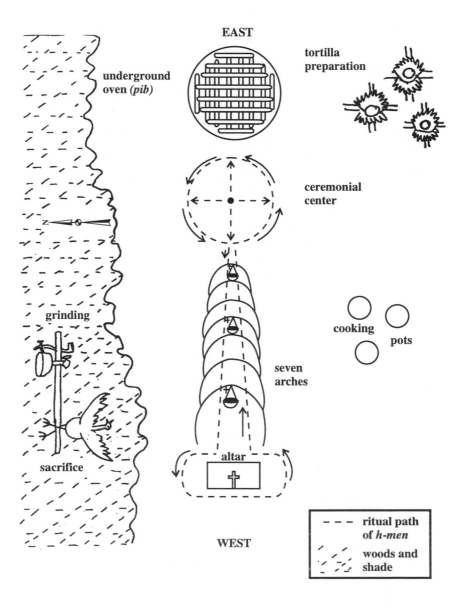

underground
oven *(pib)*

EAST

tortilla
preparation

ceremonial
center

grinding

cooking

pots

seven
arches

sacrifice

altar

WEST

- - - ritual path
of *h-men*

woods and
shade

these men took the cooked turkeys from the pots and began to cut up the meat. They and Don Pedro finished preparing the ritual foods.

The final offering of food was made in front of the wooden cross, on the altar, in the most elaborate of the rituals. The women and children of the hamlet assembled to watch it. Don Pedro stretched out his hands over the foods and made long, earnest petitions in Maya to the Lords of the Winds. An old man mimicked thunder and little boys made the sound of frogs. All the men who were heads of household in the community took turns blessing the food with the sign of the cross and each prayed in Maya.

After a respectful period during which the Lords of the Winds partook of the *gracia* (divine grace) of the offerings, the food was divided among all the families. Everyone ate a portion there and each family was given some to take home. This final division was accompanied by tired discussions concerning the distribution of foods, which by custom should be relative to family contribution, including work done during the preparations, monetary contributions for the purchase of some ingredients, and contributions of other ingredients for the ritual meal. People were tired, cross, and somewhat intoxicated. They argued, but not for long. I was given food to take home to my adopted family. Don Pedro and the sponsors cleaned up the area and buried the turkey feathers, intestines, and other inedible parts, with some pieces of the ritual foods. This was an offering to the Lord of the Earth, who must not be forgotten at the end of any ritual involving sacrifice. One of the sponsors took Don Pedro and me home in a pickup truck.

ANCIENT COSMOLOGY IN THE *TUTI WAH*

The various ritual actions of the rain ceremony are timed and oriented to critical points in the path of the sun. East and west are associated with sunrise and sunset. North and south are associated with changes in the daily path of the sun during the tropical year, with its cycle of wet and dry seasons. North is associated with the summer solstice and long days, south with winter solstice and short days. Sunrise and sunset positions move to the north until summer solstice and to the south after it.

In the *tuti wah* in Nohyaxché, the table that served as the altar was carefully oriented so that "the sun will travel down the center of it." Its length was north-south, so that the sun's path conceptually cut across its center, moving from east to west. The wood in the *pib* was carefully arranged, with the first layer going east-west, the second north-south, and so on. These are the directions to which a traditional Pichuleño orients his fields. He begins in the northeast corner, walks west like the sun during the day, following his morning shadow. At the northwest corner he begins to move toward the south, as the sun's daily path does after summer solstice, during the growing season of the corn. Arriving at the southwest corner, he returns to the east, as the sun does each morning. At the southeast corner, he begins to move north, like the sun's daily path after winter solstice, when the agricultural season is over.

The sun is associated with social order, white, noon, and summer solstice among the Chamula (Gossen 1984, 1986a) and the K'iche' of the highland Maya (Earle 1986). Among the books of *Chilam Balam* is the *Chilam Balam of Chumayel*, in which social order, the sun, and the color white are linked in symbolic imagery (Edmonson 1986). The sun is associated with order and the construction of order, as it structures both cycles of time and the directions of the world by means of its path through the sky. Thus it was symbolically appropriate that in Nohyaxché the construction of ritual foods occurred in full sunlight, both the making of tortilla bundles and the cooking of the soups. Food preparation that involved destruction occurred in the shade, both the grinding of condiments and the sacrifice of turkeys.

In Classic Maya iconography, the dark underworld is associated with death, disintegration, decay, the raw forces of creation, and fertility, which comes from organic decay. In the life cycle of human beings and plants, and by analogy of the sun, death (sunset, autumn equinox, west) is followed by decay and degeneration (darkness, underworld, sun's nadir, midnight), eventual rebirth (sunrise, spring equinox, east), and a new period of growth and maturity (upper world, sun's zenith, noon). Grinding is a cultural form of disintegration just as sacrifice is a cultural form of death. Turkeys must be sacrificed and corn must be ground before either can be cooked and eaten and thus transformed into living human beings. The pole to which both the turkeys and the grinding mills were attached was placed in the shade and ran east-west. On the pole, the mechanical grinder for grinding the corn, the squash seeds, and the condiments was east of the place used for sacrificing the turkeys. This placement suggests that grinding is more closely associated with transformation (rebirth, dawn) than with death. In the creation myth of the Maya K'iche', the *Popol Vuh*, the Lords of the Dead grind up the bones of the hero twins and throw them into water, which regenerates them, allowing them to rise in the east, carrying the sun and the moon (D. Tedlock 1985). In recent interpretations of Classic iconography and hieroglyphs, the cyclic rebirth of gods and kings are associated with the rebirth of corn plants as well as with the movements of planets, the path of the sun and the phases of the moon (Freidel, Schele, and Parker 1993:276–285).

The foods prepared for the Lords of the Winds are made of the same corn and water as the daily meals of Pichuleños, with the addition of sacrificed poultry, rum, honey, and other ingredients normally used only for special occasions. The main ingredient is the staple corn, which is eaten at all meals in the form of tamales or tortillas and consumed in beverage form (*pozole*) between meals. Corn for daily use is soaked in slaked lime to soften the outer shell of the kernels so that it can be rinsed off; then the corn is washed in three changes of water and put on to boil until soft enough for grinding.

Corn was prepared in the usual manner for the ritual tortillas of the *tuti wah* ceremony, but corn for both the *sak-ha'* beverage and the *k'ol* soup is prepared in a different manner. The outer shell is not removed by soaking in slaked lime and so the kernels must be boiled much longer before becoming soft enough to grind into dough. I was told that the reason for the different process is that the slaked lime turns the corn yellow, and the *sak-ha'* and *k'ol* need to be white. Yellow has many associations with death, decomposition, and the underworld. Lime also comes from the earth and is prepared by burning in a pit. Excluding lime keeps the corn in a category appropriate for the Wind Lords of the white, celestial world. Both *k'ol* and *sak-ha'* are prepared above the earth, in pots under the sky.

The corn itself is a cultural product par excellence in that corn plants will not grow from seed without human intervention to release the kernels from the ear. Corn is believed to be a gift from God the Father. Its critical growth period is between May and August,[14] when the sun is highest in the sky and its light is intensely white. The use of white corn without lime in offerings cooked under the sky is thus quite appropriate as an offering for celestial beings.

In the ceremony, after the tortilla dough had been prepared and some squash seeds had been ground, wrappings were prepared for the tortillas. For each wrapping a man placed two strips of bark from the *majagua (Hibiscus tiliaceus)* on the ground about five inches apart, from east to west. On top of them he placed two more strips, from north to south, forming a square where the four strips crossed. The corners of this square were tied with small loops of bark, like the tied corners of vertical and horizontal poles of a house frame and like the corners of a cornfield and the corners of the world where the Wind Lords are. Then the man placed a palm leaf (*Sabal mauritiformis*) over the tied vine square, with its "fingers pointing east, where the rains come from," and its stem toward him. He placed a second leaf to overlap the first, with its stem to the east, "fingers pointing west."[15]   Thirteen of these pairs of leaves were placed on their prepared bark strips, ready to receive the *tuti wah.*

Each *tuti wah* was made by flattening a large ball of dough (about six inches across) and then pressing down with the fingers from near the center out to the edge, while turning the tortilla in a circle, producing a tortilla about ten inches across and a half inch thick. This process left a raised disk about three inches across in the center, with "rays" coming out from it to the edge. Eventually this "sun" was patted flat, but its image was "in the *tuti wah.*" In this region, women daily make smaller tortillas in the same way. Men do occasionally make tortillas on non-ritual occasions, but only *gorditas*, the fatter ones made by the simpler method of pressing a small ball of dough on the palm of one hand with the fingers of the other, giving it a quarter turn, and pressing again until it forms a fairly flat disk. The ritual *tuti wahs* thus combine male and female aspects: they are made by men in the manner normally used by women but in a different size, indicating ritual significance.

The tortillas were stacked in thirteen piles of thirteen layers each with reddish, ground squash seeds in between each layer and the stacks placed on its *guano* leaves and *majagua* strips. Don Pedro counted the layers and patted the stacks down to about three to four inches thick. He then poked four holes in the top of each, with his finger, which roughly corresponded to the corners of the bark strips underneath the palm leaves and were "for the four corners, the four Lords, the four Winds." A final hole was made in the center to represent the center of the sky. He poured white rum, *agua bendita* (holy water), into the holes, wrapped the stacks in the palm fronds and tied them with the bark strips.

Thirteen packages of thirteen tortillas were prepared "for the thirteen layers of the sky." Don Pedro described them to me in the following way: "The sun is born in the morning in the red east and climbs the layers of the sky to his father, San José,[16] who lives on the highest, the seventh level. After noon, the sun goes down the other side of the steps, or levels, to die in the west." In response to further questioning he described the layers as levels of a pyramid, the east side of each layer is a step in the ascent of the sun while the west side of that layer is a step in its descent; the seventh layer forms the top of the pyramid. From the top there are six "steps" down, forming a total of thirteen steps in the daily path of the sun as it ascends and descends the sky pyramid. Each layer of the pyramid is the home of a Christian saint as well as certain sacred beings in the sky, such as clouds, rain, comets, the moon, planets, and stars.

Don Pedro fashioned the dough remaining from the tortillas into the shape of a swaddled baby. An "operation" was made in its "stomach," into which he poured the remaining reddish brown seed paste mixed with the remaining ritual *sak-ha'* and rum. Then the baby was closed up again and referred to as the *t'up*, a Maya word used to refer to the last child of a family. Holes were poked for *los ojos, el corazón, y el ombligo* (the eyes, heart, and umbilicus), into which more rum was poured. Finally, the *t'up* was wrapped in palm leaves and tied like the packages of thirteen tortillas.

While the stacks of tortillas and the corn baby (made from corn soaked in lime water) were cooked underground in the west, in the *pib*, the turkey soups were being prepared in large vats to the north, with the steam and fragrance rising up to the sky. As birds, turkeys are associated with flying, and thus with the sky. They are fed the *sak-ha'* before they are sacrificed, further intensifying their connections with the sky and the north. The male of the local domestic turkey is black, like the desired rain clouds.

In addition to symbolic associations with colors and directions, the turkeys also form meaningful connections with various aspects of daily life. Domesticated turkeys are commonly found in the house yard, and a related wild species (*pavo de monte, Agriocharis ocellata*) is still found in this area. Even these wild turkeys are strongly associated with human activity because they are attracted by the cornfields scattered throughout the second-growth forest, where they are hunted.

The poultry used in sacrifice carries further connotations of symbiosis with nature, in that the nests of wild birds (including wild turkeys and parrots) are often discovered in the process of clearing and burning the fields. The young from these nests are brought home and raised, along with domesticated varieties of ducks, chickens, turkeys, and pigeons. The poultry of the house yard ranges freely outside the walls during the day, returning for corn, water, and a safe place to roost at night. Birds with a tendency to wander soon have the longest feathers on one wing cut, which causes them to fly in circles. Thus the boundaries between managed wild resources and domesticated species, between nature and culture, are not rigid.[17] Humanity, animals, and plants are all part of the same cosmic system.

Both tom and hen turkeys should be offered in the rain ceremony, but the total should be an odd number, *non*. In the ceremony I observed there were two hens and one tom. The number of containers of *sak-ha'* offered to the Wind Lords is also always odd, as are the number of ears of corn offered at the first harvest. Other offerings are made in pairs: white and red soups, a plate of meat and a plate of breads, cacao beans and chile peppers. The participation of pairs and odd numbers in ritual appears to be significant. The pairs may symbolize the east-and-west and north-and-south dualities of the horizontal plane of the cosmos. The odd numbers may represent the vertical direction of Maya cosmogony, where the number of layers is always *non*. There are three basic layers: sky, earth, and underworld. The sky has thirteen levels and the underworld has nine. From the point of view of the sun or moon climbing the levels, there are seven going up from the earth, and five going down from the earth. All of these numbers are *non*.

The seven arches also had cosmological significance. They were said to be "arches like the rainbow." They were covered with halves of coconut fronds with their "fingers pointing down, like the rain." The a special vine across the tops of the arches was referred to as *cable de la corriente* (the cable of the current). It was said that, "like an electric wire, it brings the current of the rain to us, the rain comes down it like the music to the radio." The crosses on the arches, like the cross on the altar table, were made of *ha'bin* (*Piscidia piscipula*), because, one man said, "They looked for the heaviest wood they could find to make the cross for Jesus Christ to carry. *Ha'bin* is the heaviest wood, when it is dry. [In contrast], ceiba is heavy when it is green, but it gets lighter when it is dry. *Ha'bin* is not heavy when it is green, but heavy when it is dry."

The crosses are because "God is there at the ends of the world, over all." However, the crosses must not be put in the center of these arches because they would block the path of the rain down the "current cable." They are placed to the south because "south is like the flowers of the dead." This statement I would interpret as an epigrammatic way of expressing the multiple meanings associated with symbols of the underworld. The vegetation dies a yellow death in the heat and dryness of the sun, in the *bochorno*, the hottest time of the year

(May, sometimes including late April and/or early June). The *bochorno* is said to call the rains, for they come when the heat is at its most unbearable. The rains are "announced by the butterfly of the woods, the queen, the yellow and black one." There are other yellow butterflies that appear with the first puddles in the roads, rising in little fluttering clouds as one approaches. The dry season both ends and begins with yellow. It begins with glorious spreads of yellow flowers, *taj* (*Vigueira dentata*), that cover the drying vegetation of fallowing farmland, just as the leaves of many trees are dying. The bees use these immense fields of flowers to create the best honey of the year, sweetening the yearly death of the agricultural season. Earlier, harvest is celebrated with the Days of the Dead, when yellow-orange marigolds decorate graves.

An additional association of the color yellow with death is that the dead, in the absence of embalming fluids, do turn yellow. The dead are mourned in the home until the next sunset, when they are buried. The environmental heat and humidity contribute to the organic processes of decay; the body sometimes begins to turn yellow before the twenty-four-hour *bix* (wake) is over. Yellow flowers, especially marigolds, are thus considered appropriate gifts to the dead.

A final association of the south with death, and thus with yellow, is the low and southerly position of the sun at noon during the beginning of the dry season (January). The sun at noon is in its most southerly position at the winter solstice, the beginning of the dry season, the time of year when the sun spends most of its time each day "in the underworld where the dead are." Thus, the south, yellow, death, and the underworld are associated on the level of the observable conditions of this season. White, in contrast, is associated with the zenith position of the sun, the summer solstice, and the rainy season. Yellow and white in the rain ceremony may thus be seen as references to the transition from the dry season to the rainy season.

Material symbols of the ceremony included yellow and white rum, referred to as "holy water." The white was reserved for the most sacred times: (1) when rum was thrown to the four directions and over head for the Lords, (2) when it was poured in the ritual breads that would later be offered to the Lords, and (3) when it was poured in the beaks of the turkeys who would be sacrificed. The yellow rum was drunk in ritualized rounds by the men periodically throughout the preparations, always at the direction of the *h-men*. It was also poured on the head of the man who was bled with the rattlesnake fang.

The altar table is placed at the west end of the ceremonial area, facing east (see Figure 4.3). East is the direction referred to as both that of the sunrise and that from which the rains come during the critical beginning months of the agricultural season. It is associated with the celestial world and with the birth, growth, and upward motion of the sun in its daily cycle. The *pib* was constructed due east of the table altar. Its smoke would help call the rain clouds. The fires for cooking the turkey soups above ground were out in a clearing under the sky, on the south side of a line drawn between the altar and the *pib*, toward the eastern end. The large tortillas were also prepared on the south side but east of the cooking fires, that is to the southeast of the ceremonial space, a direction associated with resurrection from the underworld. They would later be cooked underground, in the *pib*. The soups were prepared entirely above the ground, exposed to the sun, which by noon would be in the northern hemisphere of the sky. To the north was the area just within the forest where the turkeys were sacrificed and the corn and seeds and condiments were ground (Figure 4.3). Shade is associated with night, decay, and the dissolution of order, which leads to fertility and regeneration.

The *h-men*'s ritual actions moved in a counterclockwise direction at most times, sometimes in the form of a cross. The seven arches stand for the seven layers of the sky pyramid, which the sun travels each day by going up its eastern side and down its western side, taking seven steps to the top and then another six steps down to the bottom, making thirteen steps altogether that the sun travels during the day, represented in the thirteen stacks of thirteen tortillas being presented to the Wind Lords.

Prayers offered along with the ritual beverages at noon and sunset and again with the ritual foods at midnight begin with a supplication to the Christian Trinity and go on to mention the saints, the local Virgins, all the nearby archeological sites, and the Lords of the Winds, who are the ones being directly asked to bring the rain. Little boys represent the sounds of four different kinds of frogs, of the four directions, and the four winds because frogs always "sing" when it rains. The sacred foods and the sacred corn beverage are offered to the Winds, along with the "holy water," the rum.

Blood sacrifice is included as a necessary ingredient in the ceremony for rain. In the *tuti wah* I observed, the *h-men* explained to me that he was curing the old man of rheumatism but that, in addition, the shedding of his blood was also absolutely essential to the rain-calling.

The turkeys used in the preparation of the ritual foods are said to be sacrificed. After ritual preparation involving incense, *sak-ha'*, and the white rum, they are killed by slitting their throats. The blood is carefully collected. This blood is kept on the altar until the time comes to add it to one of the ceremonial soups, along with the livers and hearts. Another red food, the ground squash seeds between the layers of tortillas, is an important part of the ceremony. According to the *h-men*, it is this substance that makes the tortillas special for this ritual, and not their large size, which is merely incidental. The name *tuti wah* refers specifically to layered tortillas with a reddish paste of squash seeds between each layer: *wah* means tortilla and *tuti* refers to the paste. .

The soups that had been prepared above the ground were made with corn that had not been soaked in lime water and thus was white. According to the *h-men*, lime causes even white corn to turn yellow, and that is why it must not be used for the corn that will become the ritual beverage, *sak-ha'*, nor that which will become the ritual soup, *k'ol*.

Red substances are combined with both the yellow cornbreads cooked underground in the *pib* and the white corn soups cooked "under the sky." One soup is red, one white. The red soup contains the blood, hearts, and livers of the turkeys. Into it are also put pieces of the cooked breads and green herbs (chives and mint). The white soup is served over the meat and is accompanied by pieces of the cornbreads. The breads express the ultimate dependence of human beings on vegetative growth (corn), which feeds both humans and animals. Corn and all other plant life in turn depends on rain. Human beings are often said to be "made of corn," since much of the daily diet is corn. The white corn beverage, *atole*, is the first food fed to children in addition to their mother's milk. Thus, babies are not only made *by* their parents but also made *of* corn.

Strengthening the multivalent symbolism involved is the cultural association of *atole* with semen. Blood is the substance which women contribute to the formation of an infant. Thus, the two soups, white and red, carry associations with semen and blood, male and female contributions to the engendering of offspring.[18] Both are made of corn broth, *k'ol*. The corn-dough baby (*t'up*) is served inside the red soup (female) whereas it is served beside the white soup (male).

Pregnant women are not to witness this ceremony, nor do they consume any of the foods from it. Their blood is believed to be contributing substance to the growth of the child in the womb. This prohibition for pregnant women also extends to nursing women, since the milk is said to be made of the mother's blood. Their presence is said to cause harm to *the women themselves,* rather than to the ceremony.

The cyclic processes involved in the return of the rains and the fertility of the earth are in some ways like the cyclic processes of human gestation. Blood and water are associated with both. The Virgin, Our Mother, is associated with the blood of the dawn birth of the sun and with sources of groundwater: cenotes, wells, and especially *aguadas*. These in turn are associated with the waters of the womb, released in childbirth. The Wind Lords, in contrast, are associated with sky water, with the rains and the sowing of crops that result in the birth of new plants from the pregnant earth. The rain of the Wind Lords also fills the reservoirs and wells of Our Mother when they have become depleted at the end of dry season. These in turn save the water and sustain life through the dry season until the rains return. The prohibition against the participation of pregnant or nursing women sets their reproductive cycles apart from the reproductive cycles of the agricultural world.

The rain ceremony calls for the cooperation of all the heads of extended families in the community. It emphasizes the need for proper behavior and peace within the community and reassures the assembled individuals about the most critical factor for their survival in this environment, the rains, without which the corn will not grow and the reservoir will not be refilled.

The anxiety concerning rain had reached a peak before the villagers of Nohyaxché decided to conduct this ceremony. For weeks most conversations had been dominated by questions, guesses, predictions, doubts about when it would rain and how long the young corn plants could last. Tension was high and people controlled their tempers with visible effort. The ceremony provided a distraction and enjoined cooperation in the hamlet.

In the village of Pich, a few extended families hired the *h-men* to conduct a similar ceremony on their land, but the village as a whole could not agree on having one. Communal participation in this ceremony once echoed the collective responsibility for maintenance of the reservoir-well-and-canal complex, which was replaced by the new government system of piped water in 1968 (Censo de Pich 1981:25).[19] Originally there was a parallelism between community responsibility for the physical maintenance of a public good, a reservoir, and community involvement in the rain ceremony. With the change in the water system, the practical grounding of the symbolic system in technological practice has been loosened. The cooperation in ceremony no longer echoes the cooperation in technical maintenance.

The traditional survival technologies involved in water maintenance, food production, and curing (see Faust 1988a:334–384) were linked to each other through the traditional cosmology. However, now that water comes from faucets, men sell corn, and women buy tortillas, the symbolic associations of water and corn are no longer as closely integrated with those of gender and social organization. The new technical system is not embedded in a symbolic system that enjoins social responsibilities for community survival. Village welfare has come to be seen as the responsibility of the government. "The government should . . ." is a frequently heard response to the current water problems.

THE MODERN SYSTEM OF WATER MANAGEMENT IN PICH

Today in Pich the government has provided a deep, drilled well, an electric pump, and a system of plastic pipe that delivers water to individual households. The new water system saves a great deal of human labor and is highly valued. It was intended to serve the domestic needs of the town. However, many of the wealthier families now use the water for irrigating fruit orchards and household gardens, watering cattle, and selling to neighboring communities. There is no mechanism by which this overuse is either monitored or paid for. This new deep well was introduced without a supporting structure of public scrutiny and accountability. There has not yet developed a supporting, symbolic system that encodes ethical judgments concerning individualistic abuse of this public good. Each household is assessed the same monthly fee no matter how much nor how little water it uses. For several years now the system has routinely run out of water during the afternoons of the dry season. Since the government introduced the system, the government is considered to be responsible for solving problems of abuse of the system by local individuals, particularly because the abusers are the local elite. The poor feel powerless to control those they depend on for jobs and emergency loans.

In addition, the national economic crisis is making it difficult to provide the anticipated deeper wells, bigger, power-driven pumps, and irrigation systems for agriculture.[20] Village-level techniques for the conservation of rainwater are potentially useful contributions to a solution of the regional water problem, which is the greatest obstacle to increased agricultural productivity throughout the Yucatán Peninsula. With a dependable water source, mechanisms for irrigation, and ecologically sound agricultural practices, this region could no doubt contribute substantially to the national economy, in addition to feeding itself. However, initial investment costs would be substantial—a factor that may prevent the political decisions necessary to following this path.[21]

Technological change could result both in improved terms of involvement with the world economy *and* in improved means for protecting the resource base from abuse, thus ensuring the patrimony of village children. New village-level technologies might combine the ancient Maya knowledge with modern forms of labor-saving machinery, ones affordable and maintainable on the scale of village finances. Small bulldozers or backhoes can be used to reconstruct eroded canals and to clean *aguadas* within 5 or 10 inches of their plastered floors. Cleaning the remainder by hand in a traditional, communal manner would protect the plastered floor. If the *aguada* work were divided and parts assigned to neighborhood committees, then the hand cleaning could be done by work parties with communal feasting afterwards. Wells within the *aguada* could once again belong to geographical sections of the village, which form social units. These units could be assessed man-days of labor to contribute to the central deep well.

The number of families that can effectively work together cooperatively may be limited. As villages grow, new *aguadas* can be dug on the edges of the newest sections of the village. If underground formations containing perched water pockets cannot be found, *chultunes* could be built.

The easiest solution may be to form new satellite communities around existing unused *aguadas*. In 1996 a group of forty young men from Pich and two neighboring communities asked for land around a large aguada in the center of the forest commons of Pich. This land formerly was the *ejido* of the community of San Juan Cantemó, which was abandoned by the few last families sometime between 1986 and 1992. These lands have not been used since then because of their distance from the public school and the clinic and because of the lack of electricity. With the growing economic crisis in Mexico, however, there is no work for young Maya men in the cities and so they are homesteading. They are asking for a road so they can get back and forth to the facilities available in Pich. There is now just a cleared path cut for lumber trucks, so rough that it requires 6 hours to traverse during dry season. A road could be built using locally available limestone rock and calcareous sand (*saskab*). Eventually their children will need a school and a clinic, and these pioneers will immediately need the road to take the sick to a clinic and agricultural produce to the main highway and the city on the flatbed trucks that once carried the hardwoods to market. This is the same process by which Chan Kom and Cobá began (Kintz 1990; Redfield and Villa Rojas 1934).

The existing *aguada* may be able to provide safe drinking water and sufficient water for other uses, as long as limits are placed on the number of people who can use it. In San Juan Cantemó, as in other reestablished Maya communities, user fees could increase with population density, encouraging newly married couples to homestead other new areas, with limited help from government agencies in getting started. Higher community (*ejido*) taxes on the sale of disappearing tropical hardwoods could provide some revenue as well as discouraging non-sustainable rates of use. Taxes could also be increased on commercial tourist establishments around archeological sites, with part of the money going to local Maya communities. In addition, fees could be charged to tourists for entering Maya communities. Guides who were members of the local communities could restrict tourist activities to areas not offensive to the communities, while helping tourists locate things of interest to them. Special facilities for tourists during fiesta days could bring in additional municipal revenue to be used for water-system maintenance and other community projects.

In the case of Pich, the advice of biologists could be sought concerning replacement of the plant cover of the *aguada* with native species and the reintroduction of native fish and other organisms needed to recreate the formerly balanced pond ecosystem. Once the original system was reproduced, the water would be appropriate for all uses with the possible exception of drinking and cooking. Testing could determine if it was clean enough to drink. If so, the drilled well could be used only as a supplement during especially dry years. Water use would still need to be monitored during the dry season; perhaps it could be metered.

NOTES

1. Early claims based on satellite and airplane imaging have been found to be exaggerated. However, several areas that have been surveyed and excavated gave clear evidence of complex systems of terraces and raised fields with drainage canals in swamps.

2. Small canals, similar to ones reported in other areas that have been excavated, were also cited as reasons for suspecting raised fields in association with this system.

3. It is possible that the associated canals contributed greater accumulations of silt, so that the bottoms were considerably lower than the other aguadas. We are not told to what depth the exploration was carried out.

4. He graciously lent to me for reference his own handwritten notes of the comments by local informants concerning this matter, taken while he was working on an archeological project.

5. In some areas, such as the Wells (Chenes, in Maya) the drainage system of low-lying hills sustains wells where water frequently is found within 6 feet of the surface.

6. Rock quarrying techniques used by the Maya have been analyzed by Folan (1982).

7. Although part of the seepage might have collected in the underground chamber, that chamber may not have received water naturally from the limestone formations immediately above it but rather from channels formed in the strata of the neighboring slopes. The majority of the seepage from the surface pond may have escaped along horizontal strata to other areas. Therefore, preventing its loss on that level would have conserved water in the system.

8. Government studies of water in the southern interior of the Yucatán Peninsula have found sulfites and chlorine exceeding the recommended limits for both human consumption and irrigation.   Nitrates and nitrites from commercial agricultural operations further contaminate the water supply, as do choliform bacteria from human and animal wastes (Batllori 1996).

9. Some scholars believe that some early Mesoamericans used magnetic stones hung from string as compasses. Polished magnetite has been found in ritual burials at Olmec sites.

10. Marilyn and Gary Gates, Abel Morales López, and William Folan agreed with my informal observations concerning possible indications of terraces, although to my knowledge these have not been mentioned in the literature. (Personal communications with Maya scholars with many years of experience in this area of Campeche: an ethnographer, a hydrologist and two archeologists.)

11. The links of this Maya water-management system to Maya symbolism, fiesta cycles, and agricultural ritual were discussed in Chapter 4 of Faust 1988a.

12. The degree to which natural events are seen as analogous to human work was made clearest to me when I complained about the nastiness of mosquitoes and was reprimanded with the reminder that biting people is, after all, the "work" of mosquitoes.

13. There is a great deal of flexibility in today's Maya rituals, in part because of the scarcity of ritual specialists and in part because of the changes in people's lives. The timing may have been more important in the past. I mention the date because it may be useful to future researchers concerned with survivals of ancient Maya archeo–astronomy.

14. In the Maya area, the sun reaches the center of the sky at noon (zenith passage) on two days of the year, one in May and one in August. During the period in between, the sun at noon is north of the center. This is in contrast to the observed movements of the sun in latitudes north of the tropics, where the sun reaches its highest point in the sky at noon on summer solstice.

15. This is also the process used in preparation of the *pibipollos*, ritual foods made for the Day of the Dead.

16. San José is presented as the father of the infant Jesus and is thus often thought of as a version or representation of God the Father.

17. Other young wild animals brought home from the fields include young deer, *tepesquintle* (a local animal somewhat similar to a raccoon), parrots, turtles, rabbits, and armadillos. The cornfields themselves attract the favorite sources of wild meat: deer, peccary, and wild turkey. Farmers ordinarily hunt adult animals around the edges of their fields. These fields are small clearings (2 to 5 acres, often less) in the second-growth forest, which supplies the favorite habitat of these animals.

18. The white and pink (reddish) plumeria blooms are seen by villagers as having sexual connotations. While this was explained to me with reference to the shape of the

flowers and the way they can be fit into each other, it may also be associated with their colors. These colors are also the preferred ones of the paper flowers used to decorate the church for the Mass celebrating a young woman's fifteenth birthday, after which she begins serious training for her responsibilities as the mother of a family and may be courted by young men (under family supervision).

19. The government-drilled well and the electric pump had been installed earlier, in the mid-1950s, as people recalled.

20. The fall in the price of petroleum from 1985 to 1987 had a devastating effect on the Mexican economy, which was already suffering an international debt crisis, in part due to rises in interest rates and devaluations of the Mexican peso relative to the dollar. When I arrived in September 1985, the peso was 250 to the dollar. When I left the following September, it was 680 to the dollar. In 1997 it fluctuates around 8,000 of the old pesos to the dollar, but the last three zeros have been eliminated in the new monetary system so that it now is approximately 8 "new pesos" to the dollar.

21. The term *legal sanction* is here being used in the way it is normally used in the anthropology of law, to refer to legitimate sanctions for violations of customary rules. The sanctions are considered "legal" (although unwritten) when they are considered by the community to be appropriate to the offense and are imposed by a recognized authority—one who may legitimately use force, if necessary, in imposing the sanction (cf. Paul Bohannan, Max Gluckman, Ian Hogbin, E. A. Hoebel, Bronislaw Malinowski, Laura Nader, Leopold Pospisil, and others).

5

Growing the Sacred Bread

Don Eus, one of my adopted brothers-in-law, is a traditional *milpero,* a man who produces his family's food, as well as some to sell, in the *milpa* cultivated by the traditional swidden system. He speaks Maya fluently and helps me learn it, despite the fact that I am very slow. He, like Celso, a younger brother-in-law who also still "makes" traditional *milpa,* eventually took me to his field, with other family members, so that I could see what they do without causing scandal and without being in danger. For me to have gone to the fields with a man who was not a member of my adopted family would have been considered an invitation to intimacy, if not rape. To have gone without taking other family members as chaperones would have been scandalous (even with a brother-in-law).

Before we ever went to the *milpa,* Don Eus described to me in great detail, and with nostalgic tenderness, the way he had learned to make *milpa* from his father when he was six years old. He explained that in the *milpa* are planted not only the sacred corn, but also beans, squash, chiles, flowers, and other useful plants. The *milpa* is referred to with respect, for it is sacred, as are the rain and the corn. Together, the corn, the rain, and the *milpa* make human life possible. One must not make noise in the *milpa* but go quietly about one's work. At times it is necessary to make a shelter and sleep there for a few weeks. Even at night, one should not joke, play music, or be disrespectful. The *aluxes (aluxitos* is the affectionate term often used for these little people in Pich)[1] will help you grow the corn and warn you where there are snakes, but you must always treat them with respect.

He told me about many adventures he had had there in the *milpa,* some with his father. One time, during the first year of his marriage, he encountered a jaguar. He was terribly frightened but he did not run; the jaguar slowly turned and walked away. One day I went with him and his wife and children to harvest the *milpa* nearest town. Don Eus showed me proudly the ears of corn from this field, the beautiful *tez abanico* flowers that he had planted there, the squash, the beans, the chiles. He proudly pointed out the birds that visited, naming them.

When I asked him what life would be like for his son, the *gordito* (a common nickname meaning the little fat one), his tone became intensely serious. He stood up straight, looked me directly in the eye and vehemently informed me, "My son will drive a tractor. He will not work in the mud like an animal, like me. He will go to school. He will not be ignorant. He will have respect [here meaning from outsiders, government officials, city people, the outside world in general]."

The traditional agricultural system is still the major source of income for many families in Pich and the major source of carbohydrates and proteins for most, through a combination of corn, beans, and squash seeds. Women also produce important components of the family diet in the house yard: fruits, vegetables, condiments, and medicinal herbs—all of which contribute vitamins and minerals. In addition, women care for pigs and poultry, which are "sacrificed" on special occasions, contributing highly concentrated animal protein to the diet. Most of the food, however, is provided by the crops grown by the men, and the major agricultural ceremonies are conducted by men.

Most of the men of Pich think of themselves as farmers, and most of them plant some land in the traditional swidden manner, cutting and burning plots of forest every two or three years. This is followed by a long fallow period (7-20 years, depending on the soil). This type of agricultural system is referred to as swidden and is common among traditional farmers throughout the tropics. In Mexico it is usually referred to as *roza-tumba-y-quema* (clearing brush, cutting trees, and burning). The plots are planted primarily with *maíz* (corn), but also with beans, squash, chile peppers, ritual flowers, and some root crops. This subsistence activity is supplemented with beekeeping, lumbering, cattle raising, carpentry, masonry, tailoring, storekeeping, work on governmental rural development projects, and—when all else fails—temporary migration to the city to work for wages. While the latter is normally a last resort for family men, it is often chosen first by young bachelors seeking to explore the world and make some money.

NEW SOURCES OF CASH

Government programs have made bulldozers available to clear hundreds of contiguous acres, for mechanized cultivation of rice and corn. These programs have offered to village farmers tractors, trucks, hybrid seeds, fertilizer, and herbicides on credit. They have also advanced (from anticipated harvest revenues) money to farmers for labor on their own fields (preparing the soil, planting, weeding, and fertilizing). Even though these sums, plus interest, were deducted from harvest revenues, they were referred to by villagers as wages. A group of village men also organized to obtain a government cattle-raising project. Cattle, barns, fences, pasture grasses, a water system, veterinarian support, and so on were all supplied on credit. The sale of young cattle would be used to pay off the debts. A related dairy project failed because of both the lack of a local market for milk and of knowledge concerning how to tame a range cow for milking.

Sawmills, plywood factories, and foreign lumber companies have bought the tropical hardwoods at increasing prices, encouraging villagers to buy chain saws and trucks. They have cut their own communally owned forest, transporting the logs to the city in their own trucks. The lumbering began in earnest in the early 1960s, when the paved highway came to Pich. The bull-dozers came in the early 1980s, although they had earlier been seen in Bonfil, a neighboring town of colonists from northern states, brought to the valley floor by a government rural development program that destroyed many acres of relic canals and raised fields in the area around the ancient Maya metropolis of Edzná (Matheny et al. 1983).

The swidden system had for many centuries sustained a human population in this difficult environment without causing desertification. The loss of access to land now used in government-managed agribusiness is, however, contributing to increasing pressures on traditional farmers to over-use the swidden fields. Other pressures are a growing population in the village center, as families live there year round in order to keep their children in school and in order to have the benefits of electricity and a water system that delivers water to household faucets. Formerly it was common for much of the village population to spend the agricultural season dispersed in small, temporary hamlets near fields that were moved every two or three years in a cyclic pattern. At that time, national lands were freely used, but they have lately been fenced off by the entrepreneurs who have bought them from the government at low prices and by the colonizing communities brought in by rural development programs of the government. These sales of government lands have been attempts by policymakers in the capital to encourage commercial agriculture and increase food production, for both a growing national population and for export, to meet national debt payments and improve the foreign exchange rate. Such policies have been a response to directives by foreign lenders, including the World Bank, which controls refinancing credits (Sandoval Palacios 1982)

All of these modernization pressures are resulting in a situation where farmers increasingly compete for land near the village and shorten the fallow time from twenty years to seven. The traditional agricultural system practiced by living Maya communities was an efficient and sustainable one, although it required access to large amounts of land per capita. Earlier, during the Preclassic and Classic, the ancient Maya supplemented their swidden practices with terraces and drained fields in some areas, providing food for greater population densities. Intensive alternatives to swidden known to local farmers are modern ones, which require access to cash or willingness to assume debt through the credit programs of the government. They also require access to new information concerning the use of the equipment. This information is gradually becoming more widespread, as government programs make both credit and training available.

There are several rich farmers and two groups of associates in Pich who had begun working with the new machinery by 1985. Even then, there were disturbing indications in neighboring ejidos of colonists that the modern alternatives were destructive of the local agricultural ecology (Sandoval Palacios 1982; Gates 1993). By the summer of 1992, the villagers themselves had become disillusioned. The big trees were gone, and the environmental protection agency would not let them cut the small, young ones. Replanting needed to be done, but there was no money to pay for the work or the trees. The mechanized fields of rice and corn had been invaded by Johnson grass and the soil had "grown tired," and unable to support good growth of crops.

At the same time that these ecological limits were being recognized, the government stopped giving credit for a farmer's work on his own fields.[2] Village men who once earned cash by cutting timber, began digging limestone rocks out of the ground, loading them on the flatbed logging trucks, and taking them to sell in the city for building materials. This work did not pay very well. There was a sadness in people's faces that was not there in 1986. Only the beekeepers and private cattle ranchers seemed to be maintaining the lifestyle they had in the 1980s.

Now that the rural development projects have not met expectations, swidden agriculture continues to be seen as fundamental to survival by most of the village poor. Those villagers who were more committed to modern ways and more educated have migrated to the city; the more traditional have resigned themselves to depending more on swidden and on the remaining local rich people, who will hire them as laborers.

ECOLOGY AND RELIGION IN TRADITIONAL SWIDDEN PRACTICES

Swidden practices are embedded in an evolving tradition of Maya cosmology. They are also appropriate to the local ecology. The fields are small and separated by forest; they are allowed to return to forest to replenish soil fertility and are then used again in a cyclical rotation. These practices are symbiotic with game (wild turkey, peccary, and deer) that prefers to eat young plants in the early stages of forest succession. Some areas of *monte alto* ("high forest")[3] were traditionally not cut, but used as sources of medicinal plants and considered the home of sacred spirits. Although some swidden farmers have recently begun to cut *monte alto,* greater deforestation has come from development programs and cattle raising.

Analysis of the ecological and cultural aspects of the traditional agricultural system reveals both continuities with the ancient Maya and potential for combination with labor-saving machinery in some new forms of technology appropriate to the local ecology. Unfortunately, the programs that have been introduced have largely ignored existing practices and villager's knowledge.

The orientation of fields, the way they are laid out in squares, and the associations with the sun and the winds all are congruent with the cosmological system of ancient Maya civilization and, indeed, are a technological analogy of the ritual symbolism. The procedures used in laying out traditional cornfields and planting them were explained and shown to me by local farmers. I examined the procedures with reference both to Maya iconography visible in the ruins and to present-day Maya symbolism in religious ritual, as these explicate and, in turn, are themselves grounded in the ancient agricultural ecology.

The following analysis of the swidden system includes an examination of its ecological rationality, of the liming of the fields that results from burning practices, and of possible reasons why the terraces and raised fields constructed by the ancient Maya are no longer used. Finally, I examine the process of modernization in this setting to identify the reasons modern methods are adopted by Maya villagers, even though many elders see them as ecologically destructive.

TIME AND SPACE IN THE SWIDDEN SYSTEM OF PICH

The traditional swidden system, *roza-tumba-y-quema,* begins any time between August and December with the measuring of a rectangular (often square) field aligned with the path of the sun.[4] After measuring and marking, the farmers, using machete and axe, cut and pile the brush. In three days, two men can cut about an acre of low, second-growth forest (approximately seven years old). After the brush has been allowed to dry for at least three months, it is burned. In 1986 the burning of fields began about April 10 and extended through the first of May, ending before the rains began. Since then, this process has begun to extend into June, as the rains are coming later. Before planting, the fields are measured and marked again, this time being subdivided into *mecates* (22 to 25 yards on a side). Planting begins when substantial rains begin to fall daily, traditionally in May, and now in June.

One man can plant 10 to 12 *mecates* a day. Four traditional varieties of corn are planted in a specific order. Weeding is normally done once for new fields and twice for fields planted a second year; the last weeding is finished by late July. In October the corn plant is "doubled," bent over at a point a little higher than its midpoint so that the top of the plant nearly reaches the ground. This turns the ears of corn upside down, hiding the top opening where the silk comes out. This effectively discourages birds and most insects and keeps rainwater out of the ears, preventing rot, as the corn dries on the plant.

Fresh corn is enjoyed in September and October and made into special seasonal dishes. By November, the corn is beginning to dry; referred to as "new corn," it is used in the preparation of special meals for the souls of the dead on October 31 and November 1. Harvest is leisurely, as there is no danger of frost, and continues through March on traditional fields. One man can harvest 3 to 8 *mecates* a day, depending on the growth of weeds and brush and the thoroughness of his harvesting efforts. The field will be used a second year and sometimes a third. When the field is reused, the old corn plants are cut and burned before the new planting.

The fields planted in this traditional system are not more than 2 to 5 acres in area and are separated by forest in various stages of regrowth. Distant areas of virgin forest was formerly respected as the home of sacred beings and prized as the habitat of certain types of medicinal plants, birds with beautiful feathers, monkeys, and other rare species of cultural importance.[5]

Cornfields are normally cleared in second-growth forest and are fallowed after two or three years of use. The forest grows inward from the borders. For the first few years, the new growth provides good browsing for wild deer, pigs, and turkeys, which are hunted for meat. After seven to twenty years, the land will have a forest cover 15 to 20 feet high. The roots of these trees bring trace minerals up from the subsoil; the leaf fall provides humus; the wood will provide fuel for burning. When regrowth has been sufficient the field will be used again. Then the brush and small trees are cut and allowed to dry thoroughly so that they will "burn hot." Some large trees are left (in part for shade and in part because they are hard to cut). The drying cut brush is cleared from a circle around each large tree to protect it from the fire. A firebreak is made around the edges of the field to protect neighboring areas of forest. The day of burning is selected carefully to assure that the slash will be very dry in order to produce a hot fire, since it is known that heat increases soil fertility.[6]

The practical is combined with ceremonial in the area of agricultural production, as it is with water management. Both activities are seen as sacred because they are essential to human life, and they sustain it through work with the natural world. As ceremonial offerings to the Lords of the Winds are made for rain, so too are they made for the success of crops.

THE SACRED BEINGS OF THE CORNFIELDS

The *milpas* are created out of the forest, which belongs to the *aluxes*. These beings are related to the Lords of the Winds but live on the earth and are their terrestial representatives. They are about three feet tall, wear no clothing except sombreros and sandals, and can either help or hurt a man working in the woods on his cornfield. They whistle as a means of communication. They very much dislike loud human noises, particularly swearing, singing, and disrespect. If the noise continues after dark, they will take action, stealing knives, machetes, matches, cups, and other small items. For those who do not make the proper ceremony in the fields with *sak-ha'*, the *aluxes* are among the instruments of the Wind Lords' displeasure.

The *aluxes* are clearly *local* beings inhabiting specific areas of land. In contrast, neither the Wind Lords nor the Rain Lords (*Chako'ob*) they carry, are conceived of as local. They have local manifestations, but are fathers, grandfathers or bosses of the *aluxes* and have responsibility for the weather of the world. They are charged with this responsibility by the One True God.

While the Lords of the Winds may withhold rain, it is the *aluxes* who directly withhold the help a man needs in his field. The *aluxes* may refuse to punish those who steal his crops, refuse to warn the farmer of snakes on his path, or refuse to warn of other dangers. *Aluxes* may even take to throwing stones and whistling from different directions, disorienting a man until he becomes lost in the bush. It is very, very easy to get lost in the bush. Cases are known in town of men who became lost when going out to find a new place to make *milpa*. Some found their way out to another town miles away. A few have never been seen again. It is said they were probably eaten by jaguars or bitten by snakes.[7]

The *aluxes* are important because they protect against real, life-threatening dangers. Many historical descriptions of private Maya ceremonies in their fields, for local deities, refer to this type of being (Farriss 1984:287–89, 317). Neighboring *milperos* and paid agricultural workers are invited to share in the consumption of *sak-ha'* following the ceremony. Such sharing extends to them the protection of the sacred *aluxes* when they are on this land. It also puts them on notice that the *aluxes* are allies of the owner and will punish theft by illness, snakebite, loss of tools, accidental injuries, losing one's way, or dying of thirst. During a ceremony that I observed, some passing Guatemalans were invited to share in the ritual beverage. The *patrón* took the precaution of explaining to them that the ceremony meant that this land and its crops would now be protected by the small ones, an explanation they immediately understood and would communicate to others in the refugee camp.

RITUAL BEFORE CLEARING OR PLANTING

The ceremonial offering of *sak-ha'* to the Lords of the Winds follows the same pattern whether it is done at the beginning of burning in a first-year *milpa*, or at the beginning of planting in a second- or third-year *milpa*.[8] It is similar to that given for the souls of the dead in that a drink is offered,[9] spirit beings are addressed, and people retire to a respectful distance, waiting for the sacred beings to take the spirit of the drink (and food, in the case of the dead), after which the drink must be carefully and respectfully consumed by the living.

At the beginning of the agricultural season, the farmer offers *sak-ha'* to the Lords of the Winds.[10] I was invited to observe one of these ceremonies by Don Milo, one of the rich village *patrones* who owned cattle and private land. He told me that many people had stopped performing agricultural ceremonies, but they would be sorry. Someday they would discover that they needed the cooperation of the *aluxitos*. In Don Milo's ceremony, *sak-ha'* was offered by placing five gourds on a wooden table made of poles cut and lashed together.[11] The table was approximately 1 meter long and 1/3 meter wide. It was oriented with the length north-south and a cross of carved sticks behind it, to the west, where the sun "dies" each evening. Directly east from this cross, a pole was stuck in the ground and a candle tied to it at the same height as the cross (see Figure 5.1). The ceremony began with the *milpero* asking for the blessings of the Catholic Trinity. Then each of the gourd vessels with *sak-ha'* was offered to the Lord of a different wind, beginning with the east and ending with the Lord of All the Winds, who is straight up, in the zenith of the sky, under the One True God. It is believed that this ceremony is necessary; it asks for the help of the Winds in growing the Maya's staple food.

The first prayers said during the ritual were Spanish Catholic prayers: the Apostle's Creed (*Credo*), Our Father (*Padre Nuestro*), and a prayer of thanks (*Las Gracias*). These were followed by Maya prayers addressed to the Winds. These prayers are presented below in Maya, Spanish, and English.[12]

> *He 'ele' kin lo' obik le sak-ha 'ba' ti te 'ex, yum iik' ku laak 'in ko 'on.*
> *(Aqui le estoy entregando el zacat a Uds., vientos que nos acom-*
> *pañan.)*
> (Here I deliver the sacred corn beverage to you, Winds that accom-
> pany us.)

> *Lak' in iik', chik' in iik', nohol iik', xaman iik', yum k'uh.*
> *(Viento del oriente, viento del poniente, viento del sur, viento del*
> *norte, jefe de los vientos.)*
> (East Wind, West Wind, South Wind, North Wind, Ruler of the
> Winds.)

> *Tin waalik ti te 'ex kaakah chaak, ha' ti' in kool.*
> *(Suplico que llueva en mi milpa para que yo logre la cosecha de*
> *maiz.)*
> (I pray you to grant me rain in my cornfield so I can produce my corn
> crop.)

After the people all retired to a respectful distance for about forty minutes, they returned to the table. The *milpero* took up the first gourd of *sak-ha'*. He knelt facing east, the direction from which come the winds that bring the rains of planting season. He then offered the following prayer in Mayan:

> *Dios bo' otik te' ex, lak' in iik', chik' in iik', nohol iik', xaman iik',*
> *yum k'uh.*
> *(Dios se lo pague a Uds., viento del oriente, viento del poniente,*
> *viento de sur, viento del norte, jefe de los vientos.)*

Figure 5.1
Ritual for Permission to Use the Land

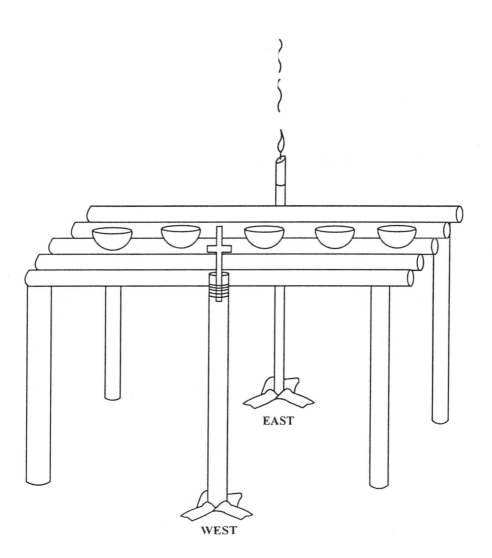

EAST

WEST

(May God reward you, East Wind, West Wind, South Wind, North Wind, Ruler of the Winds.)

He then dipped the sacred herb, rue, frequently used in processions for the saints and in the traditional healing ceremonies, in the *sak-ha'*. Holding the rue in his right hand, moving with a rapid arm and wrist motion, he flung the *sak-ha'* 6 to 7 meters into the distance—to the east, west, south, and north, and then directly overhead. The ruler or chief of the four Winds resides overhead. The cardinal directions are the location of the four Winds and are related to the path of the sun, as it rises in the east and sets in the west, with the south on its left and north on its right. South is also associated with the completion of the agricultural cycle and north with its beginning, as the sun is farthest south at the winter solstice, moving north until summer solstice. This east-west, south-north pairing will later be mirrored in the procedures for measuring and marking the field. In some rituals done by the *h-men* of Pich, and in other Mesoamerican rituals, circular motion refers to the sun's path, reflecting concepts of time and space related to the sun's cycles (Hunt 1977:72; Gossen 1984:35–53; Sosa 1986:260; Hanks 1990:388).

After the offering to local beings, the remaining *sak-ha'* was divided among those present and consumed. None was wasted, since that would have been disrespectful. The ritual is believed to induce good rainfall for the crops, to protect them from wind damage, to "cure" them so that anyone who steals them will become ill, and to protect the farmer from danger in his work.

Don Milo told me that this was the right way to do this ceremony. He had learned it from his father and would pass it down to his sons, who shared with him the work of farming these fields. He died of a heart attack in 1989, and his two sons that farm do, indeed, continue to make these agricultural ceremonies in the family fields. The eldest son was sent to the city to be educated as a veterinarian. He comes home to the village frequently on week-ends and gives advice about the family's cattle herd, but he does not himself make *milpa*. He does agree, however, that it is important to do the rituals for the *aluxitos*.

MEASURING AND MARKING FOR BURNING

The ceremony performed for the Wind Lords (and indirectly for the *aluxes*) is followed by the clearing of firebreaks around the field—the first step in the process of cutting the forest. These firebreak boundaries are aligned to the sun. The surveying procedure begins in the northeast corner of the prospective field. On the ground a space is cleared of brush and rocks. Then four sticks are cut to an equal length, approximately two feet long. Then two other sticks somewhat longer are cut. The first four are tied at their ends to form a square. The other two are crossed, connecting the corners to the center. I was told that this ensures getting the square perfectly equal on all four sides, with perfectly square corners.

The *milpero* stands with his back to the rising sun and places the square on the ground in front of him. He drives a long straight pole into the ground at the northeast corner and uses its shadow to align another stick due west. The prepared square is then adjusted so that its northern side is aligned with these two sticks, with the square to the south or left of the line. This may be of importance in interpretations of Maya ritual symbolism, in which there are frequent references to the left hand of the sun as the south (Vogt 1976:16; Hunt 1977:72; and Gossen 1974:33–35).

The vertical stick in the northeast corner of the square reaches just below the eye level of the *milpero*, who bends over to sight along it. The top of this stick is creased with a machete in the form of a cross. Two thin, straight green twigs are cut and placed as a horizontal cross on the top of the stick, as a surveyor's tool. That is aligned with the stick at the northwest corner of the square. Then the helper, the companion of the *milpero*, takes another straight stick and ties a rag to the top. He walks straight ahead approximately twenty feet, using a five-foot stick or a string to measure the distance, and places the stake. The *milpero* signals his helper with hand motions until that third stick is lined up with the first two. The *milpero*, using his green twigs as a sighting device, is the final authority on when the pole is in the right place. The process is repeated with all the poles aligned until the north side of the milpa has been laid out. When the north edge of the field has been formed, the *milpero* joins his assistant in the northwest corner, and the same process is repeated towards the left, or south.

Piles of three white rocks are put around the base of each stick. The flags at the top of the sticks form boundary markers, visible at a distance, a sign of the limits of one's field. In the event the sticks burn in the fire later, the rocks remain to mark the boundary. The 20–25 foot markers formed by this process will later form the corners of mecates.

The mecates are measured with a rod or string said to be "4 meters" (~13 feet). These devices are measured by 6 hand spans, each of which is said to be a meter but actually equal approximately 1 meter, 10 to 15 centimeters, or 44 to 46 inches. Thus, the measuring tool is about 15 feet long. The rod or string is used end to end five times on each side of the mecate, resulting in a mecate which has "20 meters" or 75 feet on each side, 5,635 square feet. Alternatively the mecate can be measured by pacing, about 32 inches to the pace, 26 paces to the mecate, or 13 double strides (left and right). The latter gives a mecate of slightly less than 21 meters, or 69 feet per side, with a little more than 4,760 square feet. Thirteen is an important number in the Maya cosmology, referring to the layers of the sky (see Figure 5.2). The thirteen left strides and thirteen right strides together as a unit of measure may refer to a man and his wife, as women are clearly associated with the left and men with the right among several highland Maya groups including the Chamula (See Figure 5.3 and Gossen 1984) and the Quiché (Earle 1986). The thirteen-layered celestial world once connected the male essence of the sky (Sky Iguana, or Itzamná)

Figure 5.2
Campeche Maya Cosmology

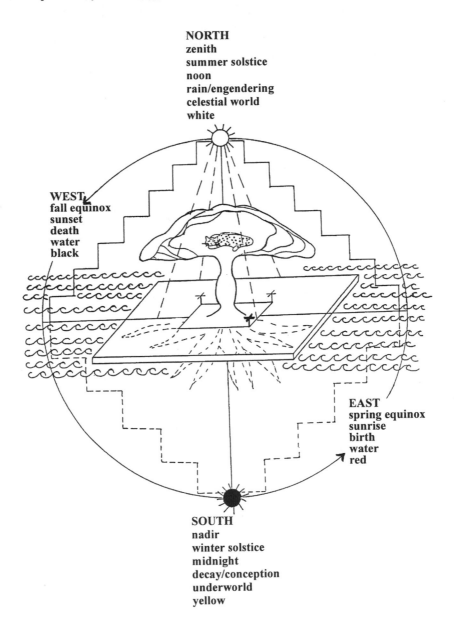

NORTH
zenith
summer solstice
noon
rain/engendering
celestial world
white

WEST
fall equinox
sunset
death
water
black

EAST
spring equinox
sunrise
birth
water
red

SOUTH
nadir
winter solstice
midnight
decay/conception
underworld
yellow

Note: Design assisted by Bea Ziggert.

Figure 5.3
Chamula Cosmology

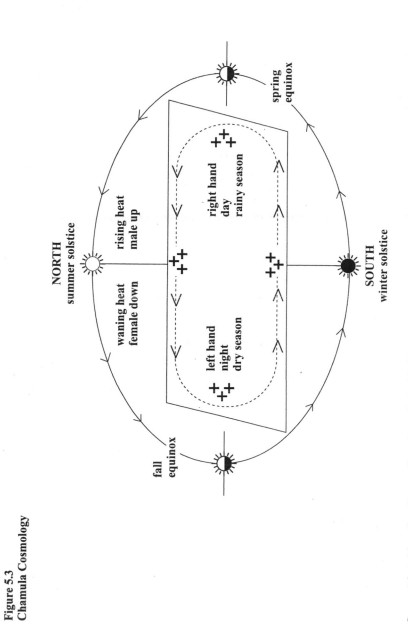

Source: Adapted from Gary Gossen, *Chamulas in the World of the Sun: Time and Space in a Maya Oral Tradition* (Prospect Heights, Ill.: Waverly Press, 1984), p. 34, Fig. 2, by permission of Gary Gossen.

with the female essence of the terrestrial world (Earth Iguana, or Ix Chel) forming Iguana House, the cosmos of the Classic Maya (Thompson 1970; Schele and Miller 1986; Kintz 1990).

This cosmically oriented, measured, and counted square of land that relates to the entire cosmos is the basic unit of land for Maya farmers. Calculations of labor owed to fellow farmers are always made in *mecates*. Planting and weeding are done by *mecate*. Yields are described in kilograms per *mecate*.

After the marking procedure is completed, the boundary is widened by about 10 feet to make a firebreak. It is cleared of twigs, brush, weeds— anything that will burn. Maya farmers recognize that on occasion a particularly nasty wind may make the fire jump this break. Unless the year is exceptionally dry, this is not a serious problem because the woods beyond the break are alive and do not burn easily. Usually, the firebreak is sufficient. To take care of those rare times when it is not, one makes a prayer and offering to the god of fire at the time of burning (usually in April).

The low forest of second growth (*monte bajo*), typically reaches about 15 to 20 feet in height. This felled brush must dry before it can be burned. I did not have the opportunity to observe a burning, but did observe the clearing process. The cut brush is heaped into piles separated by clearings of approximately 30 feet, each pile being about twice as high as a man and three times as wide as it is high. The two men I observed working for four hours cut a 120 by 120 foot section of second-growth forest. They said they would cut a hectare that week. Other men indicated that this was a respectable amount of work for the time period, considering that other tasks must also be accomplished.

In May the fields are prepared for planting. The previous marking of the external boundaries with sticks and piles of stones facilitates this process, but the markers have to be found and the sticks realigned, as many have been disturbed or burned in the fire. The laying out of the *mecates* within the field follows. Great care is taken to ensure the lines are straight and oriented properly to the sun. The reason given for this laying out of the field in *mecates* is that one must live in God's world, where His sun creates order.

From an outsider's perspective, the practical result of laying out the fields in this manner is that they are all oriented the same way. I wondered if this might be useful in fields that are contiguous, as intensively cultivated, irrigated fields might have been in Edzná, according to the research and interpretations of Matheny et al. (1983). There is no other benefit that I can discern, using my "practical" standards. The seeds are not placed in rows, as they are in Veracruz where corn is aligned with the north wind (Morales López 1986), so that the first plant will be both supported by the second and shelter it from the hurricane winds that arrive during the latter stages of growth (September through November).

The fields in Puebla reported by Tichy (1981) were also oriented in a precise manner, corresponding to the orientation of colonial churches. He noted that this orientation was associated with the direction of sunrise on dates of critical importance in the agricultural cycle and considered it a manifestation of religious rituals. However, since the technology used in the laying out of fields depends on using the sun and shadows, the orientation may be an artifact of the surveying techniques, which are practiced at a particular time of year for reasons associated with local climate.

Every *milpero* knows exactly how many *mecates* he has sown in the bush. He generally makes *milpa* with brothers or brothers-in-law, sons and nephews. It is considered advisable to plant several men's *milpa*s together because that way less is lost to animals. The relationship of periphery to volume is well understood. The larger the square the less boundary per surface unit (square meter) and wild animals eat at the boundary. This is not all bad because one can hunt them and thus obtain meat. But it is not good if they eat too much; therefore it is better to reduce boundaries by planting contiguous fields. At the same time, it is wise for each man to reduce his risk by planting *milpa* in several places, since it does not rain *parejo*, evenly.[13] Each man plants in several locations with each field normally adjoining a field or two of his relatives or friends, referred to as *compañeros* (companions). Two of my adopted brothers-in-law described this process to me over several evenings of conversation in the home of Don Pablo and Doña María. Both still make *milpa* in this traditional way every year, with the help of their sons and a brother in one case and a *compadre* in the other. Don Pablo no longer makes *milpa*, but he agreed with the description.

MEASURING AND MARKING FOR PLANTING

The measuring procedures used for marking out the fields and clearing a fire-break around them are similar to those used to prepare for the planting, except that the latter mark off the interior of the field into *mecates*. I did not find a socially acceptable way to observe agricultural practices until after this measuring and marking was done. However, it was recreated for me in the field by one of my brothers-in-law, when I was finally allowed to go with him to photograph the planting process. We were accompanied by his teen-age daughter and two younger sons. The grandmother had not felt physically up to the two-hour trip on a mule-drawn wooden cart and there had been considerable discussion about whether or not it was acceptable for me to go without her.

When we arrived, the field had been cleared; patches of white and black ash lay between stumps and emerging morning glory vines. Each square *mecate* had been laid out with reference to the path of the sun. Celso explained the process to me; he had gone in the same counterclockwise direction used for "binding" in many Maya rituals (Sosa 1986:260; Hanks 1990:388). The measuring process includes checking internal points against each other as well as against the previously established boundary markers (see Figure 5.4).

Figure 5.4
Measuring and Marking for Planting

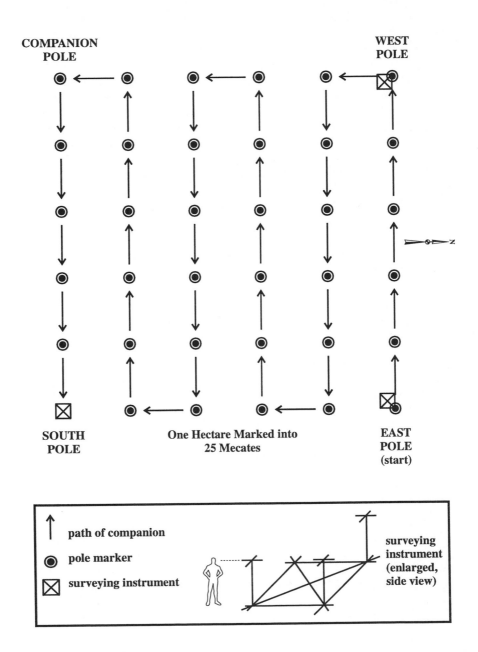

COMPANION
POLE

WEST
POLE

SOUTH
POLE

One Hectare Marked into
25 Mecates

EAST
POLE
(start)

↑   path of companion

◉   pole marker

⊠   surveying instrument

surveying
instrument
(enlarged,
side view)

Celso constructed anew, for me to photograph, the same square with diagonal cross sticks on the ground and then placed a vertical stick topped with a green cross, which I had been told was used in the measuring of the field boundaries before burning. The surveying square was placed in the northeast corner. I was told that the *milpero's* assistant goes initially west, checking the boundary markers and replacing poles at each *mecate* (26 paces, 70 feet) along the north edge of the cornfield until reaching its western boundary. Because of variation in the terrain and the burn, finding the stone markers can be difficult. The *milpero* guides him by sighting along his green surveying cross. Having replaced the poles on one side, the assistant then goes back to the northeast corner and walks to the south, checking markers and replacing poles, with supervision by the *milpero*. They usually ignore the southwest corner at this time. (I was told, "Well, some people do put a stick there, too, before beginning to mark *mecates*, but it is not really necessary.") The assistant then returns to the northeast corner to collect additional poles and proceeds with the *milpero* and the surveying square to the northwest corner, where they check and replace missing poles along the west boundary of the field. Having marked the northern, eastern, and western boundaries of the field in *mecates*, they now establish the edges of each internal *mecate*, marking their corners with poles. To do this, they start at the northeast corner of the *milpa*, go to the west boundary, placing markers every 26 paces, then repeat this along the next row from west to east and so forth. The milpero then proceeds to check the north-south alignment of each marker, and finally sights along diagonals on a final check. Now each side of each *mecate* faces a cardinal direction.

Each of the corner poles of the *milpa* has a name. The northeast corner pole is called "North Pole," the northwest corner is called "West Pole" or "Companion of the North Pole," the southwest corner is "South Pole." The remaining pole is at the southeast corner and is called either East Pole or "Companion of the South Pole." It is not as critical as the other three points that (together with the right-angles in each of their squares) determines the orientation of the rectangular field. When Celso was explaining to me how he laid out his field, I did not recognize the connections with the sun's path throughout the year. It was more than a year later when I realized that the path of the assistant as he moves through the field, laying out the markers for each *mecate* corner, is isomorphic with the path of the sun, moving from east to west during the day, from west back to east every night in the Underworld. The movement from the northern boundary toward the southern boundary takes place through consecutive, east-west zigzags, which replicate the path of the sun from the summer solstice (June 21) to the winter solstice (December 21). This is the half of the year during which the crops grow, mature, and are harvested (see Figure 5.5). Summer solstice is the day when a man's fields are normally planted and sprouting, after which he anxiously awaits the rains.

The human path involved in marking the field precedes and prefigures the path the sun will take following the planting. This undulating east-west,

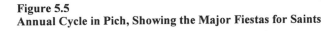

Figure 5.5
Annual Cycle in Pich, Showing the Major Fiestas for Saints

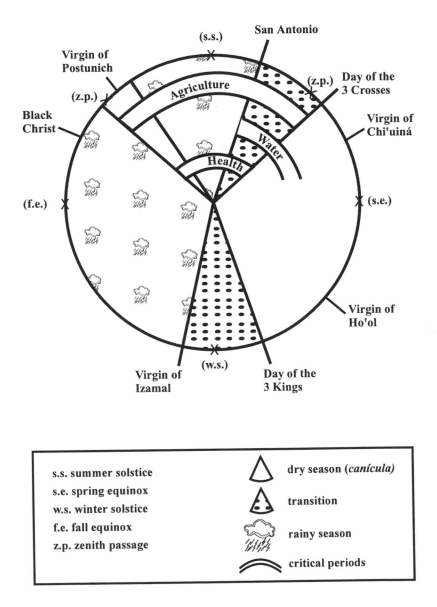

west-east movement toward the south following the summer solstice is correlated with the desired coming of the rains and is perceived as being like the movement of a snake, which also undulates from side to side as it moves forward. Throughout this area the symbols in the facades of ancient Maya buildings (Chenes style) show associations of earth serpents, borders of path-like undulating designs, sky bands associated with the path of the sun, rain gods, and corn (Morales and Faust 1986).

After the marking process, the *mecates* are each sown individually, in the shape of a squared-off spiral—a design frequently seen in the decorations of Maya buildings throughout this area, particularly on Puuc-style buildings like those at Uxmal. (See Figure 5.6). I both watched and participated in this sowing. The sower begins in the northeast corner of the *mecate*, with his left hand on the south side holding the pointed planting stick and his right hand taking seeds out of the bag slung on his right shoulder. He starts off down the field: two steps, dig the stick in firmly, pull it up, and put in five corn seeds and however many bean and squash seeds came with them. The proportion of beans and squash seeds added to each measure of corn is set by custom. To one sack of corn (70 to 80 kilograms) are added 3–4 kilograms of beans and 2–3 kilograms of squash. These are mixed before coming to the field. After the seeds have been put in the hole, the soil will fall back in on top of its own accord, if the burn has been good. There is no need to step on it. The sowing is done in a rhythmic motion, covering ground surprisingly quickly.

It is not easy, however, to learn how to do this sowing. I was criticized roundly for taking steps that were too big or too small, for not having the seed ready in my right hand when the planting stick came up, and so on. Women help with harvest, but women do not ordinarily plant: my attempting to do so was an enormous joke—talked about for days afterward, usually mercifully out of my hearing. Sowing seed with the pointed stick is seen as analogous to impregnating a woman, which contributed to the humor of my attempt at sowing. When asked why a *mecate* is planted in this squared spiral design, Celso replied that there were two reasons: (1) this shape on the ground draws the rains, and (2) one can be sure that each planting hole is lined up properly with its neighbor, and with the *milpa* and the sun. He always begins in the northeast corner, following the line between sticks marking the *mecate*, turning left at each corner until approaching the beginning point, where he turns left again at about a distance of two strides from the initial corner. Then, he takes two strides and lines up the next planting hole straight across from the companion hole on the northern boundary line, and so forth. He again turns two steps before he would be back on the *mecate* boundary, the western one, continuing in that manner in ever smaller squares until he arrives in the center. Each hole should line up with all the others so that the corn will form straight lines running both parallel to the edges of the *mecate* itself and diagonally to its corners. When one *mecate* is finished, he begins again at the northeast corner of the next, moving from the eastern edge of the *milpa* to its western boundary,

Figure 5.6
The Path for Milpa Planting

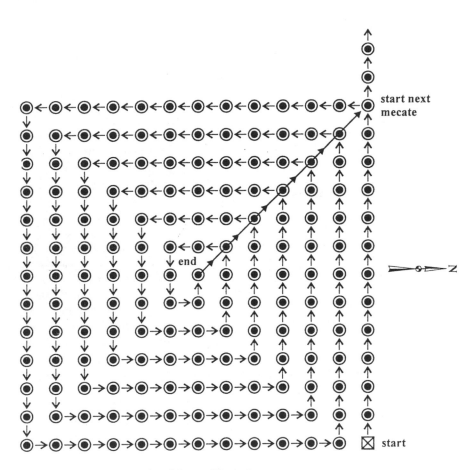

One Mecate Planted

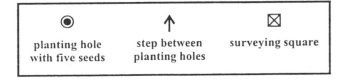

and back again from west to east until the *mecates* have all been planted. "It is beautiful work, isn't it?" he said softly.

The first two rows of *mecates* are sown with the late, yellow variety of corn, *xnuk nal amarillo*. They are followed by two rows of the early, yellow variety *sak tux amarillo;* two more of the early, white variety *sak tux blanco;* and, finally, four rows of the late, white variety, *xnuk nal blanco*. These eight rows of mecates comprise 4 hectares of corn. Normally, another field will then be planted in another location. Some are planted at lower elevations. High fields will drain well in case of too much rain; low fields will not suffer as much from drought. Every farmer plants at least one new field every year, in addition to replanting one or more.

PREDICTING THE HARVEST

Predictions are made concerning when the rains will begin, and whether or not they will bring too much or too little water, in order to assess how much of what kind of corn to plant where, as well as how soon to begin planting. Pichuleños have a complicated system of prediction called the *cabañuelas*, based on the daily weather in January. The weather in early May is another indicator of subsequent weather, while the first song of the local nightingale (*ruiseñor* in Spanish; *xk'ok'* in Maya) is said to precede the rains by seven weeks. Some people also look for certain kinds of moths or butterflies or the sounds of particular species of frogs.

Another predictor is the quantity of seeds produced by the *ha'bin* (*Piscidia piscipula*) tree in June and July. The *ha'bin* is the native tree whose wood is used to make the crosses put on the outdoor altars for agricultural ceremonies. Don Pedro, the *h-men*, explained the reason for choosing this tree: the wood is easy to cut when green, but is very heavy when dry. He thought a while and then added that the Jews picked this wood to make the cross because they wanted Christ to suffer in carrying it.

THE HARVEST SEASON

In the house yard, the first ears of corn harvested are cooked and then ritually hung up in a tree as a presentation to the Wind Lords. The number of ears is not said to be very important as long as it is *non*, an odd number. This is similar to the requirement that the number of breads and beverages in ritual presentations be *non*.[14] The cooked ears are hung in a tree or from the house roof, a little above people's heads. This presentation is similar to the offering of *sak-ha'* in hanging gourds to prevent or cure illness and also in the rain ceremony. My informants said no one knows why it must be an uneven number or why the ears of corn and the ritual beverage are placed where they are, other than that their grandparents told them that is what the spirit beings want.

I was told that after the presentation of the corn to the Wind Lords, a ceremony similar to the one at the beginning of the agricultural season may be held to thank the Wind Lords for giving good rains for the crop. However, in the ceremonies I saw, after the offering of the first ears, others were boiled or roasted in the coals and enjoyed by everyone. Both tortillas and *pozole* were made out of the tender, fresh corn during the next few weeks.

Gradually the corn in the fields begins to harden and dry. By November, it must be soaked and ground, being too hard to eat .fresh. Usually some corn is left from the year before but its taste is inferior to the current-year's corn and it is not used to make ritual foods. For the Days of the Dead (October 31 for dead children and November 1 for dead adults) two dishes are made from the dough of this new dried corn: one with freshly harvested black beans and a second with chicken in a red, *achiote* (anatto, *Bixa orellana*) sauce. Both are cooked underground in the *pib*.

SOCIAL ORGANIZATION

A relatively complex social organization can be presumed for the Classic, based on the ceremonial architecture (Webster and Kirker 1995), the intensive agricultural practices (Siemens 1978; Turner 1978, 1983; Denevan 1982; Siemens, Hebda, and Heimo 1996; Culbert 1996), and the water management systems (Matheny and Gurr 1979; Matheny et al. 1983; Domínguez Carrasco 1993). The complexity and sophistication of these systems required specialization, planning, and coordination. Research in historical records from the sixteenth century indicates that a complex political organization was still managing trade relations, tribute payments and public works in the first years after European contact in the Acalán area south of Pich (Scholes and Roys 1968; G. Jones 1982). Oral histories indicate that as recently as the 1960s a village system of political organization maintained, protected, and cleaned the water system of Pich. Knowledge of this system survives, but residents today rely on the government-provided well and pump to send water through pipes to their homes. In contrast, the traditional agricultural system is still in operation. It, like the water system, depends on cooperation. However, the cooperation is limited to *milpa* "*compañeros*," a group of two or three men who clear, burn, plant, and harvest their contiguous swidden fields, assisting one another on the basis of a balanced reciprocity. A father with teen-age sons works with them; as these mature and he ages, they form a team. The brothers gradually begin bringing their little sons. When the sons of the brothers are old ehough, their fathers will complete the cycle, separating to work with their sons. When brothers are lacking or have migrated, cousins, brothers-in-law or *compadres* may substitute.

The size of a cleared area for the fields of *compañeros* is no more than 9 acres (4 hectares), with each man having 2.2 acres (a hectare) or less. Each group of compañeros traditionally has fields in at least two different areas, one in low-lying land and the other in higher land. In some areas, the fields are substantially smaller due to variations in topography and soils. This arrangement of contiguous fields planted by small groups of milperos has a number of advantages: (1) planting a larger area results in less loss to wild animals; (2) each farmer (with his companion) can still plant fields in several areas reducing risk from both drought and flooding, and (3) a *compañero* can save the life of a farmer in case of snakebite, an encounter with a jaguar, or an accident.

The relationships of *milpa compañeros* are generally reinforced by multi-stranded relationships among their wives, who often share meals, help one another with child care, and support one another in emergencies. These are the nuclei of extended family groups, which unite for healing ceremonies and fiesta celebrations. The men who farm together also conduct their agricultural rituals together, sharing costs in time, labor, and money to buy the necessary ingredients.

After listening to a talk by one of the visiting agricultural experts (*técnicos*) on the advantages of cooperative groups and the necessity of forming them in order to receive government credits for mechanization, one *milpero*'s wife told me hopelessly that the men would never be able to do it because they do not know how to work in any groups except families, a prediction which has proven true. This is an indication of relatively recent culture loss, since ethnohistoric documents from 1557 to 1851 written in Yucatec Mayan indicate that the community-level, indigenous political organization (*cah*) remained strong among the Maya of the Yucatán peninsula (Restall 1995), in contrast to the nearly complete loss among Náhuatl speakers in the Valley of Mexico by 1650 (Friedlander 1975). This Maya community organization may have survived in part because of weaker colonial controls resulting from the lack of incentives: there were no valuable metals in the peninsula, and the lowland ecosystem was less hospitable to Europeans, their agriculture, and their domestic animals (Clendinnen 1987; Crosby 1972, 1986). On the positive side, the continuing need for collective management of rainwater for dry-season use may have provided a material base for a form of organization that was also socially and politically useful for political and cultural resistance. The loss of that water system in the last thirty years has occurred simultaneously with the imposition of national government projects and greater integration with national and international markets. Increasingly, the political organization of the village is determined by national policy, rather than Maya custom.

SWIDDEN ECOLOGY AND THE COMMONS

In traditional Maya swidden, all land planted is distinctly referred to as private property—for *this* season, for *this* harvest. The land is collectively held in that it may not be alienated and others may hunt there during the long fallow cycle; but the milpero who planted it continues to have exclusive rights to collect fruits and harvest tubers there, for it is he who made the long-term investment

in planting trees and root crops. Although the *ejido* land is community property, agricultural fields within it are not managed collectively; decision making
concerning the agricultural process is the right of the individual in charge of a
particular field. Labor is often exchanged, but decision making is the preroga-
tive of the temporary "owner" of the field being worked.

The *milpa* will be used a second year, possibly a third, and then it will be
moved. This man, his sons, or someone else will burn and plant this land again,
eight or twelve or twenty years in the future. They do not fell the distant virgin
timber to make *milpa* in Pich; they only fell those valuable old trees in order to
sell the lumber in Campeche. For *milpa* there is secondary forest, which is
much easier to clear. Also, there is a lingering sense among the traditional
elders that the high forest should not be cut because of the spirit beings.

The preferred place for traditional fields is among the rocks, on the slopes.
Bishop Landa describes the same preference in 1500s: "Yucatán is a land of
less soil than any I know, . . . on the earthy ground where it is to be found, no
trees grow, but only grass. But where they sow over the stony parts they secure
crops, and all the trees grow, some of them marvelously large and beautiful.
The cause I think is that more moisture is preserved among the stones than in
the earth" (Landa 1978:92). Since the white stones reflect the sun's heat,
leaving the earth under the rocks relatively cool, it is likely that moisture is thus
protected from evaporation in the high temperatures of the peninsula's agricultural season (normally over 100 degrees Fahrenheit). In addition, milperos
have told me that the roots grasp the stones, reducing the likelihood of uproot-
ing by the frequent strong winds from the Caribbean hurricanes that are
common when the corn ears are ripening and drying

Landa describes the social organization of agricultural work as follows:

> For each married man and his wife it was their custom to plant a space of
> 400 feet, which was called *hun vinic* [one man], a plot measured with a 20
> foot rod, 20 in breadth and 20 in length. The Indians have the excellent
> custom of helping each other in all their work. . . . The lands today are in
> common, and whoever occupies a place first, holds it; they sow in different
> places so that if the crop is short in one, another will make it up. When they
> work the land they do no more than gather the brush and burn it before
> sowing. From the middle of January to April they care for the land and then
> plant when the rains come. Then carrying a small sack on the shoulders they
> make a hole in the ground with a stick, dropping in five or six grains, and
> covering them with the same stick. When it rains, it is marvelous how they
> grow. (Landa 1978:38–39)

The description clearly could refer to the agricultural practices and ecology of
today's traditional Maya. One *mecate* probably did not feed one man and his
wife even then, but it and its produce may have been referred to as belonging
to one man and his wife. The *mecate* today is a unit, the produce of which
belongs to a single married couple. The labor is shared with others, but the man

to whom it belongs decides when the poles are lined up right and directs those who come to help him. He will reciprocate, helping his companions with their fields. However, there is no confusion concerning who is in charge of any one *mecate* or who owns the food harvested on it. That harvest is given to the wife for preparation of the family's meals.

BURNING: SOIL AND LIME

The timing of the burning of a Maya swidden field is critical. On the one hand, an additional weeding would become necessary if too much time elapsed between the burning and the rains that make the planted corn sprout. On the other hand, if one waits too late to burn, the first rains may wet the bush and cause it to burn poorly.

A good burn is essential to the success of an agricultural season for two reasons. First, it is important to have the surface free of wild vegetation and ready for planting, but it is important to save useful trees, including those which produce good shade for a rest from work in the hot sun. The cut and dried brush is carefully removed from around the trunks of these trees. Everywhere else an intense, thorough burn loosens and enriches the soil, kills insects and their eggs as well as weed seeds, and turns accumulated organic matter into a fine ash, which the rains wash into the soil. Second, when the burning is really hot, a substantial amount of limestone is converted to quick lime, which washes into the soil, increasing alkalinity.

Liming is important in this tropical region. Matheny and his colleagues have pointed out that limestone leaches out of soils far more quickly in the tropics than in temperate areas, due to the effects of heat and moisture on the organic processes involved (Matheny et al. 1983:18–26). Maintaining optimal alkalinity levels for crops is critical, as it affects their growth rate, their ability to compete with surrounding weeds, and their ability to absorb nutrients from the soil (Allaway 1975).

Research by Gary Gates (1985–1986) shows a loss of alkalinity in the ejido of Bonfil, an area of the Valley of Edzná used to settle new colonists from overpopulated northern areas in the 1970s. The new *ejido* was given drainage canals, irrigation systems, and machinery for growing rice. Gates found that the pH level fell from 6.5 to 5.0, and lower in places, despite the use of recommended fertilizers. A pH of 6.0 to 7.0 is optimal for corn. Gates said the new colonists did not recognize decreasing alkalinity as a potential problem, nor did the agricultural experts who advise the *ejido*. People say that the weeds have become unmanageable over the last fifteen years and the soil has "worn out." People insist they are using more and more fertilizer and getting lower yields; but if they do not use fertilizer, the soil will no longer produce at all. They see this condition as a type of addiction, related to human addictions to substances such as heroin or cocaine. According to Gates, at least part of this problem is probably due to the leaching of lime out of the soil.

Local agricultural experts I have talked with insisted that the soil was tested at the beginning of their development project and it does not need lime. They do not recognize that limestone can leach out, decreasing soil alkalinity. The soils of this valley have a fair amount of clay and no limestone rock near the surface (Matheny et al. 1983). Therefore the limestone particles present in the soil at the beginning of the project in 1973 had probably eroded from the rocky sides of the valley, accumulating over the centuries during which the valley was not used for agricultural purposes. Pichuleños have traditionally preferred to plant between the rocks on sloping, hilly land rather than on the valley floor. The rice project finally was abandoned by the 1990s in part because of the difficulty of working with the present-day acidic soils with their high clay content (Gates 1994:151–163).

LIME AND PRE-HISPANIC INTENSIVE AGRICULTURE

In the archeological site of Edzná, Matheny and his colleagues found no limestone subsoil and very few, widely separated, small outcroppings of limestone rock. According to their analysis, the soil is acidic with a fair amount of clay, especially near the canals. They postulate that the canal water leached lime from soils whose limestone subsoil had already eroded, due to the natural geological progression of karst topography (Matheny, et al. 1983; see also Ward, Weidie and Back 1985). Loss of lime could have been accelerated by intensive, irrigated crop production, eventually resulting in soil that would not continue adequately to support corn crops.

According to Antoine, Skarie, and Bloom (1982:234–235), before the Preclassic a thin layer of limestone marl was deposited in many areas of the peninsula by a temporary rise in sea level, resulting in fertile soils for Maya agriculture. This layer could have leached out by the Late Classic in areas of intensive use, resulting in increased reliance on hillside swidden with short fallow to feed a population that was growing exponentially, at the rate of 0.45–0.58 percent per annum from A.D. 600 to 800 (Culbert and Rice 1990:310). Effects of the resulting deforestation could have combined with global warming to produce severe local climate change. Such an intersection of decline in the resource base with an overshoot of carrying capacity are the conditions that precipitate the replacement of homeostatic cultural mechanisms with deviation-amplyfying ones in preindustrial cultures (Zubrow 1972).

Evidence from other sites supports the importance of lime to Maya cornfields. David Freidel and Vernon Scarborough report that ancient Maya canals in Cerros, Belize were lined with a limestone gravel fill and banked with a layer of *sascab* (a locally available, powdery form of limestone rock), in which were set uncut boulders of limestone rock (1982:140–42). Water flowing over these surfaces would no doubt have dissolved them gradually, making the canal water more alkaline. Either hand irrigation or the placement of canal bottom sediments as a fertilizing mulch on associated raised fields would have transferred the lime to the drained fields (Freidel and Scarborough 1982:147–148), maintaining a sufficiently alkaline soil for growing corn intensively.

Another technique possibly used in ancient Maya intensive agriculture is mulching; this can affect pH depending on the materials used for mulch. In the Yalahau area of northern Quintana Roo, Scott Fedick (1995b:3) has found Maya rock constructions in cross-channel alignments, implying management of water levels in the natural depressions. He suggests that these may have "functioned as check-dams to slow the rush of rainwater runoff into cultivated areas. . . . [They may also have facilitated] the buildup of sediments . . . which could have been used for cultivation." In another report Fedick (1995a) describes chemical analysis of the abundant periphyton found in these depressions as indicating that it would have been an excellent natural fertilizer to use on wetland soils.

It is entirely possible that the effects of either the mulch as fertilizer or the lime water on the soils of the irrigated fields were not understood by the ancient Maya.[15] They may have simply used the mulch to retain moisture and the abundant, locally available limestone as a convenient construction material to retard erosion. It certainly is true that today the Maya do not understand the role of lime in their diet. Corn is soaked in lime water to soften the outer husk so that it may be cooked more quickly. The fact that this practice allows calcium to be absorbed into the corn itself is not perceived, nor is there any perception of the dietary need for calcium.[16]

The ancient Maya did have a way of measuring soil pH, by observing the type of weeds growing in the soil. Present-day Maya farmers identify soil types in part by the vegetation, and they recognize stages of plant succession following the abandonment of cornfields. The fact that cornfields are said to be abandoned because of increases in weed growth may be a good indication of increasing acidity, making the growth of corn more difficult, while favoring weed growth (Gates 1985–1986). This may normally occur after either the second or the third year of use, at which point the field is abandoned and a new section of second-growth forest is burned. A sufficiently hot fire to produce significant quantities of lime requires the burning of fairly large trees—which is a timing factor in the swidden cycle.

The shift in location of major sites from Classic to Postclassic times (from southern lowlands to the northern area of the peninsula) may be a shift from regions of greater rainfall but exhausted soils, to ones of richer soils with water scarcity problems. If, as has been postulated by some archeologists, the growth of northern centers is due to the movement of Maya populations from the abandoned Petén sites of the Classic period, this migration may have been precipitated by the exhaustion of lime. Deevey et al. have described other possible degrading effects of intensive agriculture on lowland, moist soils (1979).

The limestone outcroppings of the northern peninsula would have been found associated with wild flora indicative of good soil for planting corn.

Although sparse rainfall is a problem, one crop of corn (and beans) can be successfully grown in normal years. When harvests were poor, either storage buildings in administrative centers or the coastal canoe trade could possibly have provided supplemental basic grains.

Evidence for prolonged drought associated with the Collapse has received a great deal of recent attention; however, the mechanisms through which a drought would have resulted in a move from areas of more rainfall to those of less are presently unknown. Perhaps the drought and soil exhaustion were both important factors resulting in severe pressure to develop complex terracing on limestone slopes, where soil pH could be maintained and rainwater conserved within terrace soils. Rainfall would then have become the new constraint on population density, and the development of rain-saving devices would have been critical. The growth of devotion to the *Chako'ob* was interpreted by Rosemary Sharp (1981) as related to concerns about rain. The ceremonies conducted in Pich by the local Maya *h-men* continue to be directed primarily to the Lords of the Winds, who bring the rains, although the One True God and the Catholic Trinity are always invoked at the beginning. The permission of God must be sought first. He must agree to their actions, but it is the Wind Lords who act.

CHANGES IN WIND AND RAIN

Alongside declining availability of lime for agriculture, variations in rainfall would have been a critical factor for population density in each ancient Maya area. Since the 1920s, tree-ring data have been used in correlations of climate with changes in sites and population densities among the ancient pueblo Indians of the southwestern United States (Woodbury 1993). Recently Hodell, Curtis, and Brenner (1995) have found evidence of prolonged drought beginning with the Late Classic in cores taken from a lake bed in the center of the Yucatán peninsula.

Changing wind patterns are well known to alter the distribution and type of rainfall, having dramatic effects on systems of intensive agriculture. Winds are critical in the Yucatán Peninsula, both because they bring the beneficial rains of the planting season and because they bring the destructive hurricanes and northern storms that can uproot and flatten the tall corn plants. This importance could explain the strong interest in winds found in Maya rituals of this area. Like many other indigenous deities, the wind and rain gods have both benevolent and malevolent aspects.

If wind patterns changed in cycles of many years, these patterns may have been recognized, because of the Maya's extraordinary dedication to documenting the passage of time. Such patterns, if they were discerned, may have affected Maya agricultural and settlement planning, as well as having been useful in determining plans for grain storage from good years in preparation for bad ones. The growing evidence for intensive, complex systems of Maya agriculture involving both terrace and canal systems makes sophisticated planning and management probable. Complex technologies in combination with high population densities are very vulnerable to external shocks, according to systems analysis (see W. R. Catton 1982; Lowe 1985).

The importance of winds in Postclassic times in the Yucatán is indicated by some of the iconography and by interpretations of architecture and city planning as symbolic systems.[17] Orientation of buildings to the local landscape and the movements of celestial bodies appears to have been important to Mesoamerican cultures (Aveni 1980, 1992; Aveni and Hartung 1981; Carlson 1981; Heyden 1981; Love 1994; and others).

The Caracol [snail] of Cozumel is a building with some indications of the importance of wind in Maya cosmology. This Postclassic building was constructed with whistles built in its roof, so that when the winds came from a particular direction, the building whistled. The whistles were made of large conch shells and the roofcomb in which they were embedded was made to look like a giant version of these shells. Their whistling function is explicitly described by Schavelzón:

> In reference to its possible function, it is evident that the whole group plays a religious role, related to the wind cult, which is indicated by the four doors of the temple, an arrangement repeated in the enlargement and its reproduction in the upper story. For its part, the great seashell, covered with other small ones that whistle when the wind blows, can offer support for this hypothesis. (Schavelzón 1985:79, author's translation)

The Caracol had doors on four sides but has a primary orientation toward the east (Caribbean), in that the seashell roofcomb is placed near the west wall, providing a larger area facing east. The eastern doorway points approximately twenty degrees north of east (Schavelzón 1985:77). Following the work of archeo-astronomers, I suggest that it may have been aligned with the sunrise at the summer solstice or at the first zenith passage of the sun, in May (see Aveni 1980, 1992).

Such a position would have been significant in Maya cosmology. The first zenith passage of the sun occurs in May, at the beginning of rainy season (or what used to be thought of as the beginning of rainy season). The summer solstice is when all crops should be planted and sprouted. After this date it is important that the rains come regularly, at least until the fall equinox. The daily rains expected during this season are brought by winds coming from the east, from the Caribbean.

Fragmentary remains of round structures similar to that at Cozumel have been noted in Mayapán and Edzná. The large, complex Caracol at Chichén Itzá may have been a variant of these. Whether or not these round structures also had acoustic decorations, like the seashells of the structure in Cozumel, is unknown.[18] These round structures appear to be associated with speakers of the Cholan Maya languages migrating east from the Tabasco and Veracruz coasts.

They carried with them myths concerning a god-king named Plumed Serpent (Quetzalcoatl, Kukulcán), who was strongly associated with wind. They also brought spear throwers for war and some Nahuatl words, indicating previous contacts with the Toltec of the Valley of Mexico.

The building and abandonment of sites, the political crises, and the fluctuations in population density reported throughout Maya history may have been, at least in part, cultural responses to cyclical changes in rainfall patterns. These cycles are obscured in the short term by the more noticeable yearly variations in rainfall, but long-term records could have been kept in association with the Maya calendar (Folan and Hyde 1985).

Research in archeo-astronomy has shown that many Mesoamerican sites were oriented to the movements and conjunctions of various celestial bodies. Some of these events occur yearly and are associated with critical points of the agricultural cycle. Others, such as the appearance and disappearance of Venus as "morning star" and "evening star" (and its position in relation to the Pleiades) have cycles encompassing many years and facilitate the measuring of periods of time larger than centuries. These cycles could thus have provided calendrical points against which to measure variations in rainfall patterns in order to determine long-term cycles.

COMPARISONS OF THE SWIDDEN SYSTEM WITH MEXICAN RURAL DEVELOPMENT PROGRAMS

The traditional swidden system is generally regarded by local government planners and agronomists as environmentally destructive, despite a great deal of research to the contrary (see Gómez-Pompa 1987; Gómez-Pompa, Flores, and Sosa 1987; Hernández Xolocotzi, Bello Baltazar, and Levy Tacher 1995; Terán and Rasmussen 1994, 1995). Concern about ecological damage from the fires is part of the rationale for disparaging the traditional system. The six local technicians (working in the areas of ecology and rural development) whom I interviewed were convinced that swidden agriculture is chiefly responsible for the destruction of the tropical forest. One of these technicians quoted Raymond Stadleman's research for the Smithsonian as the authoritative proof. Stadleman's work, however, was done in northwest Guatemala (1940). Morris Steggerda, who worked in the Yucatán peninsula, commented on the basis of his own observations that "I have never found, however, that *milpa* fires were likely to spread, even in unprotected areas" (Steggerda 1941:96). Fires do, no doubt, occasionally get out of hand, as they also do in the national forests of the United States of America. However, the Maya farmers I observed and spoke with are quite careful with their firebreaks.

Another reason given by government officials for their negative evaluation of the traditional system is that the corn seed that is used year after year is old and "degenerated." A local agricultural expert insisted to me that the native seed corn planted by the traditional farmers is dirty and full of insects and that its yield keeps declining every year. There seems to be some confusion here between the generational patterns of stable local varieties and the consequence of planting second-generation seeds from hybrid varieties (these are not stable, producing a great variety of phenotypes) rather than buying the new hybrid seed each year. The traditional local varieties are known to withstand drought better, according to the same expert, but he still recommends that farmers plant only the hybrid seeds, because they are "more efficient." They produce a greater yield (if it rains enough).

Perhaps some of the official disdain for traditional methods is due to an excess of respect for northern scientists and the products of their research in temperate zone agriculture. Perhaps it has something to do with a development process that is funded from without and makes profits available to the local decision-making elite in return for the importation of foreign technologies (see Sandoval Palacios 1982). The cost of such participation in Pich has been the destruction of a local agroforestry system that once supported a healthy and productive rural population. Systems were adopted in the 1980s which have facilitated the short-term provisioning of lumber, cattle, and rice to a world system run by international finance capital (Wallerstein 1976, 1980; Sandoval Palacios 1982; Brannon and Joseph 1991; Gates 1994). The lumber and rice are already failing. The raising of cattle employs few people and much land; it also allows some already wealthy individuals to make more money.

A trend toward a later rainy season has been observed during the 1990s—delaying the planting from May to June. Whether this is a normal, long-term drought cycle or evidence of the beginning stages of desertification is not known. Neither is it known if the change is due only to local factors or also to global warming (see Schlesinger 1991).

In contrast to the swidden method of clearing small tracts surrounded by forest, new government programs involve bulldozing tracts of forest hundreds of acres in extension. Habitat is lost to wild life. The winds of the dry season blow the soil from these bare fields, churned up by mechanical cultivators. When these expanses of land are abandoned due to soil exhaustion, the forest will not easily reclaim them as it did the small plots of swidden farmers.

Many local development workers believe that "permanent farming" with tractors and fertilizers will reduce the total amount of destruction to the forest because new fields will not have to be cleared by the same farmer each year. They do not well understand the cyclical nature of swidden agriculture.[19] It is true that this type of agriculture requires more land available per person for the rotation of fields, making it problematic in conditions of growing population pressure. However, it does not deplete soil fertility in any permanent way, unless farmers have access to too little land to allow for sufficient periods of fallow.

In the early 1980s the plans of the government were to use modern methods continuously for four or five years with fertilizers and then convert the exhausted fields to pasture for cattle (Sandoval Palacios 1982:114). This conversion may have increased foreign exchange to pay international debts, but it risks erosion and desertification. It employs few rural workers and does not contribute to meeting the basic needs of the local population or of the country as a whole (Sandoval Palacios 1982: 30–60; Gates 1994:136–137).

Raising beef is an extremely inefficient way to provide animal protein, using many more times the acreage per pound of protein than do chickens or pigs. In addition, the combination of corn and beans in the traditional Maya diet appears to supply essential amino acids. Animal protein may be a supplement, but only of major importance for the special protein needs of the injured or ill, and those women who are pregnant or nursing.

Traditionally the special needs of the ill or injured have been supplied by rituals involving the killing and eating of chickens or turkeys, while it is believed absolutely necessary to give pregnant and nursing women any food they want. Wild game is occasionally available, pork is common, and beef is sometimes served, although generally cattle are kept as an investment to be eventually exported or sold to urban Mexican markets. The poor often say that the cows are "eating" both the cornfields of the poor and the tropical forest (*comen las milpas y el monte*). Certainly they are replacing both. Ambivalence concerning cattle can be seen in the *loh*, a Maya ceremony done for the blessing and "curing" of pasture. The head, hide, and hooves of a sacrificed young bull are arranged to look like a live animal lying on the ground. Children play at dominating it and dress it with a hat, before it is ritually buried with a sacrificed chicken, that is treated with far more respect.

Despite the drawbacks and the lack of preexisting skills in the needed social organization, Pichuleños responded positively to the government incentives for the new system. The first group of associates to obtain a tractor from government loans solved its initial problems and was meeting weekly in the summer of 1986 with an adviser from the Agricultural Brigade. They were improving their reading skills; some were learning to read for the first time. They were all learning to keep accounts, figure interest rates on loans, and fill out the government forms for the credit they were receiving and would have to pay back. Some members of the group had previously learned organization skills in the locally managed Presbyterian church, where accounts are kept and read publicly every month to the congregation and where decisions are made either in committees or in open meetings. The skills developed in this religious organization were being transferred to the agricultural project.

The associates of the agricultural group expressed confidence that a collective form of organization would enable them to get ahead. They were not informed about the likelihood that the soil would become exhausted and believed that their new techniques would enable them to farm this land permanently. By 1992 most had become discouraged, but a few were working hard with a government advisor, learning to plow under crop residues and rotate crops, as well as using chemical fertilizer, herbicides, and hybrid seeds. Those who continued work with the tractor had other sources of income in the village (bees, cattle, a store, etc.); those lacking such resources generally had migrated to a city. The collective organization had disintegrated into several loose factions, composed of related patrilineages.

TRADITIONAL AGRICULTURE AND THE NATIONAL ECONOMY

On a first-year, traditional cornfield, Pichuleños hope for a harvest of native corn approximating 4,000 pounds per hectare. The second-year fields yield approximately 2,400 pounds per hectare. In a dry year (one out of three, normally; but in the years from 1986 to 1992 it has become two out of three, according to village talk), the yield for a second-year field would be only 1,200 pounds. One man can normally harvest nine sacks of corn a day. The native corn yields one sack of corn kernels for every two sacks of corn on the cob, whereas the hybrid corn yields only one to three. Each sack of corn kernels weighs about 150 pounds. The nine sacks of a normal day's work yield 1,300 pounds a day. In 1986 good, native corn was selling at 27 old pesos the pound, which meant that a man picking nine sacks in a day could net out 13,000 pesos (after paying 5 pesos per pound to have it mechanically shucked from the cob and 250 pesos for each of the sacks). If he hired labor for harvesting, he would pay 1,200 to 1,800 old pesos a day. The agricultural wage was officially 1,600 pesos per day. Although many were accepting 1,200 pesos in order to obtain work in the off-season, during harvest it was sometimes necessary for farmers to pay 200 pesos the sack of harvested ears, or an average of 1,800 per day (when the exchange rate was changing from 250 pesos the U.S. dollar to $500 pesos).

In 1985 the Comisión Nacional para Subsistencia Popular (CONASUPO, National Commission for Popular Subsistence), a government agency which maintains subsidized stores, had paid only 18 pesos per pound for corn when the going price was 45 pesos in the local markets for the hybrid corn and 53 for good, native corn. (CONASUPO will not pay more for better-quality corn.) Those who had received government assistance during the growing season were required to sell their corn to the CONASUPO at its low price. From the payment for their harvest was deducted the amount they had been previously given as advances (or credits). These were given to buy seed, fertilizer, herbicides and pesticides. In addition, "credit" was given as a kind of salary, according to the number of days of work done during the growing season. All these credits had to be repaid, with interest, from harvest income, unless the crop was declared a loss (more than half of the expected harvest lost).

HINTS FROM THE ARCHEOLOGICAL AND HISTORICAL DATA

It increasingly seems that the Classic Maya made use of *bajos* (depressions with clay soils which become seasonal swamps during the rainy season) and tropical forests as well as rocky slopes to grow food. They managed multiple-use forest preserves, silviculture, intensive irrigation systems, and swidden. They did so with complex methods of public administration that relied both on protection of the "commons" and individual accountability and incentives, until something caused the system to come apart in a descending spiral. Unfortunately, that ninth-century Collapse, rather than being compared to a structurally similar one of Ancient Rome (Adams and Smith 1977; Antonio 1979), has generally been seen as proof of the inadequacy of autochthonous methods. The negative political consequences of this view for today's Maya have been pointed out by Richard Wilk (1984). The elite of the peninsula are, in general, more interested in the Aztec than the Maya, because they see the Aztec as a successful civilization, until defeated by the Spanish. The Maya are seen by many as incompetents.

One of the sources of misunderstandings of the Maya is the sparse population found by nineteenth-century explorers in the lowlands of Yucatán and Guatemala. These populations should not, however, be thought of as the result of the Collapse. J. E. S. Thompson's (1970) review of the historical documentation made it very clear that the Yucatán Peninsula and the adjoining areas of neighboring Veracruz, Tabasco, and Chiapas were well-populated at the time of the Conquest. More recently Freidel and Scarborough (1982) have reviewed the sixteenth century literature concerning raised fields and canals, commercial agriculture and trade in the Peninsula and neighboring Tabasco. Prudence Rice's (1987) analisis of data from William Bullard's and other's excavations on Macanché Island shows that even in the Petén, in the center of the Collapse, and despite clear evidence for serious cultural disruptions, there were continuing high population densities from the ninth to the seventeenth centuries in many areas near lakes and rivers. This is in accord with a number of other studies done in the Petén lake region which have been summarized by Donald S. Rice and Prudence Rice (1990:123–148). The decline of some of the cities of the Petén was clearly not the end of dense Maya populations. The sparse Maya population found by nineteenth-century archeologists and explorers was partially the result of sixteenth-century Conquest, which introduced new diseases and imposed an economic system of agricultural technology and trade brought from a different ecological system. More recently, modernization has included the cutting of tropical hardwoods and the establishment of henequen and sugar plantations.

Conditions of life on the haciendas often did not promote population growth. Yaquis and Africans were forcibly brought to the peninsula to supplement the local labor force. Large areas of the peninsula were considered unhealthy; a non-endemic strain of malaria may have been the primary cause for low population densities between the time of early colonization and the introduction of modern malaria-control techniques in the later part of this century.

Poor communication concerning both the traditional agricultural techniques and the local ecosystems to which they were adapted probably also contributed to the initial population decline and the low population levels existing until quite recently. Similar communication difficulties continue to disrupt relationships between practitioners of a functioning and rational autochthonous agricultural system and those who want to bring it into "a better relationship with the world economic system," in order to "improve its productivity, and the economic welfare of the people." Today Pich is overpopulated for the area closes to town that can conveniently be used for swidden. However, a reversion to Classic Period technologies, terraces, canals, etc. would permit greater population density, albeit at a personally unacceptable labor cost, given the present price of corn. Government could subsidize the high initial investment costs, including the use of appropriate machinery. The more complex, intensive systems of the pre-Columbian Maya were probably built as state projects, as well.

THE PRESENT-DAY POLITICAL CONTEXT

The confusion of collective management with communism, on the one hand, and of individual accountability with capitalist imperialism, on the other, have beclouded the issues. Perhaps what we need to ask is not, Why did some Classic Maya cities collapse? but How did Classic and Postclassic Maya societies sustain themselves for so many centuries with such a dense population in this tropical, karst environment—without the aid of either draft animals or the wheel, let alone electricity or petroleum?

Periodically calls are made to reconstruct ancient Maya agricultural systems (see Lambert, Siemens, and Arnason 1984). The response of both planners and farmers is frequently an objection concerning the amount of work required, work that will not be soon compensated, as the benefits are long term. Terracing is hard work and so is digging canals. The construction of the system requires some technical competence, administrative organization, and a political climate of trust. Labor investments in land require trust that the latter benefits can be appropriated by the investors—the family who puts in labor and/or capital, that ownership will not be manipulated into the hands of outsiders once the productive improvements are made. Such investments also require trust that one's neighbors can be relied upon to construct and maintain their share of the system.

In addition, increased productivity is also intimately tied to profits. There is no incentive to produce more than you consume if the profits will be appropriated by middlemen or agencies in the system. Traditional Maya farmers can and do accumulate capital and invest it in productive resources. They do it all the time, usually far more efficiently than most city dwellers, including some of their own kin. They do not invest accumulated capital in maids or travel or clothes. They invest it in those things that, they say, are realistically most likely to return a profit on investment with a low security risk, for example, education, tractors, trucks, refrigerators (one sells cold drinks and ice to neighbors), sewing machines, and privately owned land.

One of the basic problems is how to motivate cooperation in projects requiring groups larger than extended families, in order to benefit by economies of scale in the external market. The experience of the first group of associates to mechanize agricultural production points to some important factors for group success: accounting skills, decision-making skills, procedures for group discussion, and the legal power to exclude free-loaders. The associates who had had previous experience with these in the organizational structure of the Presbyterian church became the leaders of the new group.

Another critical factor for intensive agricultural programs is marketing arrangements. The amount of return for labor invested in 1985–1986 was generally agreed to be less for crops than for either lumbering or hunting. When people are questioned regarding the newly enforced government restrictions on hunting deer and cutting lumber, the usual response is, "They are trying to force us to grow more corn for the city, for the government." Lumber and venison can be sold for higher profits in the city than can corn, although it is acknowledged that deer and good timber are becoming scarcer.

In addition to the above problems, the technology that would make intensive farming sustainable in this ecological and political environment has not yet become available to today's Maya farmer. Determining how the ancient Maya supported dense populations in this area for many centuries could contribute to the development of an appropriate modern technology. With electrical and petroleum-powered machinery, trucks for transportation, chemical methods for testing the soil, we ought to be able to do better than produce rice for ten to fifteen years, switching to cattle raising afterwards. The rice was not even double-cropped. Most of the drainage ditches were not connected with any irrigation system, so the majority of the rice was at the mercy of the rains. Yet the ancient Maya apparently used this valley intensively, not for a few decades, but for centuries.

It is conceivable that the old intensive system failed for lack of lime. Apparently, the new system suffered from a similar depletion due to the effects of leaching on the little lime that had accumulated, but it will take more than liming the fields to create an intensive system of agroforestry that can be relatively resilient in the peninsula. It will require a supportive political environment for agricultural production, one that can structure both incentives and accountability, while providing effective sanctions to protect one of the most fundamental public goods, local ecosystems which can provide renewable resources. These problems are not the concern of the tropical world alone. The tropics provide a means of understanding what is taking place in temperate zones, where the organic processes involved in both the building and the destruction of soil humus operate more slowly.

FUTURE POSSIBILITIES

The traditional swidden system of present-day Pich is one that has many advantages but that requires a great deal of land per farmer. The long fallow period required on the limestone slopes means that much land must be held in fallow, which places a limit on population growth. However, with 69,000 hectares (2.471 acres per hectare) of land for a population of 1,500 that is not a problem of immediate concern to most Pichuleños. Nevertheless, desirable land close to the village is scarce and people do over-use it, sometimes shortening the fallow period to seven years or even five. One of the incentives for this over-use is the public school. Children cannot both attend school and help with the fields unless the fields are close to town. Formerly during rainy season whole extended families went to the woods to grow their food, living in homes built near the widely scattered *aguadas*. During the dry season they would return to the village center, for this was the time of community festivities and construction. They initially arrived in town for the Days of the Dead, returning to the *rancherías* for harvest until January 6, when the Three Kings, "call us to work." Construction then began on houses, public buildings, and roads. May 3 is the Day of the Three Green Crosses, who are regarded as Holy Persons, like the Three Kings. Their day used to herald the return of the rains and the beginning of the agricultural season, which now begins in June.

Today Pichuleños express concern about the overuse of land near the village, but also desire to obtain cash in order to buy the things they now desire to own and in order to educate their children so that they will not be "ignorant." They want their children to have a *chance*, if possible, to become doctors or engineers. (It is interesting that they have adopted the English word, *chance*, rather than any word in Maya or Spanish for the idea of individual opportunity to get ahead.) If their desires for progress and their competition to use the local resource base are not to result in destruction of that resource base, information needs to be made available concerning the long-term effects of various alternative means of improving production. Training in accounting, soil testing, committee work, budgeting, and administration is needed along with agricultural technologies appropriate to the local ecology. The respect for the natural world and for community that is expressed in ritual could be channeled through appropriate local administrative techniques in order to enable Pichuleños to protect the *ejido*'s resources for their children's use. Information concerning forest management and political mechanisms for controlling abuses are both necessary.

Until recently, the village view of the future had been one of great faith in the miracles of imported, expensive, technology, although the old traditions are dear to people's hearts and regrets are frequently expressed concerning the effects of the changes on the local forest. Frequently bewailed is the loss of community "togetherness," as is loss of "respect" (for elders).

Yearning for the respect that comes with modernization, Don Eus wanted to see his youngest son on a tractor. Unfortunately, given the local ecology (with its soil and water problems), modern agribusiness has only an illusion to offer him. Ten years later his youngest son is still helping him wiith the milpa while struggling to attend middle school; periodically he thinks about moving to the city. The Mexican archeologist who identified the potsherds in Pich as Late Classic found a job for one of the older sons digging with an archeological project in Calakmul. Another son was put in the reform school for stealing from village *ricos*.

The government project the father joined and worked hard for in 1986 has not provided the *chance*. The government has not yet been able to find any sustainable agricultural system that improves on the traditional productivity per acre for more than ten years. A rich person may raise a number of cattle and sell them for a good profit, but the amount of plant food and the land area required for this mode of production are very high, resulting in the destruction of large areas of forest. Cattle raising will only worsen the problem of subsistence for the village as a whole—let alone the problem of finding a way to participate in the global market sufficiently to buy televisions, blenders, and bicycles. Nonetheless, many small farmers try to imitate the *ricos*, buying one or two cows.

Among government planners in Campeche, subsistence agriculture itself has had a bad name, representing "backwardness and poverty." Self-sufficiency in basic grains was dimly viewed while the petro-dollars were abundant. With the 1990s have come a deepening debt crisis, the devaluation of the peso, continuing low prices for petroleum, high urban migration rates, an indigenous rebellion in Chiapas, political unrest, growing unemployment (associated by many with the North American Free Trade Agreement), signs of possible desertification, and increasing rates of contamination of ground water by agrochemicals banned in other countries. These may be gradually altering the willingness of policy makers to examine their assumptions concerning progress.

It is no longer easy to buy imported basic grains[20] with which to feed a population that will continue to grow for another generation, as Mexico goes through its demographic transition. Each woman is only having two or three children, but the number of women reaching reproductive age will continue to grow for another fifteen to twenty years. The result is continuing population growth, in many areas beyond the carrying capacity of swidden agriculture, intersecting in Campeche with immigration from even more densely populated areas and with growing desires to participate in the modern market on terms that allow for real improvements in family life. These trends are potentially explosive ones, particularly as villagers become more influenced by modern media and more experienced in travel and communication with others in similar circumstances.

Poor communication concerning the existing agricultural ecology probably contributed to the initial population decline following the Conquest and the low population levels existing until quite recently. Similar communication difficulties continue to disrupt relationships between practitioners of a functioning and rational autochthonous agricultural system and those who are trying to "improve its productivity, and the economic welfare of the people."

NOTES

1. The proper Mayan plural would be *aluxo'ob*; however, the Hispanicized plural *aluxes* (or *aluxitos*) is the term most commonly used in Pich.

2. Later it did begin to give some incentives for planting.

3. This type of vegetation is described by local botanists as old secondary growth, semi-dry tropical forest of medium height.

4. The brush may be cut as late as February and will still dry in time to be burned in April; however, it is considered easier to cut when it is green (during the rainy season).

5. Thorstein Veblen has done an ethnographic study of the continuing, traditional techniques of forest conservation in a more isolated, highland Maya community, Totonicapán, Guatemala (Veblen 1975).

6. I initially saw this belief as a curious superstition; later I encountered sufficient additional information to formulate a hypothesis concerning how heat might result in soil fertility, from a Western scientific perspective. This will be explained below.

7. A jaguar was killed by local farmers the first year I was in Pich. Two others were sighted. The cattle ranchers are taking turns stalking one this year. Jaguars, other large cats, and a wide variety of dangerous snakes are commonly seen during the dry season. I have personally seen both a boa constrictor that was at least 6 feet long and a small coral snake. From a bus I saw a rattlesnake that appeared to be about 10 feet long. Snakebite is feared, especially if one is alone. There is a well-known herb that can counteract snakebite (*contrahierba, Acalypha arvensis*), but the victim needs to lie still while his companions find the herb and bring it to him. Alone he dies.

8. This ceremony has been reported by many other researchers in the area, including Robert Redfield and Alfonso Villa Rojas (1934) and Steggerda (1941), although its connections with the ceiba have not been previously analyzed as reflecting the local ecology.

9. For the dead, food as well as drink is prepared. Food is also prepared in the ceremony for the rain gods that is performed in time of drought. Turkeys are sacrificed and cooked along with special breads baked underground with ground squash seeds and other condiments.

10. *Sak-ha'* is a ceremonial beverage made of corn. Its preparation is described in Chapter 4.

11. The gourd used is called a *jícara* in Spanish and a *luch* in Maya (*Cresentia cujete*). It grows on a tree. It is split in half lengthwise and boiled, detaching the interior fruit. Then, the hull is dried in the sun. This hull is traditionally used for serving beverages and soups. It is also used to dip water from a bucket when bathing and to splash water on dishes and clothes when washing them. It is an all-purpose utensil of the traditional Maya household.

12. The Maya spelling was given me by the farmer and later corrected using the *Diccionario Maya* (Barrera 1991), with assistance from Miguel Angel Flores Vera. The Spanish translation is that of the farmer. The English translation I have provided.

13. It is said that since they began cutting down the forest in the valley, the rains have become even more inconsistent.

14. Likewise, the number of children a woman bears should be *non*. The number of turkeys to be sacrificed is always *non*, as are the number of years between a ceremony asking for healing from a chronic illness and one giving thanks for the healing. The last in a sequence ending with an odd number is the *t'up*. The last child in the family is always the *t'up*. The last bread to be made for the rain-calling ceremony is *t'up*. The last ear of corn to be offered in thanks is *t'up*.

15. I am referring to them as irrigated; however, it is also true that they are drained fields. In this climate, although a field may benefit from irrigation in dry periods, it may also need drainage during rainy periods. This is particularly true of fields in low-lying areas such as the valley floor surrounding the site of Edzná.

16. Programs in nutrition in the schools emphasize the protein content of milk, not its calcium content. No sources of calcium in the traditional local diet are taught in the schools. A good diet is defined by the educational system as one that is not produced locally. The fruit illustrations frequently contain fruits from temperate zones not available on a village budget and certainly not produced locally. Modernizing households sometimes use commercially ground corn meal which can be mixed with water and made into tortillas. Some of these preparations reportedly have lime added, others do not. I was unable to find out about the calcium content of the corn meal distributed to the Guatemalan refugees before their first crop of corn. Their own production continues to be supplemented by such commercially ground corn, possibly without lime added. The poor condition of children's teeth is locally dismissed by doctors as a general result of ignorance and poor nutrition, not lack of calcium in their diet.

17. See Agrest and Gandelsonas (1973) for a development of the idea of a semiotics of architecture.

18. Throughout the Maya area such shells are highly prized and often found as decorations in private homes. With the fall of the empire, such portable prizes may well have been looted from rooftops.

19. This observation is based on interviews with eight government officials involved in the planning of rural development programs, including three employed at high levels in agencies concerned with ecology.

20. The peso continues to decline in value relative to the U.S. dollar. As this goes to press the exchange rate is 7.75 pesos to the dollar. These are "new pesos," each one worth one thousand of the former pesos. This change was made because of the high rates of inflation. In 1985, when I arrived in Pich, the exchange rate was 250 old pesos to the US dollar. In today's pesos that would be a quarter of a peso per U.S. dollar as compared with the present rate of nearly 8 "new" pesos (8,000 old pesos) to the dollar; in eleven years the peso's value compared to the dollar has decreased by a factor of 32.

6

The Plumed Serpent, Rural Development, and the Future of the Biosphere

Maya religious cosmology is a comprehensive model of the locally observable universe, a cognitive model symbolically expressed in Maya ritual. It is grounded in the special ecology of the Maya area, with its karst topography and a tropical climate that includes alternating dry and rainy seasons. This environment is a difficult one for water management and agriculture. The Maya developed special forms of social organization to constrain the striving of individuals within the limits of local resources. Ritual symbolism reinforced the social organization while emphasizing systemic properties of the local ecology.

Maya ritual and folklore have encoded and preserved ancient understandings of the local ecology and climate. Seasons, temperatures, rainfall patterns, soils, subsoils, and topography vary widely within the Maya area—as does the symbolism associated with them. The Earth Lord is a more important deity in the earthquake-prone highlands of Guatemala than in the tectonically stable Yucatán Peninsula, where a long dry season and recurrent hurricanes give more salience to the Rain Lords (*Chaaques*) and the Wind Lords (*Dueños de los Vientos*), who bring the "Holy Rain." Transformations of Maya technologies through history have been guided by principles rooted in Maya cosmology. This process is similar to the grounding of Maya political movements in the traditional cosmology, which has been documented by Victoria Bricker (1981), Gary Gossen (l986a:5–7; 1986b, 1994), and Duncan Earle (1986). Gossen has found key themes that form a template that has been repeatedly used throughout Mesoamerica to generate new political organization and action, in response to the necessities of new situations (Gossen 1986a:5–7; 1994). The key themes include the concept of time-and-space as integrated dimensions and a mapping of the cosmos according to gender (Figure 5.3). I have found local variations of these as well as a correspondence among the human life cycle, the seasons of the year, the cycle of plant growth, and the daily and yearly cycles of the sun including the solstices and equinoxes (see Figure 6.1 as well as Figures 5.2 and 5.5).

MALE AND FEMALE SYMBOLISM

In Pich, women are strongly associated with blood, through their menses. This association is noticeable in talk among women, especially in phrases that refer to their blood "coming down." The concept may be indicated by a downward hand motion. An adolescent woman who is about to have her first period is said to be in a delicate condition because her blood is "about to come down." The condition of a woman's blood during menstruation is considered a sign of her internal health (see Faust 1988a:392–96 and forthcoming).

During pregnancy the baby is said to be formed in part by the woman's blood. This fact is simply "obvious" since the blood no longer "comes down." After birth the mother breastfeeds her baby, but the milk of a woman is said to be "blood." *(Puro sangre de la mama chupaba. Leche de la Cristiana es sangre.)* This analogy may reflect the observed connection between lactation and delay in the return of menstruation, the blood being conceived of as having been converted to mother's milk.

The man's semen contains seed, but it also "nourishes the growing child in the womb as we are nourished by *atole*," a corn gruel. Within six months after birth the child is offered sips of white *atole* made from the corn grown by Father, but prepared and served by Mother. "Parents customarily help the child with pure *atole*—with sugar or plain—the food of the Christian." *(Le ayudan a puro atole—con azucar o simple—el alimento del cristiana.)* It is for these reasons that, "No matter how much my in-laws do for me, I will never owe them more than I owe my parents, who have given me life itself. For this I will always be in their debt."

Ties of kinship are through both blood and food. Especially strong ties are expressed not only to biological parents but also to older siblings who fed younger ones when parents were ill, had to work, or had died. Adults also express great gratitude and respect for adoptive parents, for those who fed them regularly as children.

By analogy the Lords of the Winds, the Virgin, and the more distant One True God (along with Jesus Christ, the Christ Child, and the saints) all created human beings and continue to sustain us by providing us with the raw materials we need: water and rain, sun, seeds, animals, stones, trees, health. In turn, we must work to plant, weed, harvest, hunt, build houses, weave, cook food, cure the sick, and obey the moral rules. But we also owe the sacred beings life itself and are obligated to show our gratitude and respect by giving them what they need, the *gracia* (both thanks and grace) of flowers, prayers, incense, candles, foods, beverages, and blood sacrificed in ritual—giving symbolically if not in

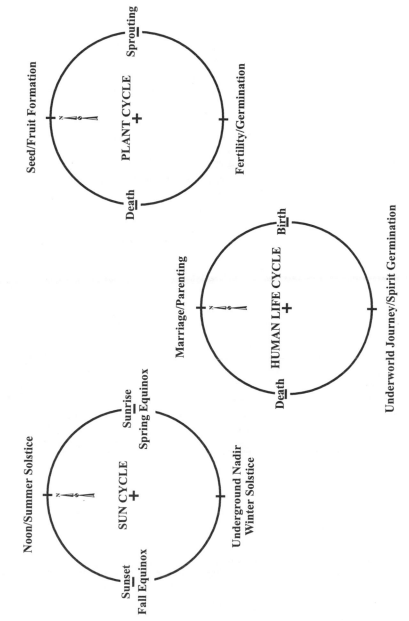

Figure 6.1
Life Cycles in Campeche Maya Cosmology

fact. These gifts are parallel to the respect and support owed by all adults to those elders who "gave them life," both by feeding them when they were children and by bringing them into existence.

Many ignore their obligations to the sacred beings, as many ignore obligations to their kin. However, when illness, drought, or bad luck strike, when anxiety is overwhelming and all the modern techniques available are of no avail, then the doubters return to the *h-men*, to the Lords of the Winds, to the Virgin, to their grandparents, and to the graves of their ancestors.

SYMBOLS, TECHNOLOGY, AND THE FAMILY

On a daily basis, the old sun dies and travels through the underworld to be reborn as the infant sun. The moon is born and dies as well and also has her monthly cycles. During lunar eclipses her blood is visible; she turns red. Curing rituals and rain calling are both timed to the position of the sun, with noon and midnight, sunrise and sunset, as critical points. The measuring, marking, and sowing of fields are begun at dawn and oriented to the path of the sun. Planting was traditionally done in association with phases of the moon as well, although few people continue to do this. The rain-calling ceremony I observed was performed at the first full moon after the summer solstice. The initial offering of *sak-ha'* to the Lords and the "curing" ceremony with the blood displayed to the sun were both done at noon. The ritual foods of the rain ceremony were presented to the Lords at night, near midnight.

The red and white ritual soups of the rain ceremony recall that pregnancy involves the formation of the child from the mother's blood and the father's semen and that even after birth the child is said to be fed by the mother's blood, which is transformed into her breastmilk, as well as being "helped" by the *atole* from the father's corn. The ritual rainbreads, including the one formed like a baby, are served inside the blood soup but on the side of the white soup—as children initially grow inside mothers and at the side of fathers. The blood soup is, however, made from the same turkey broth and white corn as the white soup, expressing the dualism of human origins. Mothers give birth but are able to do so and to live because they eat the foods produced by the earth, through the labor of men (growing crops) and women (cooking and caring for domestic animals as well as kitchen gardens). Children, though born and nursed by mothers' bodies, grow to adulthood only by the cultural work of men and women in growing, preparing, and serving food.

As women turn to Our Mother for aid in childbirth difficulties and in healing the sick, so men turn to the Lords of the Winds for help with the growing of crops. The Virgin Mother is associated with the moon, with ground water, childbirth, healing, and death. The Lords of the Winds bring the holy, fertilizing rain for the growing of crops. Our Father is associated with these lords, with the sun, and with the crucified Jesus, who died and rose from the dead to ascend into the sky, like the sun. The Virgin Mother is the mother of us all, the mother of Jesus Christ, perhaps the wife of God, perhaps his daughter—anyhow a part of God. They are all in God: the Lords of the Winds and the Virgins of Izamal, Ho'ol, Chi'uina', Pustunich, and so on, who stand for, or perhaps *are*, the younger sisters of Our Mother, represented by the moon (see Faust 1988a:181–197 and forthcoming).

Maya religious concepts are not clearly delineated. They are as multivalent and interpenetrating as the Trinity and the Eucharist. Their mysteries are understood in explicit detail more by the ritual specialist than by the laity, but, as in all religious practice, the experience of them is essentially ineffable.

For the Maya of Pich, traditional religious experience has been the *gracia* of a pattern of everyday life, a pattern created by the interdependencies of men and women with each other and with the plants, animals, climate, rock, and soil in a traditional agrarian ecology—one in which the structure of our relationships with one another and with the biosphere is simple enough to be grasped through religious symbolism (see Figure 6.1).

This symbolism validates the traditional sex roles of the family structure and the work roles involved in the survival technologies of water, food, and healing. It presents a model of the cosmos in which those technologies operated (and to some extent still operate) to sustain human life. It is given expression in the ritual practices still associated with calling rain, food production, and healing.

This symbolism has potential for being combined with modern scientific understandings of ecosystems, machinery, chemistry, biology, and so on. The combination could be helpful to the creation of authentic, rural development. Symbolic systems can combine with political organization to guide everyday behavior patterns in ways that will protect the resources of the planet from overuse and pollution, for the sake of future generations. Many other researchers have advocated combining indigenous knowledge and management procedures with scientific information to plan for conservation of resources as well as improvement in the health and economic security of rural communities (e.g. Rappaport 1984; Posey 1985; MacCay and Acheson 1987; Toledo 1987; Altieri 1987; Ostrom 1992; Pinkerton 1994; Chandler 1994; Anderson 1995 and 1996; and Frazier forthcoming). Other researchers have rejected representations of indigenous knowledge of the environment as based on claims of mystical omniscience, at one extreme, and at the other extreme there has been a rejection of such knowledge on the basis of archeological evidence of some environmental destruction caused by preindustrial societies. The authors listed here, however, have recognized that past errors do not invalidate knowledge gained through the experience of interacting with a local environment for many generations.

SACRED TECHNOLOGIES AND ENVIRONMENTAL ETHICS

Maya cosmology makes explicit the connections between the self and the universe. It does so by drawing attention to the intersection of age and sex in the cycles of life, connecting these to the seasons of the earth and the cycles of the sun and moon. Human sexual intercourse is thus interpreted as a symbol for the generation of the universe by male and female creative forces. The use of such symbolism in motivating individuals to protect their environment is aided by a social system of accountability that works in small, rather isolated communities that provide most of their own subsistence needs from local resources. The symbolism and values have survived technical and social changes, but have not been sufficiently strong to protect villagers from the temptations and pressures of a rapidly increasing integration into the world economy.

Maya symbols help individuals understand their connections with one another and the environment. The economic and social pressures of modern life are breaking down the protective barriers of this integrated conceptual system even as the Maya's tropical forest home is being bulldozed by national, rural development projects. Although fragile in the face of modern technology, the ancient concepts of the Maya can yet provide us with a model for understanding human life beyond the dichotomies of (1) individual competition versus obedience to the state and (2) economic growth versus hands-off conservation. The technologies and cosmology which the Maya evolved over many centuries in a fragile ecosystem may provide post-industrial civilization with some new ways of conceptualizing the "discordant harmonies" that humans compose interacting with nature (Botkin 1990).

A VILLAGE MODEL OF THE BIOSPHERE AND THE WORLD ECONOMY

The traditional system of Maya symbols has been analyzed in relation to Maya core values and the local ecosystem. The village's cosmology is a model of a reality that is being rapidly degraded today. The cosmology formed a template that guided decisions concerning resource use during times when such decisions were not as pressured by external factors. It not only contains knowledge of the surrounding ecosystem, weather patterns, and movements of the stars, but also facilitates adoption of innovations. It is a model for behavior in that it conceptualizes gender, social and biological reproduction, interdependency, responsibility, and accountability in relation to both the natural world and to social rules.

This Maya "model of reality and for behavior" (Geertz 1973) is not dichotomous. It focuses on connections, cycles, and interdependencies. Compared with European culture at the time of the Conquest, it lacked some kinds of precision in instrumentation and technologies for using non-human energy sources. Europeans had developed these and used them in a powerful military technology, which enabled them to impose their system and define Maya culture as inferior. Maya culture, however, is not intrinsically opposed to the adoption of new technological devices. It can be readily combined with them, as was documented for the highland Maya by Nash (1961). Introducing new technologies in a manner that allows flexible adaptation to the local agrarian ecology with its social and cosmological systems would seem to be advisable—before deforestation further affects local and global weather cycles. Maya agrarian ecosystems are not obstructions to change; rather they are an adaptation to a particular ecology and a set of cultural values. Among those values is an emphasis on imbrication, the combining of parts into systems, the bringing together of the present with the past and the human world with the biosystems that sustain it. Maya traditions can also, if given the opportunity, help create a form of rural development that includes resource management and the conservation of biodiversity

CULTURAL PLURALISM, ENVIRONMENTAL PROTECTION, AND PROGRESS?

Many Pichuleños have been struggling for decades to find a meaningful way of both living as a community and passing on environmental resources to the next generation, while also benefiting from exchanges with the larger national and international community. Between 1992 and 1996, Pichuleños were beginning to lose hope as their efforts resulted repeatedly in the exhaustion of resources. Some of the elders try to advise their own adult children to return to swidden agriculture as a way of life. They are struggling to maintain a sense of the cosmological meaning of human life while maintaining resources needed for future generations. They would like to be able to use new technologies to make life somewhat more secure from danger and somewhat more comfortable for themselves and their children, but so far they have not found a way to do this without overusing resources that will be needed by the grandchildren.

Some of the village elders are worried about preserving their reservoir, their wells, their multicropped fields, and some of their healing practices—not out of fear or superstition but out of knowledge of the local situation. They wish to test the new carefully in their environment and adopt what appears to work, without damaging the resource base.

Government programs have provided incentives and incomplete information. This combination has made it difficult for the people of Pich to manage their resources. Their failures have come not from irrational thinking but from a lack of scientific information, instruments, and training in their use, which could have allowed them to assess the long-term consequences of certain types of resource use. Lack of training and information concerning the side effects and long-term impacts of new technologies have combined with social institutions that were not adequate to protect public goods from new incentives and tools for exploitation.

Pichuleños make the same types of mistakes we in the United States have made with DDT and amphetamines. These products accomplish their purposes in an impressive manner, and the long-term dangers are not at all obvious to the user. There are other areas where the detrimental consequences of new practices are readily observable, but the social structure is not organized in a manner that can easily stop them. This is true both of misuse of the new government water system and of the lumbering activities in the communally owned forest. The latter problem is similar to that faced early in this century in the United States with the threatened destruction of the redwood forests of the West Coast. The State of Oregon has had similar problems in the last decade in its struggles both to protect its few remaining ancient forests and to structure truly sustainable forestry practices. Loggers in both Campeche and Oregon blame the local environmental protection agency and refuse to believe that they will run out of logs. New technologies, new markets, and new opportunities require new forms of social control.

In 1985 Pichuleños tended to define the changes experienced by the village as "progress" and were committed to continuing the process. The community as a whole was actively engaged in trying to acquire more of the goods associated with the modern, industrial world. It also avidly consumed information regarding that world. Today, however, people are anxious, concerned, and frightened by the negative aspects that have accompanied the desirable ones. Increased drinking problems, family violence, village factions, and juvenile delinquency are among the bad effects. The last includes sniffing glue, stealing, breaking into empty homes, and attempted rape. The reduction of income from logging, the drought, and the failure of the mechanized cultivation of rice have combined to make people wonder if this is the time that the Plumed Serpent will come out of the sea to punish humans for not obeying the wisdom of the ancestors.

At times those persons most exposed to the city culture blame village "backwardness" and "ignorance" for all the social and economic problems. The more traditional blame the changes on the loss of morality and respect, both for the authority of elders and for the traditional religion. Some see the losses as part of a modernization process that replaces obedience to true values with the desire for ephemeral material things.

Don Jesús summarized the situation by telling me that his children will not listen to him anymore and that he is just waiting to die, there in front of his television set. He in fact did maintain handsome fields with a variety of fruit trees, flowers that he sold, manioc plants, and other useful perennials, in addition to planting his traditional cornfield. He has not outwardly "retired" from the life of a traditional Maya farmer. He is not burdened by rural poverty, having a refrigerator as well as a television. He owns private land and 400 heads of cattle, which his son helps him tend.

His grandfather made a living selling dyewood. His father sold tree sap for chewing gum. Don Jesús bought his first truck in 1939 ("an old, cheap one") and then in 1951 was able to buy a 1948 Ford truck. He took water by truck to sell to settlements that ran out during the dry season. In 1986 his son was using the truck, cutting wood and hauling water to the refugee camp and other villages. Despite this economic success, by 1986 his disappointment with modern life was deeper than that of most people with whom I talked. His children would not listen and he did not know what was going to happen to this world.

Don Tacho, equally disillusioned with modernity, has decided actively to reject it, for the most part, although he does own a truck and a black-and-white television (both of which have seen many years of service). This man refuses to allow his wife or daughter-in-law to purchase factory-made tortillas. The women in his family wear clean, beautifully embroidered *huipiles* (traditional dresses of white cloth with embroidered flowers around the neck and the hem). He has an abundance of domestic animals and large quantities of his own native corn stored in the traditional storehouses. His goal is to buy more of his own land, outside of the *ejido*.[1] He trusts no authority except the Lords of the Winds and their assistants (*aluxes*), the saints, and God. He distrusts priests and will not go to Mass. He does not drink because "that is how rich people exploit farmers."

He maintains an extended family household, with his wife, grown sons, a daughter-in-law, and grandchildren. He owns a small herd of cattle that are kept corralled near his home, where he can watch over them. His sons chafe under his restrictions, working for wages when they can find work, supplementing the family's cash income and providing themselves with spending money, but this man is not waiting to die. He has carefully constructed plans for the future. He keeps himself informed by means of radio, television, and newspapers. He is busy with strategies for defending himself and his family and building long-term economic security. He is attentive to the needs of his wife and daughter-in-law and sometimes helps them with household chores, as do many Maya husbands. He is clearly the authority figure in the household, but he also teaches everyone in the family the reasons for his decisions. Lessons include stories of horrible disasters that befell others who chose different ways to live. He has committed to memory an astonishing amount of oral history, including the stories of his parents and grandparents, who lived on a neighboring hacienda, "before the Mexican Revolution ended that slavery." He was once president of the village and knows something about Mexican law as it applies to the village. He also knows a great deal about the local plants and animals and the "strange things that happen."

Don Tacho's family is healthy, well fed, and secure, if sometimes annoyed at his restrictions on spending. The children generally eat wild and domestic fruit, rather than store-bought candy and soda. His grown sons do buy those things in the local stores when he is not there and sometimes drink a few beers. However, their father's logic is convincing as he points to examples of poverty throughout the village. The sons are also kept busy maintaining, improving, and expanding the joint family holdings when they do not work for wages. The irrefutable security of their father's resource base compared to the unpredictability of wage labor opportunities is constantly pointed out in the advice and stories of the old man:

Not a single village stores its own corn any more here in Campeche.[2] The government orders it all taken away. If you do try to keep your own corn, there are so many who don't have any they will steal it. Thieves and robbers.

God is punishing us for not storing our own corn. That is why there is scarcity now.

In order for the corn not to get old, it must be stored in its husks. That way it doesn't get old.

Because they don't want to dedicate themselves to growing corn, but rather to cutting wood, there is scarcity. God does not want the wood cut.

They get money and get drunk, and live poor. They live more poorly than those who cultivate corn. God pays you when you produce in your cornfield. He gives you food: corn, beans, squash, tomatoes, other foods. [The cornfield is multicropped, with a large variety of food plants.] You don't have to buy any.

Those truckers [owners of logging trucks] pay the workers and then sell them booze. Mexico is number one in sale of alcohol in the whole world.

Alcohol and tobacco. If I see that something is bad for me, I don't do it. I don't need a companion to tell me not to do it. One ought to think about his own welfare, in order to live in this world. Blame it on friends? If I see that my friend is offering me alcohol, he is not my friend. Chicken stew, if he is your friend.

The man who works for wages has nothing in his house. The wealthy take advantage of the poor that don't have their own food [from their own fields]. Even though they pay them cheap, they get it back selling them beer.

If God helps you grow corn, it's yours. There is nobody who can take it away from you. Anybody will give you land.

They are abandoning agriculture. They don't want to work their own fields. They are working like slaves. Before there was slavery. It's the same structure. The rich pay the poor whatever they feel like.

The crisis [national crisis of debt and low price for petroleum exports] did not come from the sky. Mexico itself is producing the crisis, through that alcohol. It is poisoning itself.

Because I am the father of that impertinent [youth]. . . . As the father, I asked, I said that he had to be put in jail. He was shooting bullets with his rifle in the village.

There are four centers of vice in this place. One cantina and three agencies [for selling beer]. They are arch millionaires, the owners. The owners are really employees of the real owners, those who make the liquor, there in Campeche. The government and the officials are all in agreement with them.

They ought to prohibit it. There is a scarcity of food. They ought not to be cutting. It is the fault of the lumbering.

It is necessary to sow crops. God donates the seeds, one has an obligation to plant them.

And the trees are gone. The good cedar, the mahogany, the *guayacán*, the *ha'bin*, the *chacte'*. Now there is not even *guano* to thatch houses or *chicle-zapote* [a tree that gives both gum for chewing and fruit to eat].

Among the problems of progress seen by Don Tacho and the two rich villagers are (1) that wealth differences are escalating; (2) people are becoming more impulsive and less responsible to one another; and (3) natural resources are being damaged. These are similar to the problems of fully industrialized countries.

Even when there is local knowledge of the increasing destruction of the tropical ecosystem, such destruction is not easily prevented within the patterns of village life that have resulted from a series of government agricultural policies and rural development programs (Hewitt de Alcántara 1981; Gates 1993). When programs are oriented toward short-term maximization of discrete factors, predictable but unintended consequences result in major costs. Long-term planning for modernization could begin with multisectoral analysis of the existing traditional technologies, as well as the local ecology, the social structure, and the belief system that have supported them.

The one-way communication flow predicated on stereotypes of peasants as ignorant and superstitious prevents decision makers from learning important information about the local system and the effects of their programs. In addition, incentives are structured and sanctions provided in such a way that any individual small farmer who desists from destructive practices will be at an economic and social disadvantage in the short term. This will decrease his status and hence his power to protect his interests in the normal conflicts of village life. Private ownership is a solution recommended by those who believe that the "tragedy of the commons" is a necessary result of collective ownership, but the recent changes being made in the Mexican *ejido* system may further undermine the ability of indigenous communities to manage the resources needed by future generations. The combination of collective ownership and individual accountability found in Maya traditional technologies is an alternative solution to the problem of the commons, one that could contribute substantially to the development of long-term agricultural policy and resource management appropriate for tropical forest environments.

The resource management problems of Pich are not a reflection of village backwardness or magical thinking but rather are a part of the problems of a world in transition. The problems Pichuleños have had with past "development" of their resources resemble global ones of industrialization of the biosphere. The village is a system, an open one, but a sufficiently small one that we can see quite clearly in it some of the interdependencies among social systems, cognitive (including symbolic) systems, and biological systems. Viewing these interdependencies from a Maya perspective can contribute to our understanding of systemic properties. The Western tendency to think dichotomously and hierarchically, competitively rather than cooperatively, impedes our awareness of systemic cycles, interdependencies, and interactions among the biological, the sociopolitical, and the symbolic. Our technical precision in analysis of linear sequences within demarcated disciplines and specialties makes it easy for us to lose sight of the relationship of human beings to one another and the natural universe, relationships symbolized in the Plumed Serpent, a representation of the universe as the matrix in which we live and out of which we are made, as we daily reconstitute our bodies with food and water taken from its recurring cycles. Maya villagers for centuries have reminded themselves of these realities through ritual symbolism.

NOTES

1. *Ejido* land cannot be "alienated"; it cannot be sold, willed, or used as security for loans). Neighboring land belongs to the national government and is available for private sale to individual farmers, who use it to produce crops. Improvements can be made on privately owned land with the knowledge that the land cannot be taken by the vagaries of local *ejido* politics. It can be securely kept against the claims of the relatively powerful *ejido* "*ricos*" It can also be willed to heirs, sold for profit, and used for collateral.

2. It is not literally true that no one stores any corn or beans. There are two relatively wealthy *patrones* who do own storehouses and store their crops for speculation, waiting to sell until prices are higher. They also store supplies for the year for their families and the families of their regular employees, who are *compadres*, fictive kin. This storage, however, is not widely known since the corn is stored inside empty houses within the land owned by the *patrón*. Traditionally, corn was stored by each family for its own future use. It was stored in the husk in racks in the houseyard or the cornfield, where it was easily seen. The practice of storing became much less common during the 1970s and 1980s; a government agency provided credits to farmers for agricultural tasks on the condition that the harvest be sold to the government, with the amount for credits and interest deducted. In the 1990s a number of alternative programs have been tried and some people are again beginning to store corn, although they complain that theft has recently become a serious problem. In addition, there are time and energy expenses of storing and losses from rodents, insects, rot, etc. Thus, many people say that storing crops is no longer "rentable"; it does not "pay."

References

Abrams, Eliot M. 1994. *How the Maya Built Their World: Energetics and Ancient Architecture*. Austin: University of Texas Press.

Acosta, Joseph de. (n.d. 1500s). *The Natural and Moral History of the Indies*. trans. Edward Grimston. New York: Burt Franklin. Quoted in Alfred W. Crosby, Jr., *The Columbian Exchange* (Westport, CT: Greenwood, 1972), 38.

Adams, Richard E. W. 1991. Nucleation of Population and Water Storage Among the Ancient Maya. *Science* 251:632.

Adams, Richard E. W., and Woodruff D. Smith. 1977. Apocalyptic Visions: The Maya Collapse and Mediaeval Europe. *Archaeology* 30:292–301.

Agrest, Diana, and Mario Gandelsonas. 1977. Semiotics and the Limits of Architecture. In *A Perfusion of Signs*, ed. T. A. Sebeok, pp. 90–120. Bloomington: Indiana University Press.

Allaway, W. H. 1975. *The Effect of Soils and Fertilizers on Human and Animal Nutrition*. Agriculture Information Bulletin No. 378. Washington, DC: United States Department of Agriculture with Cornell University Agricultural Experiment Station.

Altieri, M. A. 1987. *Agroecology: The Scientific Basis of Alternative Agriculture*. Boulder, CO: Westview.

Anderson, Eugene. 1995. The Kitchen Gardens of Chunhuhub. Ponencia en el Tercer Congreso de Mayistas, Chetumal, Quintana Roo, México.

———. 1996. *Ecologies of the Heart*. New York, NY: Oxford University Press.

Andrews, Anthony P. 1983. *Maya Salt Production and Trade*. Tucson: University of Arizona Press.

Andrews, Anthony, and C. Robles. 1985. Chichén Itzá and Cobá: An Itzá-Maya Standoff in Early Postclassic Yucatán. In *The Lowland Maya Postclassic.*, ed. D. Chase and P. M. Rice, pp. 62–72. Austin: University of Texas Press.

Andrews, George F. 1969. *Edzná, Campeche, Mexico: Settlement Patterns and Monumental Architecture*. Eugene: University of Oregon.

Antoine, Pierre P., Richard L. Skarie, and Paul R. Bloom. 1982. The Origin of Raised Fields near San Antonio, Belize: An Alternative Hypothesis. In *Maya Subsistence: Studies in Memory of Dennis Puleston*, ed. Kent V. Flannery, pp. 227–236. New York: Academic Press.

Antonio, Robert J. 1979. The Contradiction of Domination and Production in Bureaucracy: The Contribution of Organizational Efficiency to the Decline of the Roman Empire. *American Sociological Review* 44:895–912.

Aranda González, Mario H. 1985. *Apuntaciones históricas y literarias del Municipio de Hopelchén, Campeche*. Campeche, México: Colección Ah Kin Pech (Programa Cultural de las Fronteras).

Aveni, Anthony. 1980. *Skywatchers of Ancient Mexico*. Austin: University of Texas Press.

———. 1992. *The Sky in Maya Literature*. New York: Oxford University Press.

Aveni, Anthony, and H. Hartung. 1981. The Observation of the Sun at the Time of Passage Through the Zenith in Mesoamerica. *Archeoastronomy* (Supp. to *J. History of Astronomy*) 3:551–570.

Ball, Joseph W. 1977. *The Archeological Ceramics of Becan, Campeche*. Middle American Research Institute, Publication 43. New Orleans: Tulane University Press.

———. 1979. Ceramics, Culture, History, and the Puuc Tradition: Some Alternative Perspectives. In *The Puuc: New Perspectives,* ed. L. Milles, pp. 18–35. Scholarly Studies in the Liberal Arts, No. 1. Pella, IA: Central College Press.

———. 1985. A Summary View. In *Arquitectura y arqueología: metodologías en la cronología de Yucatán*, Études Mesoamericaines Series II, vol. 8, pp. 85–88. México DF: Centre d'Études Mexicaines et Centramericaines.

Barrera Rubio, Alfredo. 1987. Obras hidráulicas en la región Puuc, Yucatán. Mérida, México: *Boletín de la Escuela de Ciencias Antropológicas de la Universidad de Yucatán* 87:3–19.

Barrera Vázquez, Alfredo, Director. [1980] 1991. *Diccionario Maya: Maya-Español, Español-Maya*. México, DF: Editorial Porrúa.

Bates, Daniel G., and Fred Plog. 1991. *Human Adaptive Strategies*. New York: McGraw Hill.

Batllori, E. 1996. Tablas de Contaminación de Agua en la Península de Yucatán. Working Paper, Proyecto Población y Desarrollo Sustentable en Yucatán, CINVESTAV, CONAPO and IIASA.

Bennett, John W. 1990. Ecosystems, Environmentalism, Resource Conservation, and Anthropological Research. In *The Ecosystem Approach in Anthropology: From Concept to Practice*, ed. Emilio F. Moran, pp. 435–457. Ann Arbor: University of Michigan Press.

Berdan, Frances F. 1982. *The Aztecs of Central Mexico*. New York: Holt, Rinehart and Winston.

Bianchine, Peter J., and Thomas A. Russo. 1995. The Role of Epidemic Infectious Diseases in the Discovery of America. In *Columbus and the New World: Medical Implications*, ed. Guy A. Settipane, pp. 11–18. Providence: OceanSide Publications.

Bodley, John H. 1994. *Cultural Anthropology: Tribes, States and the Global System.* Mountain View, CA: Mayfield Publishing Company.

Bonor Villarejo, Juan Luis. 1987. Aproximación al estudio de las fuentes de agua en la antigua ciudad maya de Oxkintok. *Boletín de la Escuela de Ciencias Antropológicas de la Universidad Autónoma de Yucatán* 87:3–19.

Boserup, Ester. 1965. *The Conditions of Agricultural Growth.* Chicago: Aldine Publishing Co.

Botkin, Daniel B. 1990. *Discordant Harmonies: A New Ecology for the 21st Century.* Oxford: Oxford University Press.

Boughey, Arthur S. 1968. *Ecology of Populations.* New York: Macmillan.

Bower, Bruce. 1991. Water Storage Spurred Growth of Maya Cities. *Science News* 139:85.

Brannon, Jeffrey T. and Gilbert M. Joseph. 1991. *Land, Labor and Capital in Modern Yucatán: Essays in Regional History and Political Economy.* Mobile: University of Alabama Press.

Brendt, Hartmut. 1979. *Peasant Work Capacity and Agricultural Development.* Occasional Papers. Berlin: German Development Institute.

Bricker, Victoria. 1981. *The Indian Christ, the Indian King: The Historical Substrate of Maya Myth and Ritual.* Austin: University of Texas Press.

Carlson, John B. 1981. A Geomantic Model for the Interpretation of Mesoamerican Sites: An Essay in Cross-Cultural Comparison. In *Mesoamerican Sites and World-Views*, ed. Elizabeth P. Benson, pp. 143–211. Washington, DC: Dumbarton Oaks, Trustees for Harvard University.

Catton, William R., Jr. 1982. *Overshoot: The Ecological Basis of Revolutionary Change.* Urbana: University of Illinois Press.

Censo de Pich. 1981. Censo socio-económico del Municipio de Campeche, Gobierno de Campeche.

Chandler, Paul. 1994. Adaptive Ecology of Traditionally Derived Agroforestry in China. *Human Ecology* 22(4):415–442.

Chase, A. F., and D. Z. Chase. 1985. Postclassic Temporal and Spatial Frames for the Lowland Maya: A Background. In *The Lowland Maya Postclassic*, ed. A. F. Chase and P. M. Rice, pp. 9–22. Austin: University of Texas Press.

Chase, A. F., and P. M. Rice, eds. 1985. *The Lowland Maya Postclassic.* Austin: University of Texas Press.

Clark, C., and M. Haswell. 1964. *The Economics of Subsistence.* London: Macmillan.

Clendinnen, Inga. 1987. *Ambivalent Conquests: Maya and Spaniard in Yucatan, 1517–1570.* Cambridge: Cambridge University Press.

Coe, Michael D. 1973. *The Maya Scribe and His World.* New York: The Grolier Club.

———. 1989. The Hero Twins: Myth and Image. In *The Vase Book: A Corpus of Rollout Photographs of Maya Vases*, vol. 1, ed. Justin Kerr, pp. 161–184. New York: Kerr and Associates.

Contreras Sánchez, Alicia del C. 1990. *Historia de una tintorea olvidada: el proceso de explotación y circulación del palo de tinte (1750–1807).* Mérida, Mexico: Universidad Autónoma de Yucatán.

Crosby, Alfred W., Jr. 1972. *The Columbian Exchange: Biological and Cultural Consequences of 1492*. Westport, CT: Greenwood Press.

———. 1986. *Ecological Imperialism*. Cambridge: Cambridge University Press.

Culbert, T. Patrick. 1977. Maya Development and Collapse: An Economic Perspective. In *Social Process in Maya Prehistory: Studies in Honor of Sir Eric Thompson*, ed. N. Hammond. London: Academic Press.

———. 1996. Agricultura Maya en los Humedales de las Tierras Bajas Mayas. Primera Conferencia Magistral. VI Encuentro de Los Investigadores de la Cultura Maya. Campeche, México: Universidad Autónoma de Campeche.

Culbert, T. P., and D. S. Rice. 1990. *Precolumbian Population History in the Maya Lowlands*. Albuquerque: University of New Mexico Press.

Deevey, E. S., D. S. Rice, P. M. Rice, H. Vaughan, M. Brenner, and M. S. Flannery. 1979. Mayan Urbanism: Impact on a Tropical Karst Environment. *Science* 206(4416):298–306.

Denevan, William M. 1982. Hydraulic Agriculture in the American Tropics: Forms, Measures, and Recent Research. In *Maya Subsistence: Studies in Memory of Dennis E. Puleston*, ed. Kent V. Flannery, pp. 181–203. New York: Academic Press.

Díaz del Castillo, Bernal. [n.d., orig. 1500s] Account of Díaz del Castillo, archival document, reproduced in *Historia Verdadera de la Conquista de la Nueva España*. México, D. F., vol. 1, chapters II–VI, 1904. Translated in Henry R. Wagner, *The Discovery of Yucatán by Francisco Hernández de Córdoba* (Whittier, CA: The Cortez Society, 1942), p. 63.

Domínguez Carrasco, María del Rosario. 1993. Calakmul, Campeche y su sistema hidráulico. *Los Investigadores de la Cultura Maya* (Campeche, México: Universidad Autónoma de Campeche) 1:42–46.

Domínguez Carrasco, María del Rosario y William J. Folan. 1995. Calakmul, México: aguadas, bajos, precipitación y asentamiento en el Petén Campechano. Paper presented in the IX Simposio de Investigaciones Arqueológicas en Guatemala.

Donkin, R. A. 1979. *Agricultural Terracing in the Aboriginal New World*. Tucson: University of Arizona Press.

Drennan, Robert D. 1988. Household Location and Compact versus Dispersed Settlement in Prehispanic Mesoamerica. In *Household and Community in the Mesoamerican Past*, ed. by Richard R. Wilk and Wendy Ashmore. Albuquerque: University of New Mexico Press.

Dumond, Carol Steichen, and Don E. Dumond, eds. 1982. *Demography and Parish Affairs in Yucatan 1797–1897: Documents from the Archivo de la Mitra Emeritense*, selected by Joaquín de Arrigunaga Peón, University of Oregon Anthropological Papers, No. 27. Eugene: Universitiy of Oregon.

Dumond, Don E. 1977. Independent Maya of the Late Nineteenth Century: Chiefdoms and Power Politics. In *Anthropology and History in Yucatán*, ed. Grant D. Jones, pp. 103–138. Austin: University of Texas Press.

———. 1986. The Metaphor of the Day in Quiché: Notes on the Nature of Everyday Life. In *Symbol and Meaning Beyond the Closed Community: Essays in*

Mesoamerican Ideas, ed. Gary H. Gossen, pp. 227–267. Albany: State University of New York Press (Institute for Mesoamerican Studies).

Ehrlich, Paul R., and Anne H. Ehrlich. 1996. *Betrayal of Science and Reason: How Anti-Environmental Rhetoric Threatens Our Future.* Washington, DC: Island Press.

Elmendorf, Mary. 1976. *Nine Mayan Women: A Village Faces Change.* New York: Schenkman Publishing.

Ewell, P. T., and D. Merrill-Sands. 1987. Milpa in Yucatan: A Long-fallow Maize System and Its Alternatives in the Maya Peasant Economy. In *Comparative Farming Systems,* ed. B. L. Turner II and S. B. Brush, pp. 95–129. New York: Guilford Press.

Farriss, Nancy M. 1984. *Maya Society Under Colonial Rule: The Collective Enterprise of Survival.* Princeton: Princeton University Press.

Faust, Betty B. 1988a. Cosmology and Changing Technologies of the Campeche-Maya. Ph.D. dissertation, Syracuse University (listed in Dissertation Abstracts 1989, copyrighted 1988).

―――. 1988b. When Is a Midwife a Witch? A Case Study from a Modernizing Maya Village. In *Women and Health: Cross-Cultural Perspectives,* ed. Patricia Whelehan. Granby, MA: Bergin and Garvey Publishers, Inc.

―――. Forthcoming. Cacao Beans and Chile Peppers in a Yucatec Maya *K'ex*: Curing a Pubescent Girl. Special Edition of *Sex Roles,* ed. Ellen Kintz.

Faust, Betty B., and Abel Morales López. 1993. La aguada en la historia oral de Pich, Campeche: Adaptaciones a variaciones de clima en un pueblo maya. Paper presented in Session 341, 13th International Congress of Anthropological and Ethnological Sciences in Mexico City.

Faust, Betty B., and John Sinton. 1991. Let's Dynamite the Salt Factory! In *Ecotourism and Resource Conservation,* Selected papers from the 1st and 2nd International Symposium on Ecotourism, vol. 2, ed. by Jon A. Kusler, pp. 602–623. Berne, NY: Association of Wetlands Managers.

Faust, P. 1993. Personal communication.

Fedick, Scott. 1995a. Ancient Maya Use of Wetlands in Northern Quintana Roo, Mexico. Paper presented at the conference Hidden Dimensions: The Cultural Significance of Wetland Archaeology, University of British Columbia, Vancouver.

―――. 1995b. Observations on Archaeological Features Within a Wetland of the El Eden Ecological Reserve, Northern Quintana Roo, Mexico. Report submitted to the Instituto Nacional de Antropología e Historia, Mexico, D. F.

Fernández Repetto, Francisco, and Genny Negroe Sierra. 1995. *Una Población perdida en la memoria: Los Negros de Yucatán.* Mérida, México: Universidad Autónoma de Yucatán.

Flannery, Kent V. 1976. *The Early Mesoamerican Village.* New York: Academic Press.

―――. 1982. *Maya Subsistence: Studies in Memory of Dennis Puleston,* ed. Kent V. Flannery. New York: Academic Press.

Flannery, Kent V., Michael Kirkby, and A. W. Williams, Jr. 1967. Farming Systems and Political Growth in Ancient Oaxaca. *Science* 158(3800):445–54.

Folan, William J. 1970. *The Open Chapel of Dzibilchaltún, Yucatán*. Middle American Research Institute, Publication 26. New Orleans: Tulane University Press.

Folan, William J., L. Fletcher, and E. Kintz. 1979. Fruit, Fiber, Bark, and Resin: Social Organization of a Maya Urban Center. *Science* 204(4394):697–701.

Folan, William J., J. Gunn, D. Eaton, and R. W. Patch. 1983. Paleoclimatological Patterning in Southern Mesoamerica. *Journal of Field Archaeology* 10:453–468.

Folan, William J., and Burma H. Hyde. 1985. Climatic Forecasting and Recording Among the Ancient and Historic Maya: An Ethnohistoric Approach to Epistemological and Paleoclimatological Patterning. In *Contributions to the Archaeology and Ethnohistory of Greater Mesoamerica*, ed. William J. Folan, pp. 15–48. Carbondale: Southern Illinois University Press.

Folan, William J., J. Kathryn Josserand, and Nicolas A. Hopkins. 1983. Una nota sobre paleoclimatología, prehistoria y diversificación lingüística de los mayas a través de los tiempos. *Información* (Campeche, México: Universidad Autónoma de Campeche) 7: 3–18.

Folan, William J., Ellen R. Kintz, and Laraine A. Fletcher. 1983. *Cobá: A Classic Maya Metropolis*. New York: Academic Press.

Folan, William J., Joyce Marcus, Sophia Pincermin, María del Rosario Domínguez Carrasco, Laraine Fletcher, and Abel Morales López. 1996. Calakmul: New Data from an Ancient Maya Capital in Campeche, Mexico. *Latin American Antiquity* 6(4):310–334.

Frazier, John G. [forthcoming, 1997]. Sustainable Development: Modern Elixir or Sack Dress? *Environmental Conservation* 24(2): [pagination in press].

Freidel, David A. 1985. New Light in the Dark Ages: A Summary of Major Themes. In *The Lowland Maya Postclassic*, ed. A. F. Chase and P. M. Rice, 285–309. Austin: University of Texas Press.

Freidel, David A., and Vernon Scarborough. 1982. Subsistence, Trade and Development of the Coastal Maya. In *Maya Subsistence: Studies in Memory of Dennis E. Puleston*, ed. K. Flannery, pp. 131–155. New York: Academic Press.

Freidel, David A., Linda Schele, and Joy Parker. 1993. *Maya Cosmos: Three Thousand Years on the Shaman's Path*. New York: William Morrow.

Friedlander, Judith. 1975. *On Being Indian in Hueyapán: A Study of Forced Identity in Contemporary Mexico*. New York: St. Martins Press.

Garrett, Wilbur E. 1989. La Ruta Maya. *National Geographic*, 176(4):424–479.

Gates, Gary. 1985–1986. Personal communications. Geologist, Simon Fraser University, Vancouver, British Columbia.

Gates, Gary, and William J. Folan. 1993. The Hydrogeologic Setting of the Aguadas in the Calakmul Biosphere, Campeche, Mexico. Paper presented in Session 341, 13th International Congress of Anthropological and Ethnological Sciences in Mexico City.

Gates, Marilyn. 1993. In *Default: Peasants, the Debt Crisis, and the Agricultural Challenge in Mexico*. Boulder, CO: Westview Press.

Geertz, Clifford. 1973. *The Interpretation of Cultures*. New York: Basic Books.

Gibbons, Whit. 1993. *Keeping All the Pieces: Perspectives on Natural History and the*

Environment. Washington, DC: Smithsonian Institution Press.

Gluckman, Max. 1965. *The Ideas in Barotse Jurisprudence.* New Haven: Yale University Press.

Gómara, López de. [n.d., orig. 1500s]. Account of López de Gómara, archival document published in *Historia de las Indias*, edition of Vedia of 1852. Translated in Henry R. Wagner, *The Discovery of Yucatán by Francisco Hernández de Córdoba* (Whittier, CA: The Cortez Society, 1942), p. 185.

Gómez de Silva Cano, Jorge Joaquín. 1981. Sociocultural Factors Impacting Community Development in the Maya Region of Campeche, Mexico. Ph.D. dissertation, United States International University.

Gómez-Pompa, Arturo. 1987. On Maya Silviculture. *Mexican Studies/Estudios Mexicanos* 3(1):1–17.

Gómez-Pompa, Arturo, Salvador Flores, and V. Sosa. 1987. The "Pet Kot": A Man-made Tropical Forest of the Maya. *Interciencia* 12(1):10–15.

Gómez-Pompa, Arturo, Andrea Kaus, Juan Jiménez-Osornio, David Bainbridge, and Veronique M. Rorive. 1993. Mexico. In *Sustainable Agriculture and the Environment in the Humid Tropics*, ed. National Research Council, pp. 483–554. Washington, DC: National Academy Press.

Gómez-Pompa, Arturo, Héctor Luis Morales, Epifanio Jiménez Ávila, and Julio Jiménez Ávila. 1982. Experiences in Traditional Hydraulic Agriculture. In *Maya Subsistence: Studies in Memory of Dennis E. Puleston*, ed. Kent V. Flannery, pp. 327–344. New York: Academic Press.

Goméz-Pompa, Arturo, C. Vazquez-Yanex, and S. Guevara. 1972. The Tropical Rain Forest: A Non-Renewable Resource. *Science* 177:762–765.

Gossen, Gary. [1974] 1984. *Chamulas in the World of the Sun: Time and Space in a Maya Oral Tradition.* Prospect Heights, IL: Waveland Press. (Original edition: Cambridge, MA: Harvard University Press.)

———. 1986a. The Chamula Festival of Games: Native Macroanalysis and Social Commentary in a Maya Carnival. In *Symbol and Meaning Beyond the Closed Community: Essays in Mesoamerican Ideas*, ed. Gary Gossen, pp. 227–267. Albany: State University of New York Press (Institute for Mesoamerican Studies).

———. 1986b. From Ethnography of Tzotzil Communication to Historical and Political Action. Paper presented in the 85th Annual Meeting of the American Anthropological Association, Philadelphia, PA.

———. 1994. From Olmecs to Zapatistas: A Once and Future History of Souls. *American Anthropologist* 6(3):553–570.

Green, Donald H. 1984. Metaphor as Process. Ph.D. dissertation, University of Texas at Austin.

Groombridge, Brian. 1992. *Global Biodiversity: Status of the Earth's Living Resources.* A Report Compiled by the World Conservation Monitoring Centre. London: Chapman and Hall.

Gunn, Joel D. 1994a. Global Climate and Regional Biocultural Diversity. In *Historical Ecology: Cultural Knowledge and Changing Landscapes*, ed. Carole L. Crumley, pp. 67–97. Santa Fe, New Mexico: School of American Research Press.

————. 1994b. Introduction: A Perspective from the Humanities-Science Boundary. *Human Ecology* 22(1):1–22.

Gunn, Joel D., and William J. Folan. 1996. Tres ríos: Una superficie de impacto climatológico global interregional para las tierras bajas de los mayas del suroeste. *Los Investigadores de la Cultura Maya* (Campeche, México: Universidad Autónoma de Campeche) 4:57–79.

Gunn, Joel D., William J. Folan, and Hubert R. Robichaux. 1994. Un análisis informativo sobre la descarga del sistema del Río Candelaria en Campeche, México: Reflexiones acerca de los paleoclimas que afectaron a los antiguos sistemas mayas en los sitios de Calakmul y El Mirador. In *Campeche Maya Colonial*, ed. William Folan Higgins, pp. 174–197. Campeche, México: Universidad Autónoma de Campeche.

Hall, Edward T. 1966. *The Hidden Dimension*. Garden City, NY: Doubleday.

Hammond, Norman. 1982. *Ancient Maya Civilization*. New Brunswick, NJ: Rutgers University Press.

Hanks, William F. 1990. *Referential Practice, Language, and Lived Space Among the Maya*. Chicago: University of Chicago Press.

Harrison, Peter D. 1977. The Rise of the Bajos and the Fall of the Maya. In *Social Process in Maya Prehistory: Studies in Memory of Sir Eric Thompson*, ed. Norman Hammond, pp. 469–508. London: Academic Press.

————. 1978. Bajos Revisited: Visual Evidence for One System of Agriculture. In *Pre-Hispanic Maya Agriculture, ed.* Peter D. Harrison and B. L. Turner II, pp. 247–254. Albuquerque: University of New Mexico Press.

Haviland, William A. 1969. A New Population Estimate for Tikal, Guatemala. *American Antiquity* 34:429–433.

Hellmuth, Nicholas. 1977. Cholti-Lacandon (Chiapas) and Peten Ytza Agriculture, Settlement Pattern and Population. In *Social Process in Maya Prehistory*, ed. Norman Hammond, pp. 421–428. New York: Academic Press.

Hernández Xolocotzi, Efraim, Eduardo Bello Baltazar, and Samuel Levy Tacher, Compilers. 1995. *La Milpa en Yucatán: Un Sistema de Producción Agrícola Tradicional*, Vols. 1 and 2. México, DF: Colegio de Postgraduados.

Hewitt de Alcantara, Cynthia. 1981. *Anthropological Perspectives on Rural Mexico*. London: Routledge and Kegan Hall.

Heyden, Doris. 1981. Caves, Gods, and Myths: World-View and Planning in Teotihuacan. In *Mesoamerican Sites and World-Views*, ed. Elizabeth P. Benson, pp. 1–40. Washington, DC: Dumbarton Oaks.

Heywood, V. H., ed. 1995. *Global Diversity Assessment*. Published for the United Nations Environment Programme. Cambridge: Cambridge University Press.

Hironymous, Michael. 1989. Personal conversation, reference to observations during linguistic fieldwork with the University of Chicago in 1974.

Hodell, David A., Jason H. Curtis, and Mark Brenner. 1995. Possible Role of Climate in the Collapse of Classic Maya Civilization. *Nature* 375(1):391–394.

Hunt, Eva. 1977. *The Transformation of the Hummingbird: Cultural Roots of a Zinacantecan Mythical Poem*. Ithaca, NY: Cornell University Press.

Huntington, Ellsworth. 1912. *Civilization and Climate.* New Haven: Yale University Press.

Jones, Ellen, and Glen Wersch. 1989. Developing a Natural Balance, *Americas* 42(2): 27–35.

Jones, Grant D. 1977. *Anthropology and History in Yucatan.* Austin: University of Texas Press.

———. 1982. Agriculture and Trade in the Colonial Period Southern Maya Lowlands. In *Maya Subsistence: Studies in Memory of Dennis E. Puleston*, ed. Kent V. Flannery, pp. 275–293. New York: Academic Press.

Joseph, Gilbert Michael. 1986. *Rediscovering the Past at Mexico's Periphery: Essays on the Modern Yucatán.* University, AL: University of Alabama Press.

Kintz, Ellen R. 1990. *Life Under the Tropical Canopy.* New York: Holt, Rinehart and Winston.

Kintz, Ellen R., and Laraine A. Fletcher. 1983. A Reconstruction of the Prehistoric Population at Cobá. In *Cobá: A Classic Maya Metropolis*, by William J. Folan, Ellen R. Kintz, and Laraine A. Fletcher, pp. 191–210. New York: Academic Press.

Lambert, J. D. H., A. H. Siemens, and J. T. Aranson. 1984. Ancient Maya Drained Field Agriculture: Its Possible Application Today in the New River Floodplain, Belize, C.A. *Agriculture, Ecosystems, and Environment* 11:67–84.

Landa, Diego de. [1566] 1978. *Yucatán Before and After the Conquest* (unabridged republication of 1937 translation with notes by William Gates). (Original title: Relación de las cosas de Yucatán). NY: Dover.

Ledec, George, and Robert Goodland. 1988. *Wildlands: Their Protection and Management in Economic Development.* Washington, DC: The World Bank.

Lees, Susan H., and Daniel G. Bates. 1990. *The Ecosystem Approach in Anthropology.* Ann Arbor: University of Michigan Press.

Leibig, Justus von. 1863. *The Natural Laws of Husbandry.* New York: D. Appleton. As referenced in Arthur S. Boughey, *Ecology of Populations* (New York: MacMillan, 1968).

León-Portilla, Miguel. 1988. *Time and Reality in the Thought of the Maya*, 2nd English edition. Norman: University of Oklahoma Press.

Levi-Strauss, Claude [1962] 1966. *The Savage Mind.* (Original title: *La Pensée Savage*). Chicago: University of Chicago Press.

Love, Bruce. 1986. Yucatec Maya Ritual: A Diachronic Perspective. Los Angeles: Ph.D. dissertation, University of California at Los Angeles.

———. 1994. *The Paris Codex: Handbook for a Maya Priest.* Austin, TX: University of Texas Press.

Lowe, John W. G. 1985. *The Dynamics of Apocalypse: A Systems Simulation of the Classic Maya Collapse.* Albuquerque: University of New Mexico Press.

MacArthur, Robert, and Joseph Connell. 1966. *Biology of Populations.* New York: John Wiley and Sons.

MacCay, Bonnie, and James M. Acheson. 1987. *The Question of the Commons: The Culture and Ecology of Communal Resources.* Tucson: University of Arizona Press.

MacNeish, Richard S. 1972. *Prehistory of the Tehuacan Valley*, vol. 4, *Chronology and Irrigation*. Austin: University of Texas Press.

Manz, Beatriz. 1988. *Refugees of a Hidden War: The Aftermath of Counterinsurgency in Guatemala*. Albany: State University of New York Press.

Martínez, Dennis. 1995. Personal communication concerning the death of elders in indigenous communities throughout the world. Annual Meeting, September 1995, Society for Ecological Restoration, Seattle, WA.

Martyr, Pindigeter. n.d. (orig. 1500s). Account of Peter Martyr, archival document, reproduced in Francis Augustus MacNutt´s translation of *De Orbe Novo, Decade IV, Books 1-2*. Quoted in Henry R. Wagner *The Discovery of Yucatán by Francisco Hernández de Córdoba* (Whittier, CA: The Cortez Society, 1942), pp. 6–11.

Matheny, Ray T. 1978. Northern Maya Lowland Water-Control Systems. In *Pre-Hispanic Maya Agriculture*, ed. Peter D. Harrison and B. L. Turner II. Albuquerque: University of New Mexico Press.

Matheny, Ray T., and Deanne L. Gurr. 1979. Ancient Hydraulic Techniques in the Chiapas Highlands. *American Scientist* 67 (4):441–449.

Matheny, Ray T., Deanne L. Gurr, Donald W. Forsyth, and F. Richard Hauck. 1983. *Investigations at Edzná, Campeche, Mexico: The Hydraulic System*. Papers of the New World Archaeological Foundation, No. 46. Provo, UT: Brigham Young University Press.

McAnany, Patricia A. 1990. Water Storage in the Puuc Region of the Northern Maya Lowlands: A Key to Population Estimates and Architectural Variability. In *Precolumbian Population History in the Maya Lowlands*, ed. T. P. Culbert and D. S. Rice, pp. 263–284. Albuquerque: University of New Mexico Press.

Meggers, Betty. 1996. Amazonia on the Eve of European Contact: Ethnohistorical, Ecological and Anthropological Perspectives. *Revista de Arqueología Americana (Journal of American Archaeology)* 8:91–115.

Miller, Mary, and Karl Taube. 1993. *The Gods and Symbols of Ancient Mexico and the Maya: An Illustrated Dictionary of Mesoamerican Religion*. New York: Thames and Hudson.

Morales López, Abel. 1985. Kitam, Campeche: Un complejo cívico-religioso en la región del Río Bec. *Información* (Campeche, México: Universidad del Sureste) 10: 30–41.

———. 1986. Personal communication. Archaeologist, Centro de Estudios Históricos y Sociales, Universidad del Sureste, Campeche, México.

———. 1989. Arqueología de salvamento en la nueva carretera a Calakmul, Municipio de Champotón, Campeche. *Información* (Campeche, México: Universidad del Sureste) 12:75–110.

Morales López, Abel, and Betty B. Sumner-Faust (Faust). 1986. Tabasqueño: Indicios de la cosmología maya en un sitio de los Chenes, Campeche, México. *Información* (Campeche, México: Universidad del Sureste) 11:9–78.

Morley, Sylvanus G. 1927. New Light on the Discovery of Yucatan and the Foundation of the New Maya Empire. *American Journal of Archaeology*, 2d series, 31(1):51–69.

————. 1946. *The Ancient Maya*. Stanford, CA: Stanford University Press.

Moulton, Forest Ray, ed. 1942. *Leibig and After Leibig: A Century of Progress in Agricultural Chemistry*. Washington, DC: American Association for the Advancement of Science. As referenced in Arthur S. Boughey, *Ecology of Populations* (New York: MacMillan, 1968).

Munro, David A. 1991. *Cuidar la tierra: Estrategias para el futuro de la vida*. Gland, Switzerland: UICN, PNUMA, and WWF.

Naranjo, Plutarco. 1995. Epidemic Hecatomb in the New World. In *Columbus and the New World: Medical Implications*, ed. Guy A. Settipane, pp. 19–24 Providence: OceanSide Publications.

Nash, Manning. 1961. The Social Context of Economic Choice in a Small Community. *Man* 61:186–191.

————. [1958] 1967. *Machine Age Maya: The Industrialization of a Guatemalan Community*. Chicago: University of Chicago Press.

Ostrom, Elinor. 1992. The Rudiments of a Theory of the Origins, Survival, and Performance of Common Property Institutions. In *Making the Commons Work: Theory, Practice and Policy*, ed. David W. Bromley et al., pp. 293–337. San Francisco: Institute for Contemporary Studies.

Pinkerton, Elinor. 1994. Summary and Conclusions. In *Folk Management in the World's Fisheries: Lessons for Modern Fisheries Management*, eds. Christopher L. Dyer and James R. McGoodwin, pp. 317–337. Niwot: University of Colorado Press.

Pohl, Mary, and Lawrence H. Feldman. 1982. The Traditional Role of Women and Animals in Lowland Maya Economy. In *Maya Subsistence: Studies in Memory of Dennis E. Puleston*, de. Kent V. Flannery, pp. 295–312. New York: Academic Press.

Pollock, Harry E. D. 1980. *The Puuc, an Architectural Survey of the Hill Country of Yucatán and Northern Campeche, Mexico*. Cambridge: Peabody Museum of Archaeology and Ethnology, Harvard University.

Posey, D. 1985. Native and Indigenous Guidelines for New Amazonian Development Strategies: Understanding Biodiversity Through Ethnoecology. In *Change in the Amazon*, ed. J. Hemming, pp. 156–181. Manchester: Manchester University Press.

Puleston, Dennis E. 1977. The Art and Archaeology of Hydraulic Agriculture in the Maya Lowlands. In *Social Process in Maya Prehistory*, ed. Norman Hammond, pp. 449–467. New York: Academic Press.

————. 1978. Terracing, Raised Fields, and Tree Cropping in the Maya Lowlands: A New Perspective on the Geography of Power. In *Prehispanic Maya Agriculture*, ed. Peter D. Harrison and B. L. Turner II, pp. 225–246. Albuquerque: University of New Mexico Press.

Rappaport, Roy. [1968] 1984. *Pigs for the Ancestors: Ritual in the Ecology of a New Guinea People*. 2nd ed. New Haven: Yale University Press.

Redfield, Robert, and Alfonso Villa Rojas. 1934. *Chan Kom: A Maya Village*, Publication 448. Washington, DC: Carnegie Institution.

Restall, Mathew Bennett. 1995. *Life and Death in a Maya Community: The Ixil*

Testaments of the 1760s. Lancaster, CA: Labyrinthos.

Rice, Donald S., and Prudence M. Rice. 1984. Collapse to Contact: Postclassic Archaeology of the Petén Maya. *Archaeology* 37(2):46–51

Rice, Prudence M. 1987. *Macanché Island, El Petén, Guatemala: Excavations, Pottery, and Artifacts*. Gainesville: University of Florida Press.

Robicsek, Francis, and Donald Hales. 1981. *The Maya Book of the Dead: The Ceramic Codex* (The Corpus of Codex Style Ceramics of the Late Classic Period). Norman: University of Oklahoma Press.

Robles, Castellanos F. 1990. *La Secuencia Cerámica de la Región de Cobá, Quintana Roo,* Serie Arqueología, Colección Científica No. 184. México, D. F.: Instituto Nacional de Antropología e Historia.

Sabloff, Jeremy A. 1995. Drought and Decline. *Nature* 375:357.

Sabloff, Jeremy A., and E. W. Andrews V., eds. 1986. *Late Lowland Maya Civilization: Classic to Postclassic*. Albuquerque: University of New Mexico Press.

Sabloff, Jeremy A., and William L. Rathje. 1975. The Rise of a Maya Merchant Class. *Scientific American* 233 (4):72–83.

Sanders, William T. 1973. The Cultural Ecology of the Lowland Maya: A Reevaluation. In *The Classic Maya Collapse*, ed. T. P. Culbert, pp. 326–365. Albuquerque: University of New Mexico Press.

———. 1976. The Agricultural History of the Basin of Mexico. In *The Valley of Mexico*, ed. Eric R. Wolf, pp. 59–67. Albuquerque: University of New Mexico Press.

Sanders, William T., Jeffrey R. Parsons, and Robert J. Santley. 1979. *The Basin of Mexico: Ecological Processes in the Evolution of a Civilization*. New York: Academic Press.

Sandoval Palacios, Juan Manuel. 1982. Development of Capitalism in Mexican Agriculture. Its Impact on the Humid Tropics: The Case of the Yohaltún Project in the Southeastern State of Campeche. Ph.D. dissertation, University of California at Los Angeles.

Sandoval Palacios, Juan Manuel, and Abel Morales López. 1982. Una aproximación metodológica para el estudio de un sistema hidráulico prehispánico en Yohaltún, Valle de Edzná, Campeche. *Boletín Escuela de Ciencias Antropológicas de la Universidad de Yucatán* 9(53):13–27.

Scarborough, Vernon L. 1992. Flow of Power: Water Reservoirs Controlled the Rise and Fall of the Ancient Maya. *The Sciences* 32:38–43.

———. 1996. Agua, paisaje y crecimiento en el desarrollo de las tierras mayas. *Los Investigadores de la Cultura Maya* (Campeche, México: Universidad Autónoma de Campeche) 4:169–186.

Scarborough, Vernon L., and Gary G. Gallopin. 1994. A Water Storage Adaptation in the Maya Lowlands. *Science* 251(4):658–662.

Schavelzón, Daniel. 1985. El caracol de Cozumel: Una pequeña maravilla de la arquitectura maya. *Cuadernos de Arquitectura Mesoamericana* (México D. F.: División de Estudio Posgrado, Facultad de Arquitectura, Universidad Nacional Autónoma de México) 5:75–81.

Schele, Linda. 1993. Afterword: A Final Word on Trees from Linda. In *Maya Cosmos: Three Thousand Years on the Shaman's Path*, by David A. Freidel, Linda Schele, and Joy Parker, pp. 393–403. New York: William Morrow.

Schele, Linda, and David Freidel. 1990. *The Forest of Kings: The Untold Story of the Ancient Maya*. New York: William Morrow.

Schele, Linda, and Mary Ellen Miller. 1986. *The Blood of Kings: Dynasty and Ritual in Maya Art*. New York: George Braziller.

Schlesinger, William H. 1991. *Biogeochemistry: An Analysis of Global Change*. San Diego: Academic Press.

Scholes, France V., and Ralph L. Roys. 1968. *The Maya Chontal Indians of Acalan-Tixchel: A Contribution to the History and Ethnography of the Yucatán Peninsula*. Norman: University of Oklahoma Press.

Scott, James C. 1985. *Weapons of the Weak: Everyday Forms of Peasant Resistance*. New Haven: Yale University Press.

Settipane, Guy A., and Thomas A. Russo. 1995. Mechanism of Disease Transmission to Native Indians. In *Columbus and the New World: Medical Implications*, ed. Guy A. Settipane, pp. 25–28. Providence: OceanSide Publications.

Sharp, Rosemary. 1981. *Chacs and Chiefs: The Iconology of Mosaic Stone Sculpture in Pre-conquest Yucatan, Mexico*, Studies in Pre-Columbian Art and Archaeology No. 24. Washington, DC: Dumbarton Oaks.

Sian Ka'an Biosphere Reserve. 1988. *UNESCO Courier*, March, pp. 8–10.

Siemens, Alfred H. 1978. Karst and the Pre-Hispanic Maya in the Southern Lowlands. In *Pre-Hispanic Maya Agriculture*, ed. Peter D. Harrison and B. L. Turner II, pp. 117–143. Albuquerque: University of New Mexico Press.

———. 1989. *Tierra Configurada*. México, D. F.: Consejo Nacional para la Cultura y las Artes.

Siemens, Alfred H., Richard J. Hebda, and Maija I. Heimo. 1996. Remontando el río, de nuevo: Nuevos hallazgos en las zonas inundables a lo largo del Río Candelaria en Campeche, *Los Investigadores de la Cultura Maya* (Campeche, México: Universidad Autónoma de Campeche) 4:32–56.

Siemens, Alfred H., and Dennis E. Puleston. 1972. Ridged Fields and Associated Features in Southern Campeche: New Perspectives on the Lowland Maya. *American Antiquity* 37(2):228–239.

Sonnenfeld, David A. 1992. Mexico's "Green Revolution," 1940–1980: Towards an Environmental History. *Environmental History Review* 16(4):29–52.

Sosa, John. 1986. The Maya Sky, the Maya World: A Symbolic Analysis of Yucatec Maya Cosmology. Ph.D. dissertation, State University of New York at Albany.

Stadelman, Raymond. 1940. *Maize Cultivation in Northwestern Guatemala*, Publication 523. Washington, DC: Carnegie Institution.

Steggerda, Morris. 1941. *Maya Indians of Yucatan*, Publication 531. Washington, DC: Carnegie Institution.

Stephens, John Lloyd. [1841]. 1949. *Incidents of Travel in Central America, Chiapas, and Yucatán*, Vols. 1 and 2 (Illus. F. Catherwood, ed. R. L. Predmore). New Brunswick, NJ: Rutgers University Press.

————. [1843] 1988. *Incidents of Travel in Yucatan,* (Illus. F. Catherwood) Vols. 1 and 2. Mexico: Panorama Editorial.

Sullivan, Paul. 1989. *Unfinished Conversations: Mayas and Foreigners Between Two Wars.* New York: Alfred A. Knopf.

Sumner-Faust, Elizabeth (Faust, Betty). 1985. Religious and Economic Externalities of American-Guatemalan Agribusiness. In *Anthropology and International Business,* ed. Hendrick Serrie, Monographs of Third World Societies, vol. 28, pp. 211–272. Williamsburg, VA: William and Mary Press.

Taylor, Griffith. 1937. *Environment, Race and Migration.* Chicago: University of Chicago Press. Quoted in John H. Bodley, *Cultural Anthropology* (Mountain View, CA: Mayfield Publishing Company, 1994), pp. 415.

Tedlock, Barbara. 1982. *Time and the Highland Maya.* Albuquerque: University of New Mexico Press.

Tedlock, Dennis. 1985. *Popol Vuh: The Definitive Edition of the Mayan Book of the Dawn of Life and the Glories of Gods and Kings,* trans. with commentary based on the ancient knowledge of the modern Quiché Maya. New York: Simon and Schuster.

Terán, Silvia, and Christian H. Rasmusssen. 1994. *La Milpa de los Mayas.* Mérida, México: Gobierno del Estado de Yucatán.

————. 1995. Genetic Diversity and Agricultural Strategy in 16th Century and Present-day Yucatecan Milpa Agriculture. *Biodiversity and Conservation* 4:363–381.

Thompson, Edward H. 1897. *The Chultunes of Labna, Yucatan,* Report of the Explorations by the Museum 1888–1889 and 1890–1891, vol. 1, no. 3. Cambridge: Peabody Museum, Harvard University.

Thompson, J. Eric S. 1970. *Maya History and Religion.* Norman: University of Oklahoma Press.

Tichy, Franz. 1981. Order and Relationship of Space and Time in Mesoamerica: Myth or Reality? In *Mesoamerican Sites and World-Views,* ed. Elizabeth P. Benson, pp. 217–258. Washington, DC: Dumbarton Oaks.

Toledo, Víctor M. 1987. Ethnoecology, Peasant Economy, and Rural Production in Mexico. Paper presented in the University of California, Berkeley. Quoted in David Patton, Ethnoecology: The Challenge of Cooperation, *Etnoecología* 1(2) (1993):5–15.

Turner, B. L., II. 1978. Ancient Agricultural Land Use in the Central Maya Lowlands. In *Prehistoric Maya Agriculture,* ed. Peter D. Harrison and B. L. Turner II, pp. 163–182. Albuquerque: University of New Mexico Press.

————. 1979. Prehispanic Terracing in the Central Maya Lowlands: Problems of Agricultural Intensification. In *Mesoamerican Archaeology and Ethnology,* ed. N. Hammond and G. R. Willey, pp. 103–113. Austin: University of Texas Press.

————. 1983. *Once Beneath the Forest: Prehistoric Terracing in the Rio Bec Region of the Maya Lowlands.* Boulder, CO: Westview Press.

————. 1990. Population Reconstruction of the Central Maya Lowlands 1000 B.C. to A.D. 1500. In *Precolumbian Population History in the Maya Lowlands,* ed. T.

Patrick Culbert and Don S. Rice, pp. 301–324. Albuquerque: University of New Mexico Press.

U.S. National Research Council. 1992. *Conserving Biodiversity: A Research Agenda for Development Agencies*. Washington, DC: National Academy Press.

Vadillo López, Claudio. 1994. *La Región del Palo de Tinte: El Partido del Carmen, Campeche*. Campeche, México: Fondo Estatal para la Cultura y las Artes.

Veblen, Thomas Thorstein. 1975. The Ecological, Cultural, and Historical Bases of Forest Preservation in Totonicapan, Guatemala. Ph.D. Dissertation, University of California at Berkeley.

Villagutierre Soto-Mayor, Juan de. [1701] 1983. *History of the Conquest of the Province of the Itzá*. Culver City, CA: Labyrinthos. (Translation from the Spanish edition of 1701.)

Vitousek, Peter M., Carla M. D'Antonio, Lloyd L. Loope, and Randy Westbrooks. 1996. Biological Invasions as Global Environmental Change. *American Scientist* 84:468–478.

Vogt, Evon S. 1976. *Tortillas for the Gods: A Symbolic Analysis of Zinacanteco Rituals*. Cambridge: Harvard University Press.

Wallerstein, Immanuel. 1976. *The Modern World-system: Capitalist Agriculture and the Origins of the European World-Economy in the Sixteenth Century*. New York: Academic Press.

———. 1980. *The Modern World-system II: Mercantilism and the Consolidation of the European World-Economy, 1600–1750*. New York: Academic Press.

Ward, W. C., A. E. Weidie, and W. Back. 1985. *Geology and Hydrogeology of the Yucatán and Quaternary Geology of Northeastern Yucatán Peninsula* (with A History of Quintana Roo by A. P. Andrews). New Orleans: New Orleans Geological Society.

Weaver, Muriel Porter. 1993. *The Aztecs, Maya, and Their Predecessors: Archaeology of Mesoamerica*, 3rd ed. San Deigo, CA: Academic Press.

Webster, David and Jennifer Kirker. 1995. Too Many Maya, Too Few Buildings: Investigating Construction Potential at Copán, Honduras. *Journal of Anthropological Research* 51:363–387.

Wilk, Richard. 1984. Households in Process: Agricultural Change and Domestic Transformation Among the Kekchi Maya of Belize. In *Households: Comparative and Historical Studies of the Domestic Group*, ed. R. McC. Netting, R. Wilk, and E. Arnould, pp. 217–244. Berkeley: University of California Press.

Wilk, Richard, and Wendy Ashmore. 1988. *Household and Community in the Mesoamerican Past*. Albuquerque: University of New Mexico Press.

Wilkinson, Robert L. 1995. Yellow Fever: Ecology, Epidemiology, and Role in the Collapse of the Classic Lowland Maya Civilization. *Medical Anthropology* 16:269–94.

Willey, Gordon R. 1978. Pre-Hispanic Maya Agriculture: A Contemporary Summation. In *Pre-Hispanic Maya Agriculture*, ed. Peter D. Harrison and B. L. Turner II, pp. Albuquerque: University of New Mexico Press.

Wolf, Eric. 1982. *Europe and the People Without History*. Berkeley: University of

California Press.

Woodbury, Richard B. 1993. *60 Years of Southwestern Archaeology: A History of the Pecos Conference.* Albuquerque: University of New Mexico Press.

Yankelovich, Daniel. 1987. Coming to Public Judgment. The 1987 Frank W. Abrams Lecture Series at Syracuse University.

Zapata Peraza, Renee Lorelei. 1985. Los chultunes de la región serrana de Yucatán. *Cuadernos de Arquitectura Mesoamericana* 5:17–24.

―――. 1987. El uso del agua y los mayas antiguos: algunos ejemplos arqueológicos. *Boletín de la Escuela de Ciencias Antropológicas de la Universidad Autónoma de Yucatán* 87:20–31.

―――. 1989. *Los chultunes: Sistemas de captación y almacenamiento de agua pluvial.* Serie Arqueología. México, D. F.: Instituto Nacional de Antropología e Historia.

Zubrow, Ezra B. W. 1972. Carrying Capacity and Dynamic Equilibrium in the Prehistoric Southwest. In *Contemporary Archaeology: A Guide to Theory and Contributions*, ed. Mark P. Leone, pp. 268–279. Carbondale: Southern Illinois University Press.

―――. 1975. *Prehistoric Carrying Capacity: A Model.* Menlo Park, CA: Cummings.

Index

About the Author

BETTY BERNICE FAUST is a Researcher and the Academic Coordinator of Human Ecology at the Centro de Investigación y de Estudios Avanzados del Instituto Politécnico Nacional in Mérida, Mexico. She is a contributor to *Women in Health* (Bergin & Garvey, 1988).

ISBN 0-89789-482-0

9 780897 894821

90000>

EAN

HARDCOVER BAR CODE